Planning Your Retirement Housing

Michael Sumichrast
Ronald G. Shafer
Marika Sumichrast

An AARP Book
published by
American Association of Retired Persons
Washington, D.C.

Scott, Foresman and Company
Lifelong Learning Division
Glenview, Illinois

Copyright © 1984
Scott, Foresman and Company, Glenview, Illinois
American Association of Retired Persons, Washington, D.C.
All Rights Reserved
Printed in the United States of America
123456-KPF-888786858483

Authorized adaptation from the edition published by Dow Jones-Irwin, Homewood, Illinois. Copyright © 1981 by Dow Jones-Irwin. All Rights Reserved.

Library of Congress Cataloging in Publication Data

Sumichrast, Michael.
   Planning your retirement housing.

   Includes index.
   1. Aged—United States—Dwellings—Planning.
2. Retirement—United States—Planning. I. Shafer,
Ronald G. II. Sumichrast, Marika. III. Title.
HD7287.92.U54S92   1982   643′.12′0240565   83-24702
ISBN 0-673-24810-0 (Scott, Foresman)

ISBN 0-673-24810-0

This publication is protected by Copyright and permission should be obtained from the publisher prior to any prohibited reproduction, storage in a retrieval system, or transmission in any form or by any means, electronic, mechanical, photocopying, recording, or otherwise. For information regarding permission, write to: Scott, Foresman and Company, 1900 East Lake Avenue, Glenview, Illinois 60025.

Contents

Preface		v
Chapter 1	Is There Life After Retirement?	1
Chapter 2	Where Will the Living Be Easiest?	9
Chapter 3	Cashing In Your Housing Assets	54
Chapter 4	Buy Now, Move Later	75
Chapter 5	Housing Options—A Home of Your Own	94
Chapter 6	More Housing Options—Renting	121
Chapter 7	Designed for Mature Living	134
Chapter 8	Keeping Up the Old Homestead	179
Chapter 9	Retirement Communities—The "Good Life"?	207
Chapter 10	Adventures in Retirement Living	228
Chapter 11	Unfinished Business	238
Notes		251
Index		253

This book is an educational and public service project of the American Association of Retired Persons which, with a membership of more than 15 million, is the largest association of middle-aged and older persons in the world today. Founded in 1958, AARP provides older Americans with a wide range of membership programs and services, including legislative representation at both federal and state levels. For further information about additional association activities, write to AARP, 1909 K Street, N.W., Washington, DC 20049.

Preface

The United States is facing a crisis in housing for older people.

There is a serious shortage of moderate-cost homes for older people to buy or rent. Many are stuck in deteriorating homes that are too big for their needs and too costly to keep up. To top it off, the designs of many homes are, as one retiree told us, "for the birds."

This shelter shortage will worsen as the maturing baby-boom generation ages into an avalanche of oldsters. By the year 2000, it is estimated that one in every eight Americans will be age 65 or older. And people are living longer, meaning we will need different types of housing for the "young-old" and the "old-old."

Adding to the worries is that neither government nor industry are facing up to the problem of housing for older people. One reason is that much of the public simply doesn't think the problems of older people apply to them. They are wrong. If there is one thing we have realized in preparing this book, it is that we will all face these problems some day. To paraphrase Pogo, we have met the elderly and—sooner or later—they are us!

There is no one solution to the housing needs of older people. This is because older people are as different—with as varied interests, needs, and dreams—as any other part of society. But there is much that must and can be done to develop better housing options for this rapidly growing group of Americans.

Some builders, government officials, and private groups are starting to respond to the housing needs of older people, and we have updated this book to include such welcome developments. But, unfortunately, most of the problems that we initially reported remain unchanged. Still needed are such changes as more houses designed for the needs of older people, improved ways to allow older homeowners to tap the increased equities of their homes, and more housing alternatives to permit older people to stay in their old neighborhoods or near their families.

The good news is that, despite the problems, millions of older Americans are finding the good life through smart planning, sheer determination, and a never-say-quit spirit. This includes finding the housing that will help them live that good life. The purpose of this book is to help you consider the many options for housing in your later years.

To do this, we solicited the views of older people on housing. They responded with more than 1,400 letters full of advice. So, in many ways, this book is written by those who know best about housing for older people, the older people themselves. We also drew from many other experts on aging and housing. And we were able to use the valuable and readable resource of stories written by reporters for The Wall Street Journal.

Our goal is to provide a detailed view of the many housing options for older Americans and the many needs that have yet to be met. It should be only the start for your research, and we have tried to include as many other sources as possible.

We want to thank the numerous people and organizations who provided us with material for this book. We especially wish to thank the American Association of Retired Persons, its communication counsel, Barry Robinson, and its housing program coordinator, Leo Baldwin, for their guidance and help.

Most of all, we want to thank the more than 1,400 older people who shared their experiences with us. It is to them that this book is dedicated.

Ronald G. Shafer
Michael Sumichrast
Marika Sumichrast

Is There Life After Retirement?

1

*Your age is only a number.
It has nothing to do with how old you are.*
Mrs. Gwen Anson Norton
Troy, Missouri

You bet there is life after retirement, and it's a good one for many Americans. One foundation to that good retirement life is a happy housing situation.

"I feel I have the almost perfect housing situation for older people," said Anna Poorman of St. Helens, Oregon. Mrs. Poorman, a widow in her 90s, planned and had built years ago a retirement bungalow that she has shared with her nearly 100-year-old brother.

"We are fortunate to be independent, but close to family and friends," she said. "We credit our long, healthful life to happy living conditions."

But the golden retirement life doesn't just happen. It requires thoughtful planning.

Wrote Mrs. Margaret Alton of Jefferson, Maryland:

"My husband and I are 63 years old. At 50 to 55 years, we decided to do something positive about approaching retirement. After much research, we decided it would be worthwhile financially, physically, and mentally to buy some land with a house on it worth restoring. We have spent the last eight years restoring Castle Hill Farm in Middletown Valley, Maryland.

"We have 40 acres, rent 36 acres of pasture and grain fields, and keep sheep, ducks, chickens, a dog, and cats on the remainder. We have 10 rooms, 5 completely restored, plus 2 full baths and 2 half-baths. Since the house was built around 1840 and not maintained, lots and lots of work has been involved. All of this keeps us busy and happy with a tremendous feeling of accomplishment.

"P.S. Nothing pleases so much as two small grandsons visiting and thinking this is the biggest and best farm in the valley."

A Housing Crisis: The Shelter Shortage

The power of positive retirement planning is echoed in more than 1,400 letters and cards sent to us by retirees from Alaska to the Virgin Islands. But these older Americans also warn that moderate-priced housing that fits the budgets of older people is becoming scarcer and scarcer. And many who remain in their big old homes face rising operating costs. As one elderly widow put it: "It's either heat or eat."

To find out exactly what kind of retirement housing people want, we went to the folks who know best—the retirees themselves. The 15-million-member American Association of Retired Persons (AARP) and several retirement communities cooperated by printing in their newsletters our requests for information about retirement housing. The result was an outpouring of cards and letters brimming with advice, complaints, and real-life retirement tales.

These letters were supplemented by a questionnaire sent to many of the letter writers, and also by special questions inserted in a consumer survey by the National Association of Home Builders of 5,000 homeowners of all ages. While these surveys didn't involve scientific samplings of all people, or of all retirees, they did provide significant insights into retirement housing needs and wants—insights and conclusions we will discuss throughout this book.

Housing Worries

A major worry of older people is where they will live—or where they can afford to live.

"The impact of inflation for me has meant remaining in my present home while I would like to relocate to another state," said Mrs. Elsie Grapentin of Cleveland, Ohio. "The unreasonably high cost of another home, whether old or new, and consequent higher real estate taxes would seriously lower the amount of money my savings and investments bring to me. I do not want to lower my lifestyle."

Or as Mr. and Mrs. Jack Parker of Caldwell, Indiana, put it: "We are thinking about buying a home, with the Lord's help. At these prices, we need all the help we can get."

Older people also have plenty of gripes about the way houses and apartments are designed.

"I have found house planning for the elderly to be unimaginative, stereotyped, and lacking in an understanding of the lifestyle requirements of older people," said Mrs. Marion G. Rudnick of Cape Neddick, Maine.

Like other retirees, she maintained that too many houses are designed with too many levels, too many steps, high shelves, inadequate storage space, and poorly planned living spaces that make life difficult for older people.

Our survey of letter writers also clearly shows that most older people do not want to live in large, high-rise buildings. And they are concerned about what they see as a trend toward high-rises for the elderly. Nearly two-thirds of those surveyed *disagreed* with the statement, "High-rises are an ideal place for senior citizens."

Older people say they fear the impersonality of high-rise living. One 60-year-old Philadelphia woman wrote: "We shudder at the thought of being a 'sardine' in a high-rise." Others conceded, though, that high-rises offer some advantages. The results of the survey questions are shown in Table 1·1.

Many older people have a still bigger worry about their future housing. "Like so many, I have a horror of nursing homes," wrote an Oklahoma woman. In fact, according to Dr. Robert Butler, former director of the National Institute of Aging, "only 5 percent of America's aged live in nursing homes. Only one in five will ever have anything to do with a nursing home."

Table 1·1

Do you agree with the following statement?

	Agree	Disagree	Don't know
1. High-rise buildings are an unsatisfactory place for senior citizens to live	40.7%	35.6%	23.7%
2. High-rise buildings for senior citizens have many advantages	38.9	38.9	22.2
3. High-rise buildings for senior citizens seem to be the trend	42.1	10.5	47.4
4. Most senior citizens prefer not to live in high-rises	41.0	13.1	45.9
5. High-rises are an ideal place for senior citizens	20.4	63.0	16.6

What Housing Do People Want?

In terms of retirement housing, most older people want homes smaller in price to fit their pocketbooks and smaller in size to meet their needs.

"Why can't some of the home builders design a small house for two people that doesn't cost a fortune and put it on a small piece of property?" asked John Finnegan of New Hyde Park, New York.

The National Association of Home Builders' consumer survey of 5,000 homeowners showed that most of them—86.2 percent—who are of pre-retirement age prefer living in detached, single-family houses close to their relatives. After age 65, these people said they still prefer to live in their own single-family units, but many would prefer smaller homes.

Table 1·2 reveals the response of people to the question, What type of home would you prefer to live in when you are over 65 years of age?

Table 1·2

	Percent distribution
Single-family detached	50.3
Townhouse	11.3
Condominium	15.9
Rent only	0.0
Not sure/don't know	22.5
Total	100.0

Whatever kind of house they live in, older people want dignity and self-respect.

"Retired people have pride. They do not want to be 'kept.' They desire to be independent and to take care of themselves," declared Eva L. Sturrock of Skokie, Illinois.

And, despite problems, your chances for doing just that are getting better than ever.

Housing Hopes

The growing number of older people will be able to lobby for greater housing opportunities. More older people will put more pressure on industry and the government to develop housing to fit their needs.

Even now, you may have more housing choices than you realized. Housing preferences are an individual matter, and we can't tell you which retirement housing situation will be best for you. But, with the help of those who already have retired, we can show the wide variety of housing options you can consider.

Many retirees stay right where they are—in the old homestead where the mortgage has a low interest rate or is paid off so that the monthly costs are relatively low.

"My neighbor and I didn't sell, and we are 'holdouts,'" happily declared Richard Bergere, a retiree who owns a 13-room Victorian home in Flushing, New York. "I live as well as people in $500,000 townhouses. But it only costs me $120 a month."

Others move to a smaller house that is easier to keep up than their old home once the kids have grown and moved away.

"I truly wish all elderly people could have as lovely and convenient home as mine—not too large or too costly, yet lovely," wrote Lena Layman of Springville, Alabama. Mrs. Layman and her husband, both in their 80s, designed and built their one-story house when they were 65 and left a seven-room, two-story house.

Many retirees in northern areas head for sunnier climes.

"When I retired, I and my wife opted for retirement in the Sunbelt from out of the cooler East. We came to Albuquerque, New Mexico in 1977 and purchased a three-bedroom home," said Joseph Stasick. "Our home is partially heated by solar, and, with the addition of a wood stove, we will be completely self-sufficient in heating energy. (We cut our own wood in the mountains.) We are completely happy with our housing."

Some retirees busy themselves in the many activities of a retirement community with other people their own ages. Mr. and Mrs. Robert Crispen, both in their 60s, bought a two-bedroom home in the retirement community of Green Valley, Arizona.

"The ideal weather, the interesting people, and the varied activities attracted us to buy after a period of renting—having lived 32 years in Long Island," Mrs. Crispen said. "The east-west exposure allows *patio living, a double garage permits Bob puttering space, a gasoline golf cart takes us to the nearby golf course or to a shopping center 11 minutes away."*

But others can't stand the thought of retirement communities.

"I feel most retirement communities are geared for the well-to-do retirees," said a Maryland retiree. *"I don't golf, swim, play tennis, shuffleboard, et cetera. I already know more hobbies than I can practice, and I feel it is all an exercise in time-killing, not worthwhile living."*

Still other older people march—or drive—to a different drummer altogether.

"We live in our bus motor home. We think it is the ideal way for retired people to live," wrote Anne Purpura, whose mailing address is Blanco, Texas. *"You can travel when you wish and have little work inside and out. A house is nothing but work and problems. As you get older, you look for less work, not more."*

Enterprising Entrepreneurship

Then there are the enterprising efforts of Ruth Pauley and a few of her friends.

"Four of us [women] in our 70s formed a partnership to build a house to our requirements . . . within the limits of our retirement incomes and resources," Mrs. Pauley wrote.

"By pooling our resources and taking out the highest mortgage the bank would grant, we started out with an initial investment by each partner of $18,000. We have since added about $1,000 each for landscaping. Our initial investment is less than the entrance fee to a good retirement setting, and we retain ownership rights in the property.

"This [plan] was in the discussion and dreaming stage for probably a year before we made up our minds to move on it. We started looking for a location in North Carolina. We wanted to be on water and we needed to be assured of good medical facilities. Our first stop was Pinehurst. That was as far as we got because we fell in love with the area from the first look.

"From then on we moved ahead rapidly, and all legal actions on the partnership were completed, the house was planned, the builder was selected, and the go-ahead signals were given.

"We planned our home with the aid of a home designer. We have within the house two bed sitting rooms with a kitchenette in each [for two of the partners]. The fullsize, three-bedroom, two baths, and full kitchen on one floor is the headquarters of two partners and serves as the entertainment area for the partnership.

"The house is equipped with every device we could envision needing in the future as illness or disability might attack us. These include one bathroom big enough for a wheelchair to enter and turn around, a chair lift on the stairs, panic buttons in baths, and handholds to assist with stiff joints and handicaps...

"The house is located just outside of Southern Pines, North Carolina, on a lake. We have a paddle boat and a sailboat and a beautiful view of lake and pines and of the birds that abound.

"We are happy here because we are ready for the quiet country life away from the pollution, traffic, and hurry of the big city," Mrs. Pauley said. "And we are able to provide a secure living in a setting of mutual help."

Housing Plans

Housing is the cornerstone of the financial planning of the majority of Americans. Your best investment, like charity, begins at home. The outlook is that a home will continue to be a good investment as well as a good way to shelter income from taxes through deductions for mortgage interest and property taxes.

That's not just our opinion. Most financial experts and many retirees agree that a home of your own is one of the best investments you can make. In our survey of people of all ages, many agreed that gold glitters and is a good investment bet. But the largest number of respondents think that the best hedge against inflation is—you guessed it—their own homes.

The results of the survey are shown in Table 1·3.

Table 1·3 Best hedges against inflation (percent of respondents)

	Total
Single-family detached home	75.1%
Townhouse	8.7
Condominium apartment	6.6
Investment in land	54.2
Vacation home	6.9
Art collection	7.3
Stamps	4.9
Gold	28.7
Silver	12.8
Diamonds	22.0
Mutual funds	9.6
Stocks	14.5
Other	7.9

And the home you own now can be your ticket to the home you want to move to later.

Housing should be part of your overall financial program in your later years. For further information on planning a retirement financial program, you can obtain a federal "Guide to Planning Your Retirement Finances" for $4.25 from the U.S. Consumer Information Center in Pueblo, Colorado. (See page 250 for instructions on ordering.)

Where Will The Living Be Easiest?

My personal determination is that I never again wish to live in an area where I have to shovel snow.
Luther L. Willard
Dallas, Texas (formerly of Worcester, Massachusetts)

It sure seems that just about everybody who retires moves away to sunny climes to escape cold weather and high costs. But in fact only about 5 percent of today's retirees have left their home states. And some experts on aging say there's no place like your current home area to spend your retirement years. But if you plan properly, you will have the flexibility to choose whether you want to stay put or to move.

Our surveys show that many people would like to move to another region of the country when they retire. But this itch to switch depends on where they live now.

The Urge to Move

We asked people this question: "When you retire, in which area of the country would you like to live?"

Nearly 95 percent of those living in the Pacific region said they'd prefer to stay right where they are, thank you; 93 percent living in the South Atlantic states said the same thing. But in the colder, northern states, the picture is vastly different.

Look at Table 2·1 and the blocks going diagonally through the middle. The first one, 44.4 percent, means that less than half the people surveyed who now live in New England would like to stay on when they retire. Only 33.3 percent of those living in the East North Central region want to stay, and only 25 percent in the West North Central states. Figure 2·1 on page 11 shows in map form the sections

Table 2.1

When you retire, in which area of the country would you like to live?

Move to

Presently live in	New England	Mid-Atlantic	E. N. Central	W. N. Central	South Atlantic	E. S. Central	W. S. Central	Mountain	Pacific
New England	44.4%				33.3%		11.1%		11.1%
Middle Atlantic	5.0	55.0%	33.3%	5.6%	25.0	5.0%	5.6	5.0%	5.0
E. N. Central			33.3%	5.6%	22.2		5.6	16.7	16.7
W. N. Central				25.0%	25.0		12.5	37.5	
South Atlantic					93.1%			6.9	
E. S. Central						75.0%	8.3	8.3	8.3
W. S. Central				6.3		6.3	75.0%		12.5
Mountain					7.7			92.3%	
Pacific						5.6			94.4%
Total percent	3.5	7.7	4.2	2.8	29.3	8.4	11.2	15.4	17.5

Figure 2·1: Census Regions

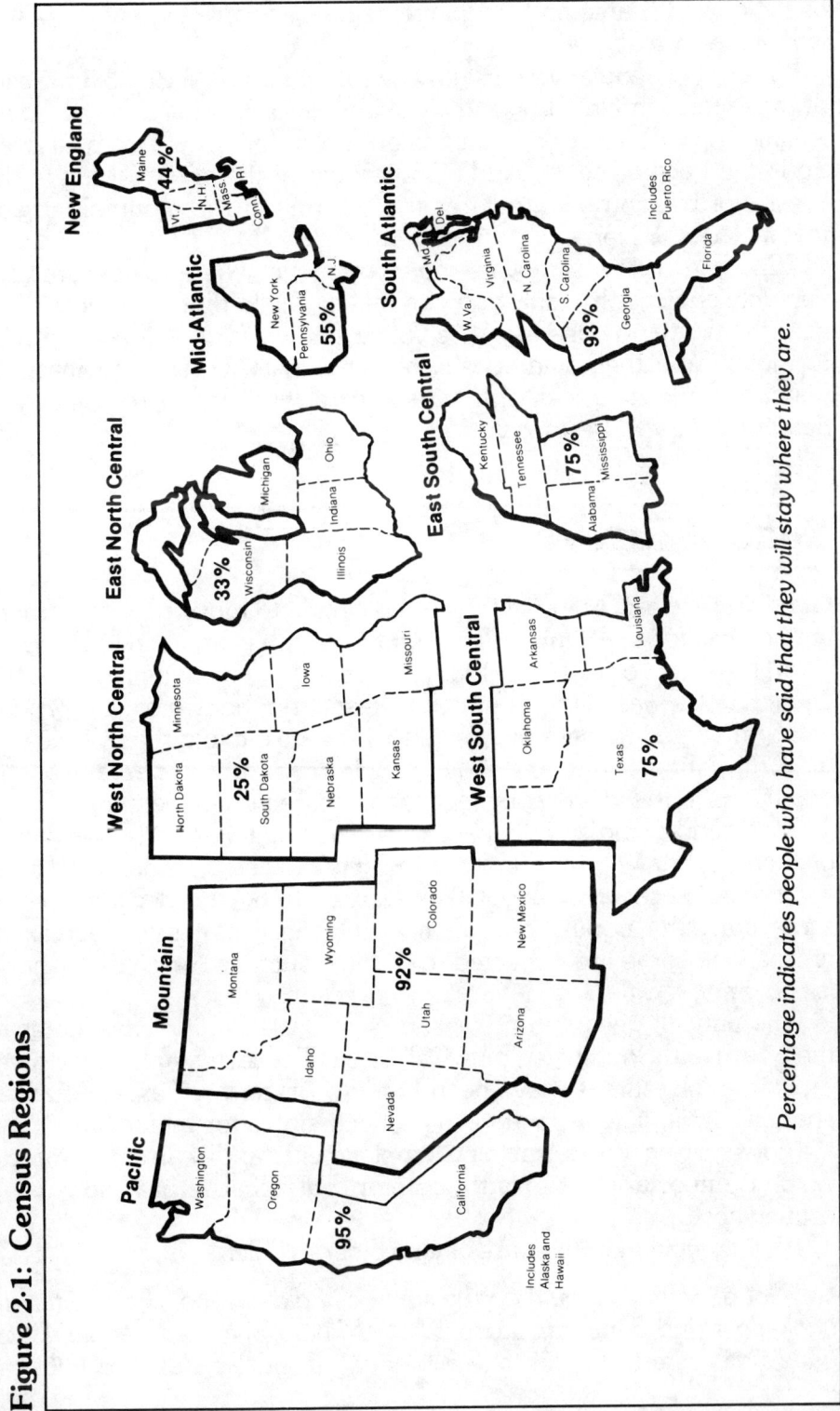

Percentage indicates people who have said that they will stay where they are.

of the United States and the percentages of people who wish to stay where they are.

Where do people want to go when they retire? Well, 33.3 percent of those folks in New England would head for Florida and the South Atlantic region, and that is a popular choice for people from all over. So is the Pacific region. And 37.5 percent of those now living in the West North Central states dream of retiring in the mountain region that includes Arizona.

Whether to stay or move—and if you move, where to go—are very personal choices that only you can make. To do that, you must compare the pros and cons of where you are now with the possible places to move—and their living costs, housing costs, leisure activities, climate, and the nearness of friends and relatives. Only then can you determine what is best for you.

Sunbelt Retirement

One thing is clear. Many of those who decide to move after retirement are heading for the Sunbelt. The run to the sun is underlined by population trends. From 1970 to 1980, the largest population growth in the United States was in the South and West. And the two biggest groups fueling that growth were people 20 to 40 years old and the over-65 set. In 1970, young adults and older people made up 36 percent of the population in these areas; by 1982, their share was 45 percent.

The trend is expected to accelerate in the 1980s. The population of such states as Arizona, Colorado, New Mexico, Florida, and Texas are projected to grow about 20 percent during the decade. At the same time, the populations of many northern states will barely increase, and some are expected to decline, such as New York, Rhode Island, and New Jersey.

The Sunbelt goes around a wide area. Basically, it means states in the South and Southwest, plus California. The fastest-growing states, especially for retirees, have been Florida, Arkansas, Texas, Arizona, and California. The attractions of Sunbelt states for many Americans are lower living costs, growing employment, and warmer climates, which is important not only for comfort but because of rapidly rising heating costs.

It's a combination that lures many older people.

"Not all retirees would do the same as I did—leave all of my family back East and come far away where I know only two people! But I have not regretted it for one moment," declared Bethune Gibson, who moved from Chevy Chase, Maryland, and bought a duplex in West Sedona, Arizona. "The sky is clear, and the air is clean. The scenery is fantastic, and I have a magnificent chunk of it just beyond my front window."

Texas is one of the fast-growing states for retirees. Lester and Mary Ruth Olson sold everything they owned in New Jersey and retired to a condominium in McAllen, Texas, in the Rio Grande Valley.

"After deciding this was the jumping-off place from the whole United States—and not knowing a soul in McAllen—I am now a born-again Texan," wrote Mrs. Olson. "We are very happy in our housing situation."

And she added these words of advice: "I must say if one is not happy in your heart and does not have a positive outlook—I've learned in my 67 years—you won't like it better in Texas than where you are now. Right on!"

Yes, may retirees find a sunny life in the Sunbelt. But there are problems, too.

Clouds over the Sunbelt

Many of the Sunbelt havens where retirees rushed are becoming overcrowded, living costs and congestion are increasing, and many are looking for new places in nearby areas or elsewhere. You may have to, also.

In Arizona, many retirees are moving into communities outside Phoenix—as refugees from the increasing Phoenix air pollution and traffic congestion.[1]

"Phoenix has become an urban nightmare," said Peter A. Dickinson, author of books about retirement havens.

As some retirees become disenchanted with the prices or the population density in the Phoenix area, some other sections of Arizona are getting increasing attention—especially farther north where the climate is more moderate.

In Florida, where 17.5 percent of the residents are retirees, movement away from popular retirement areas is accelerating. Sarasota is typical of the Gulf Coast retirement areas that have become too crowded to suit many retirees.

One 70-year-old widow who moved to Sarasota from Ann Arbor, Michigan, complained of the "overcrowded and overpriced" conditions. She planned to move to a smaller community in Florida.

"I'm fleeing all those little old ladies with their curly white hair who go watch Fred Waring and the Pennsylvanians at the city auditorium," said the woman, who has curly white hair and is short but stocky.

Of course, Phoenix, Sarasota, and other Sunbelt cities are still popular or they wouldn't be so congested. But many places are starting to attract the eyes of retirees.

Other Popular Retirement Places

Florida, Arizona, and California no longer own the retirement market. As these national magnets for the elderly become saturated, smaller regional retirement centers are attracting more retirees.[2]

The lake-dotted Ozark region of northern Arkansas and southwest Missouri is drawing large numbers of older migrants. So are the southern shore of New Jersey and the several coastal and valley communities of the Pacific Northwest. These places are often a day's drive from friends and relatives left behind.

"It's a less expensive move in terms of emotions and money," said Jeanne Biggar, a gerontologist at the University of Virginia. "As the national centers wear themselves out, you're going to see more and more regional centers."

The Ozark region is becoming a prime retirement center for people from such midwestern states as Illinois, Iowa, and Nebraska. Word of mouth brings them to the area for vacations; many return for good.

"It's really a neighborhood movement in the Ozarks," said Mrs. Biggar.

A U.S. Census survey ranked Arkansas second only to Florida in percentage of a population aged 65 and older. The Arkansas figure was 13.7 percent. In Baxter County, which includes the Ozarks, the proportion exceeds 28 percent. By 1990, the Census Bureau projects that the percentage of people 65 or older will rise to 19.5 percent of Florida's population, and to 14.4 percent in Arkansas (see Table 2·2).

Like the Ozarks, parts of Texas are becoming retirement centers for midwesterners. The Rio Grande Valley along the Mexican border draws "snowbirds" who come for the winter months and eventually return to retire.

The lake country north of Houston and the hills around Austin and San Antonio are popular, too. Similarly, Washington State's Olympic Peninsula and communities west of the Cascade Range in Oregon are destinations for disenchanted Californians, while the south shore of

Table 2·2 Population 65 years of age or over

State	1980	1990	State	1980	1990
Alabama	11.4%	12.6%	Montana	11.0%	12.4%
Alaska	2.7	3.7	Nebraska	12.9	13.1
Arizona	11.2	12.9	Nevada	8.7	10.7
Arkansas	13.7	14.4	New Hampshire	11.2	11.7
California	10.5	11.9	New Jersey	11.4	12.7
Colorado	8.8	9.9	New Mexico	9.0	10.8
Connecticut	11.4	12.9	New York	11.9	12.6
Delaware	9.3	10.8	North Carolina	10.0	11.6
District of Columbia	10.5	10.9	North Dakota	12.7	14.0
Florida	17.5	19.5	Ohio	10.6	11.7
Georgia	9.3	10.0	Oklahoma	12.8	13.3
Hawaii	7.8	10.0	Oregon	12.2	13.1
Idaho	10.6	11.8	Pennsylvania	12.7	14.3
Illinois	10.8	11.4	Rhode Island	12.8	13.7
Indiana	10.5	13.0	South Carolina	9.1	10.6
Iowa	13.2	13.8	South Dakota	13.4	14.7
Kansas	13.1	13.7	Tennessee	11.3	12.4
Kentucky	11.4	12.8	Texas	10.0	10.8
Louisiana	9.8	10.7	Utah	8.1	9.0
Maine	12.3	13.0	Vermont	11.1	11.2
Maryland	9.0	10.4	Virginia	9.4	11.0
Massachusetts	12.0	12.7	Washington	10.8	11.4
Michigan	9.4	10.2	West Virginia	12.0	14.1
Minnesota	11.6	11.7	Wisconsin	11.8	12.3
Mississippi	11.4	11.8	Wyoming	9.8	11.4
Missouri	12.9	13.1			

New Jersey appeals to New York-area retirees and northern-bred retirees from Florida.

The "Hayseed Revolution"

Many retirees are moving out of big cities and heading for the country or the small towns. You might not think anyone would leave Hawaii and retire to a farm on the mainland. But that's exactly what Theresa Mueller and her husband did.

"My husband took early retirement [at age] 54. We decided to move back to the mainland. We scouted the West Coast and found our present home," 8½ acres in Eddyville, Oregon. "While we are still in our young 60s, we are enjoying our rural life with horses, cats, and garden," Mrs. Mueller said.

Their move illustrates a recent trend in Americans' quest for ideal retirement havens.[3] "We're seeing a 'back to the village' movement among a growing number of retirees," said Sanford R. Goodkin, chairman of Goodkin Research Corporation, a national real estate consulting firm. Mr. Goodkin and others refer to the trend as a budding "hayseed revolution."

In California, many retirees have moved into smaller homes, apartments, or mobile homes in more rural and desert areas of the state. Some have gone to towns in Oregon and Arizona. Population movements also are occurring in Arizona and Florida, the most popular Sunbelt retirement states.

In Florida, the back-to-the-village movement is accelerating despite continued popularity of Sun City-type retirement communities. On Florida's west coast, which attracts people from Michigan, Ohio, and Illinois, who tend to prefer single-family homes, the retiree population shift is particularly noticeable. The trend is northward from crowded St. Petersburg and Tampa to North Pinellas and Pasco County.

The Best Bets

The hayseed revolution squares with some experts' advice on America's top retirement values. Peter A. Dickinson, author of the book *Sunbelt Retirement* and other retirement books, spent three years combing the United States for the best retirement areas.

In an analysis of top retirement sites, Mr. Dickinson used these criteria:

> *Climate:* temperatures average 66 degrees and humidity 55 percent on most days. *Cost of living:* retired couples living for less than $10,000 a year and paying less than 8 percent of their income for state and local taxes. *Housing:* a variety of two-bedroom units available for less than $40,000. *Medical facilities:* hospital rooms that cost less than $133 a day, and at least one doctor for every 750 persons. *Recreation and culture:* ample facilities. *Special senior services:* transportation and low-cost hot-meal programs.

Using these criteria, Mr. Dickinson picks the best small towns in rural areas, usually not too far from a larger city. In his opinion, these small towns offer the best retirement values in the nation:

> *Tyron, North Carolina,* a town of 6,000 that is 30 miles south of Asheville in the Appalachian highlands; *Mount Dora, Florida,* a town of 7,000 that is 25 miles north of Orlando in central Florida; *Fairhope, Alabama,* a town of 7,400 on the eastern shore of Mobile Bay, about 20 miles north of Mobile; *Prescott, Arizona,* a town of 12,000 in central Arizona that escapes the

southern Arizona heat; *Covington, Louisiana,* a town of 10,000 north of Lake Ponchartrain and about 30 miles north of New Orleans.

For more details on these and other good retirement towns, look for Mr. Dickinson's books at your bookstore or library.

Big Help for Small Cities

Another source for finding the best little place to settle down is a newsletter called *SmallTown USA* begun in 1977 by Leonard de Geus of Ridgecrest, California, a devotée of small-town living. Each of the 6 issues printed annually profiles a town with a population of between 5,000 and 25,000 people.

"People are looking for a way to upgrade their lifestyle," Mr. de Geus said. "People from big cities are coming down to find a dream. A small town is that dream, that Shangri-la."

He and his wife, Beverly, write the reports on specific small towns after visiting them. And the reports contain the bad aspects with the good "to show it the way it really is," Mr. de Geus said. Copies of his newsletter are available for $5, and yearly subscriptions for $30. Write: *SmallTown USA,* Woods Creek Press, P.O. Box 339-WW, Ridgecrest, CA 93555.

Small-Town Attractions

In the last several years, more people have been moving to small towns and rural areas than to big cities, reversing a historical pattern, and older people have been in the vanguard.[4]

The numbers are relatively small, but the trend is there nevertheless. Between 1975 and 1980, one million people aged 55 or over moved from urban areas to rural areas, while less than half that number moved the other way. In 1980, 6.5 million people 65 or over lived in rural areas, up from 5.4 million 10 years before.

The shift, experts say, results from the crowds, crime, and high costs in the cities and the neighborliness, tranquility, and low costs in rural areas.

In Guion, Arkansas, where most of the town's 200 or so people are 65 or older, home prices are roughly half what they are in Little Rock, the state's metropolis, more than 100 miles away; and property taxes are about 40 percent of Little Rock's. The White River is one of the best in the United States for trout fishing. And nearly everyone has a vegetable garden to help keep food costs down. Clothing costs are lower because outside of church, there isn't much to dress up for. Crime is almost nonexistent.

Beyond such practical matters, there is the satisfaction of seeing the Ozark hills emerge ghostlike from the morning mist and disappear in the orange haze of the sunset.

Sometimes it is hard to find suitable houses in small towns. Few new houses are being built and the old stock often isn't what it used to be. But the alternative can be an exciting and satisfying one: building or remodeling an old house.

"My wife and I sold our house in Louisville, Kentucky, and bought a small, unkempt farm house (shack) here in Danville, Kentucky," wrote Arthur Leche. *"We have remodeled and added to it with the equity we got in selling our Louisville house—and it is now an approximately 8-room, very comfortable house,"* he said proudly.

City Lights Still Call

In all this talk of retiring to the countryside, you don't want to overlook the attraction of big cities.

"I am in my second year of retirement and love it, and I am staying put in the center of Philadelphia in a studio apartment," wrote Gladys Scott. *"I go out and can walk a mile to the Art Museum of the University of Pennsylvania, a couple of miles to Independence Mall and its surrounding attractions, more blocks to stores and shops. I can sit in one of many small parks and 'people watch.' I can go in and out several times a day if the spirit moves me and can relax in between with my shoes off.*

"It's a stimulating atmosphere and certainly not confining," she wrote. *"I'm afraid if I moved to a retirement community I would vegetate."* As for costs, *"In 1975, I was paying $234 for this apartment. Now, I'm paying $335. But I rationalize that I now need less of other things and I do love center-city living."*

Living in or near a big city has plenty to offer retirees. Think of having the time to see Broadway shows in New York, going to baseball games in cities with major league teams, or visiting historic sites, many of them free of charge. The drawbacks to city living are well known—high cost, congestion, and, depending on where you live, crime. Indeed, crime can be a problem even in smaller cities.

One retiree, who lives with his wife in downtown Wheeling, West Virginia, said, *"We have been threatened by gang members, my wife stoned, and our property damaged. Our property value has declined appreciably. I am on a fixed income and in poor health, and we live a fearful existence."*

Fans of city living contend that urban life can be not only safe but economical and convenient.

"We are five minutes away from subways, and buses stop on our corner. This saves me $6,000 a year!" in auto and transportation costs, asserted Richard Bergere, who retired in his Victorian mansion in Flushing, New York. *"Because I'm surrounded by apartments, my heating bill is cut in half. My taxes are low, and I can rent out rooms if worse comes to worse."*

Mr. and Mrs. Raymond Erfle moved back to Philadelphia after living for a while in a retirement community 26 miles from the city. They found that commuting to the city to visit family and friends was just too much trouble.

"While city living is somewhat higher, we eliminated the car," Mr. Erfle said. *"We rent a small auto when we need one—say, once or twice a week. The cost is less than one-half that of owning one. Everything else is within walking distance. Taxes are higher, household operating costs are less.*

"If anything happens to either of us, all the necessities are within two city blocks," he added. *"Same is true of historical, cultural, and entertainment places."*

For one reason or another, it's expected that many retirees will live in metropolitan areas, mainly in suburban areas. The number of suburban households headed by someone 65 or older rose 18.7 percent between 1975 and 1980, according to the Census Bureau; most live in housing built at the time of World War II.

"Suburban areas can be expected to be the location choice of an increasing share of the elderly population over the next 10 to 20 years," said a report by the Urban Institute. As a result, suburban areas will face "increasing demands for facilities, housing, and housing-related services" for these older persons.

Before you plan to move or to stay put, though, evaluate the options. You may find some places stack up better for you than others.

Chase's Choices

When it comes to evaluating living conditions for retirees in different states, some of the work has been done for you. It's a study called "Ranking States According to Their Attractiveness for Retirement." And it was done for *Money Magazine* by Chase Econometrics, a subsidiary of Chase Manhattan Bank in New York.

The study evaluated 10 factors: unemployment rate, nonmanufacturing employment growth, ratio of elderly to working-age population, property tax load, living costs, housing availability, growth of retired population, weather conditions, utility rates, and metropolination.

The state that came out on top may surprise you. It was Utah. Next came Louisiana, South Carolina, Nevada, and Texas. The lowest retirement rating went to Massachusetts.

The complete list is in Table 2·3.

"Not surprisingly," the Chase study said, "the states which ranked high tended to be in the South and West, while the states which ranked low were in the Northeast.

"The highest ranking states were those with low property taxes and living costs, low unemployment with growing economies, warm weather, plus low utility rates and good housing availability. Low ranking states were just the opposite."

Chase issued a caveat about the results:

> First, it is clear that *every* state has good retirement locations, and that *any* state can be attractive to a given retiree. Our study is only intended to show which states from a purely economic, weather, and demographic sense are the most desirable for the average retiree.
>
> The fact that the change of seasons, the location of other family members, the availability of mass transit, or other such factors may be of more importance is not and cannot be included without great difficulty and arbitrary judgments. We confined our analysis to strictly measurable, well-defined factors which we felt to be important to the average retiree.

It's up to you to make the choices regarding personal needs and the lifestyle you want in your retirement living. But in your planning, you need to look closely, too, at the hard facts: What can you get for your house if you decide to sell? What will it cost to buy another? Wherever you consider living, what is the cost of living and taxes? What will be the access to hospitals, shopping, and leisure activities? All these and more are factors to consider.

Let's start.

Where Will the Living Be Cheapest?

You will have to do some investigating to find the living costs in specific areas that interest you. But there are some general guides each year. The Bureau of Labor Statistics (BLS) issued until 1983 cost-of-living estimates for retirees in 40 metropolitan areas across the United

Table 2·3 — States ranked by relative attractiveness to retirees (excludes Alaska and Hawaii)

Ranking	State name	Rating
1	Utah	305
2	Louisiana	295
3	South Carolina	280
4	Nevada	260
5	Texas	230
6	New Mexico	200
7	Alabama	185
8	Arizona	175
9	Florida	160
10	Georgia	155
11	Colorado	140
12	North Carolina	110
13	Tennessee	100
14	Kentucky	88
15	Virginia	75
16	Washington	40
17	California	35
18	Oklahoma	30
19	Maryland	−5
20	Idaho	−15
21	Oregon	−15
22	Kansas	−20
23	Arkansas	−63
24	Mississippi	−70
25	West Virginia	−103
26	Wyoming	−130
27	Nebraska	−138
28	Ohio	−160
29	Wisconsin	−170
30	Delaware	−195
31	Indiana	−195
32	Illinois	−223
33	Missouri	−225
34	Pennsylvania	−230
35	South Dakota	−235
36	Iowa	−240
37	Michigan	−245
38	Montana	−250
39	Minnesota	−265
40	North Dakota	−280
41	Connecticut	−285
42	New Hampshire	−300
43	New York	−355
44	Rhode Island	−373
45	Vermont	−385
46	New Jersey	−390
47	Maine	−428
48	Massachusetts	−498

Source: Chase Econometrics, "Ranking of States According to Their Attractiveness for Retirement."

States. The BLS provides three retirement budgets—low, intermediate, and high. The budget includes cost of food, housing, transportation, clothing, medical, and personal items, but not personal income tax payments.

Based on the figures released in fall 1982, the costliest place for a retired couple to live in the continental United States was the Boston area, with an intermediate budget of $11,925, compared with the national urban average of $10,226. Next highest were the metropolitan areas of New York, Seattle, Washington, D.C., San Francisco, and Buffalo.

The cheapest place to live was Atlanta, Georgia, with an intermediate budget for retirees of $9,516. The next lowest-cost metropolitan areas were Dallas, San Diego, Kansas City, Houston, and Denver.

The cheapest region in which to live is the South. And costs in nonmetropolitan areas (an intermediate budget of $9,203) were considerably below those for metropolitan areas.

Table 2·4 on pages 23–26 gives the estimated annual costs for retirees on intermediate budgets in 40 metropolitan areas.

Cost Caveats on the BLS

A few points need to be made about the BLS figures. For one, they provide only an estimate of true living costs for retirees in a particular area. Second, they don't include many of the areas that attract retirees. For example, no metro areas are included from Florida or Arizona. Finally, some of the costs, notably homeownership costs, are understated for someone who plans to move to certain areas.

For instance, the table shows that retirees in Los Angeles, San Francisco, San Diego, and Honolulu enjoy relatively low homeownership costs. That may be true for some retirees who already live in those areas and purchased their homes many years ago. But the table doesn't take into account the cost of buying a home now. And those cities rank among the highest-priced cities in the nation when it comes to housing.

Moreover, the homeownership costs for retirees in California reflect the impact of Proposition 13, which sharply slashed property taxes in the state.

"It's always difficult to move elsewhere because of the higher cost and the fact that under Proposition 13, if you move, the new owner is reassessed at a substantially higher rate," wrote George Goody, of Oceanside, California.

With those caveats in mind, let's examine more closely the housing-cost figures.

Table 2.4 Annual costs of an intermediate budget for a retired couple, autumn 1981

Area	Total budget	Family consumption Total consumption	Food Total	Food at Home	Food away from Home	Housing Total	Shelter Total	Renter costs	Home-owner costs	House furnishings & operations
Urban United States	$10226	$9611	$2898	$2569	$329	$3393	$2198	$2130	$2235	$1194
Metropolitan areas	10568	9932	2935	2587	348	3622	2343	2297	2367	1279
Nonmetropolitan areas	9203	8650	2787	2515	273	2708	1767	1633	1840	941
Northeast										
Boston, Mass.	11925	11208	2966	2653	313	4785	3434	2893	3726	1351
Buffalo, N.Y.	10744	10098	2958	2661	297	3667	2393	2089	2557	1274
New York–Northeastern N.J.	11623	10924	3284	2831	453	4620	3245	2569	3609	1375
Philadelphia, Pa.–N.J.	10646	10006	3223	2744	479	3710	2477	2177	2638	1233
Pittsburgh, Pa.	10503	9871	3018	2667	351	3396	2160	1854	2324	1236
Nonmetropolitan areas	10318	9697	2940	2630	310	3462	2569	2226	2753	893
North Central:										
Chicago, Ill.–Northwestern Ind.	10070	9464	2853	2569	284	3270	2063	2224	1976	1207
Cincinnati, Ohio–Ky.–Ind.	10038	9434	2942	2649	293	3108	1950	1733	2067	1158
Cleveland, Ohio	10500	9868	2908	2538	370	3458	2316	2207	2375	1142
Detroit, Mich.	10395	9770	2908	2602	306	3525	2338	2229	2396	1187
Kansas City, Mo.–Kans.	9978	9378	2826	2532	294	3024	1782	1721	1815	1242
Milwaukee, Wis.	10673	10031	2804	2448	356	3699	2451	2222	2574	1248
Minneapolis–St. Paul, Minn.	10121	9512	2760	2433	327	3351	2071	2378	1905	1280

(continued)

Table 2-4 (continued)

Area	Total budget	Total consumption	Family consumption									
			Food				Housing				
			Total	Food at Home	Food away from Home	Total	Total	Shelter		Home-owner costs	House furnishings & operations
								Total	Renter costs		

Area	Total budget	Total consumption	Food Total	Food at Home	Food away from Home	Total	Housing Total	Shelter Total	Renter costs	Homeowner costs	House furnishings & operations
North Central (continued):											
St. Louis, Mo.–Ill.	$10108	$9500	$3018	$2698	$320	$3118	$1822	$1796	$1836	$1296
Nonmetropolitan areas	9298	8739	2759	2502	257	2801	1898	1877	1910	903
South:											
Atlanta, Ga.	9516	8944	2801	2454	347	2669	1444	1709	1301	1225
Baltimore, Md.	10051	9446	2724	2388	336	3368	1894	2172	1744	1474
Dallas, Tex.	9768	9180	2726	2381	345	3033	1901	2100	1794	1132
Houston, Tex.	9996	9395	2877	2488	389	3055	1851	1758	1901	1204
Washington, D.C.–Md.–Va.	11000	10338	2977	2665	312	3769	2414	2513	2361	1355
Nonmetropolitan areas	8801	8272	2767	2495	272	2440	1466	1276	1568	974
West:											
Denver, Colo.	10028	9425	2716	2404	312	3197	1811	1846	1792	1386
Los Angeles–Long Beach, Calif.	10238	9622	2824	2458	366	3243	1995	2783	1570	1248
San Diego, Calif.	9827	9236	2746	2334	412	3008	1903	2380	1646	1105
San Francisco–Oakland, Calif.	10921	10264	2904	2578	326	3604	2159	2816	1805	1445
Seattle-Everett, Wash.	11343	10661	2939	2563	376	4077	2621	3033	2399	1456
Honolulu, Hawaii	12157	11426	3890	3531	359	3827	2356	3293	1851	1471
Nonmetropolitan areas	9529	8956	2791	2512	279	2835	1886	1908	1874	949
Anchorage, Alaska	12900	12124	3343	2970	373	4661	3035	3981	2525	1626

(continued)

Table 2-4 (continued)

Area	Family consumption					Other items
	Transportation	Clothing	Personal care	Medical care	Other family consumption	
Urban United States	$1073	$409	$290	$1091	$457	$615
Metropolitan areas	1089	416	283	1097	491	636
Nonmetropolitan areas	1027	389	310	1074	355	553
Northeast:						
Boston, Mass.	1148	451	267	1056	535	717
Buffalo, N.Y.	1212	488	271	1017	485	646
New York–Northwestern Ind.	775	364	293	1084	504	699
Philadelphia, Pa.–N.J.	960	293	244	1091	485	640
Pittsburgh, Pa.	1238	397	258	1084	480	632
Nonmetropolitan areas	1136	435	305	1057	362	621
North Central:						
Chicago, Ill.–Northwestern Ind.	1037	382	261	1109	552	606
Cincinnati, Ohio-Ky.-Ind.	1061	495	247	1092	489	604
Cleveland, Ohio	1161	450	330	1051	510	632
Detroit, Mich.	1129	375	282	1070	481	625
Kansas City, Mo.–Kans.	1139	439	328	1126	496	600
Milwaukee, Wis.	1186	484	284	1083	491	642
Minneapolis–St. Paul, Minn.	1138	432	294	1036	501	609
St. Louis, Mo.–Ill.	1189	395	265	1062	453	608
Nonmetropolitan areas	991	446	329	1052	361	559

(continued)

Table 2-4 (continued)

Area	Family consumption					Other items
	Transportation	Clothing	Personal care	Medical care	Other family consumption	
South:						
Atlanta, Ga.	$1177	$456	$269	$1076	$496	$572
Baltimore, Md.	1146	395	282	1053	478	605
Dallas, Tex.	1184	373	272	1136	456	588
Houston, Tex.	1095	443	320	1158	447	601
Washington, D.C.-Md.-Va.	1168	430	349	1122	523	662
Nonmetropolitan areas	1027	320	288	1086	344	529
West:						
Denver, Colo.	1170	518	285	1066	473	603
Los Angeles-Long Beach, Calif.	1276	376	280	1191	432	616
San Diego, Calif.	1203	383	265	1156	475	591
San Francisco-Oakland, Calif.	1300	446	342	1175	493	657
Seattle-Everett, Wash.	1201	448	333	1135	528	682
Honolulu, Hawaii	1293	428	323	1120	545	731
Nonmetropolitan areas	1013	484	357	1100	376	573
Anchorage, Alaska	1330	531	513	1326	420	776

Housing Costs

If you are considering renting, the BLS budgets provide some clues to where rents are comparatively lowest. Look at the column showing "renter costs" in the intermediate budget for a retired couple (Table 2-4). You'll see that the budget shows nine metropolitan areas with rent costs below the national average. They are Atlanta (the cheapest), Kansas City, Cincinnati, Houston, St. Louis, Denver, Pittsburgh, Buffalo, and Dallas. In general, the South is the cheapest region for rents.

The highest rental places are the metro areas of Anchorage, Alaska, and Honolulu, Hawaii. In the continental United States, the highest-rent neighborhoods are in Seattle, Boston, San Francisco, Los Angeles, New York, and Washington, D.C.

When it comes to homeownership costs, the budget shows that the cheapest place is, again, Atlanta. Next come Los Angeles, San Diego, Baltimore, Denver, and Dallas. As indicated previously, the figures for the California cities are misleading for retirees moving into the state.

The highest-cost cities, according to the BLS, are Boston, New York, Philadelphia, and Kansas City.

In the table, homeownership costs include property taxes, insurance, water, trash disposal, heating fuel, electricity, and home repairs. A major cost is the property taxes, which vary widely. The nation's highest property taxes are in Massachusetts, where taxpayers rebelled in 1980 by voting a Proposition-13-type tax cut. The lowest property taxes are in Alabama and Louisiana. Just remember that areas with low taxes also may provide fewer services.

You should check the property-tax rates in the areas where you contemplate retiring. As a guide, Table 2-5 lists some per-capita property taxes for selected metropolitan areas. The per-capita tax shows the amount of taxes paid for each person living in an area, not actual tax payments. From the numbers, you can get an indication of comparative property-tax burdens.

Where are housing prices the highest and the lowest? Table 2-6 shows you the highest- and lowest-priced housing cities in the United States, as of 1983.

More on Taxes

Nobody likes to pay taxes, and one silver lining in growing older is that you often don't have to pay as many. Many states and cities offer tax breaks to older residents, and you should be on the lookout for

Table 2·5 Per-capita property taxes for selected SMSAs,* 1977–1978, 1978–1979, 1979–1980

	Per-capita property tax (in dollars)		
	1977–78	*1978–79*	*1979–80*
Alabama			
Birmingham	$ 88.12	$102.33	$116.38
Arizona			
Phoenix	276.98	299.67	284.58
California			
Anaheim–Santa Ana–Garden Grove	456.51	254.02	262.65
Los Angeles–Long Beach	508.35	250.98	232.37
Riverside–San Bernardino–Ontario	417.93	226.22	239.11
Sacramento	407.68	211.36	213.55
San Diego	376.24	210.86	211.86
San Francisco–Oakland	580.26	286.24	293.25
San Jose	502.92	255.97	268.88
Colorado			
Denver–Boulder	330.18	357.20	337.34
Connecticut			
Bridgeport	519.73	557.69	568.92
Hartford	453.19	461.47	487.67
New Haven	403.78	422.06	426.90
Delaware			
Wilmington, Del.–N.J.–Md.	194.10	217.66	219.31
District of Columbia			
Washington, D.C.–Md.–Va.	358.91	364.84	381.07
Florida			
Fort Lauderdale–Hollywood	253.36	280.78	234.72
Jacksonville	166.00	188.61	172.37
Miami	286.39	329.84	293.61
Orlando	210.36	240.12	201.33
Tampa–St. Petersburg	183.05	196.94	176.44
Georgia			
Atlanta	290.16	303.80	287.33
Hawaii			
Honolulu	168.17	188.13	190.07
Illinois			
Chicago	361.81	380.32	395.88
Indiana			
Gary–Hammond–East Chicago	330.54	293.91	352.98
Indianapolis	271.12	274.33	248.02
Kentucky			
Louisville, Ky.–Ind.	132.81	153.27	154.26
Louisiana			
New Orleans	100.67	105.87	121.73

(continued)

*Standard Metropolitan Statistical Areas

Table 2·5 (continued)

	Per-capita property tax (in dollars)		
	1977–78	*1978–79*	*1979–80*
Maryland			
Baltimore	$227.54	$222.67	$236.50
Massachusetts			
Boston	587.93	597.75	654.37
Springfield	420.37	419.77	412.48
Worcester	402.37	397.93	413.48
Michigan			
Detroit	387.86	408.66	457.85
Flint	290.17	329.87	357.85
Grand Rapids	260.79	293.09	316.58
Minnesota			
Minneapolis–St. Paul, Minn.–Wis.	358.64	376.71	375.67
Missouri			
Kansas City, Mo.–Kans	258.87	275.65	281.50
St. Louis, Mo.–Ill.	233.68	241.25	255.21
Nebraska			
Omaha, Nebr.–Iowa	328.37	355.96	362.75
New Jersey			
Jersey City	369.25	433.24	402.51
Newark	539.20	554.20	552.85
New Brunswick–Perth Amboy–Sayreville	475.08	503.47	513.15
New York			
Albany–Schenectady–Troy	341.91	357.34	373.11
Buffalo	361.23	367.86	408.94
Nassau–Suffolk	692.98	715.25	782.13
New York, N.Y.–N.J.	493.79	493.38	518.08
Rochester	401.21	398.97	408.07
Syracuse	361.87	386.77	399.17
North Carolina			
Charlotte–Gastonia	221.70	238.20	239.27
Greensboro–Winston Salem–High Point	174.64	202.71	208.32
Ohio			
Akron	236.92	267.26	305.85
Cincinnati, Ohio–Ky.–Ind.	228.81	226.12	301.37
Cleveland	322.53	318.39	376.97
Columbus	200.04	247.27	253.28
Dayton	230.61	243.67	256.41
Toledo, Ohio–Mich.	247.65	278.35	285.02
Youngstown–Warren	215.89	214.52	227.27
Oklahoma			
Oklahoma City	155.64	176.70	162.35
Tulsa	177.58	193.13	185.48

(continued)

Table 2·5 (continued)

	Per-capita property tax (in dollars)		
	1977-78	*1978-79*	*1979-80*
Oregon			
Portland, Ore.-Wash.	$373.71	$384.16	$382.86
Pennsylvania			
Allentown-Bethlehem-Easton, Pa.-N.J.	268.13	286.92	292.47
Northeast Pennsylvania	156.84	179.31	190.07
Philadelphia, Pa.-N.J.	294.61	298.95	310.07
Pittsburgh	246.77	262.55	283.69
Rhode Island			
Providence	359.13	390.69	408.60
Tennessee			
Memphis, Tenn.-Ark.-Miss.	194.10	209.68	211.12
Nashville-Davidson	175.96	188.17	178.74
Texas			
Dallas-Fort Worth	284.48	295.07	283.10
Houston	343.02	405.33	396.90
San Antonio	167.75	178.83	173.57
Utah			
Salt Lake City-Ogden	207.62	254.45	245.83
Virginia			
Norfolk-Virginia Beach-Portsmouth, Va.-N.C.	158.88	170.58	176.33
Richmond	239.46	260.88	403.31
Washington			
Seattle-Everett	239.57	239.44	199.13
Wisconsin			
Milwaukee	313.48	401.88	395.36

Source: U.S. Department of Commerce, Bureau of the Census, "Local Government and Finances in Selected Metropolitan Areas and Large Counties: 1978-79 and 1979-80, Table 3.

these benefits. By one estimate, more than half of all older people pay higher taxes than are required because they fail to claim exemptions and other tax privileges to which they are entitled.

One attraction of Florida besides the sun is the state's tax breaks for older people. Florida is one of the few states that doesn't have a state income tax, and it is about the only state that doesn't have a state inheritance tax. In addition, the state sales tax doesn't apply to apartment rents, utility bills, prescription drugs, and disability appliances. And homeowners over age 65 get a break on their property taxes.

"After one year's residence, the state of Florida gives a $5,000 homestead exemption, which is taken from the assessed valuation of

Table 2·6 Most and least expensive cities in the United States by housing cost for Quarter I 1973, Quarter I 1982, and Quarter I 1983

Most Expensive

	Quarter I 1973		Quarter I 1982*		Quarter I 1983	
1.	Honolulu, HI	$72,000	San Francisco, CA	$138,100	San Francisco, CA	$139,600
2.	Los Angeles, CA	53,600	Washington, D.C.	123,400	Los Angeles, CA	133,100
3.	Miami, FL	46,700	Los Angeles, CA	121,500	Washington, D.C.	120,700
4.	New York, NY	45,900	San Diego, CA	118,300	San Diego, CA	118,300
5.	Washington, D.C.	43,100	Dallas–Ft. Worth, TX	114,500	Honolulu, HI	116,000
6.	Milwaukee, WI	41,700	Phoenix, AR	108,900	New York, NY	108,600
7.	Kansas City, MO	40,500	New York, NY	101,200	Dallas–Ft. Worth, TX	105,100
8.	Boston, MA	39,700	Miami, FL	100,800	Denver, CO	104,900
9.	Louisville, KY	39,100	Houston, TX	98,700	Houston, TX	102,900
10.	San Francisco, CA	36,200	Tampa, FL	97,600	Seattle, WA	90,200

Least Expensive

	Quarter I 1973		Quarter I 1982*		Quarter I 1983	
1.	St. Louis, MO	$23,500	Louisville, KY	$ 57,500	Louisville, KY	$ 55,800
2.	Portland, OR	26,100	Rochester, NY	57,900	Greensboro, NC	56,700
3.	Baltimore, MD	27,100	Philadelphia, PA	62,900	Pittsburgh, PA	57,500
4.	Pittsburgh, PA	28,200	St. Louis, MO	65,900	Philadelphia, PA	64,400
5.	Rochester, NY	28,700	Boston, MA	67,300	Portland, OR	65,100
6.	Philadelphia, PA	30,600	Greensboro, NC	67,400	Columbus, OH	69,300
7.	Tampa, FL	30,700	Cleveland, OH	73,200	St. Louis, MO	72,900
8.	Denver, CO	31,100	Pittsburgh, PA	75,400	Cleveland, OH	73,200
9.	Cleveland, OH	31,200	Detroit, MI	80,600	Rochester, NY	73,800
10.	Seattle, WA	31,300	Minneapolis, MN	83,200	Kansas City, MO	74,300

*Data for Honolulu, HI for Quarter I 1982 was not available.

Note: Data for Quarter I 1973 was based on existing home prices only, while Quarter I 1982 and 1983 were based on a combination of both new and existing home prices.

Source: Federal Home Loan Bank Board; Compiled by NAHB Economics Division.

the property. After five years, we will be eligible for another $5,000 exemption," said Clarice Johnsen of Dunedin, Florida. Mrs. Johnsen and her husband Herbert moved from Nassau County, New York, and bought a condominium in Dunedin in 1975. "Our taxes for real estate average $280 a year, which is a big difference from over $1,100 in New York," she said.

Low Taxes in Texas

Low taxes are a major factor in the rapid growth rate of Texas. The Lone Star State has no state income tax, most of its cities have relatively low tax assessments, the cost of living runs about 12 percent below the national average, and unemployment usually stands substantially below the nationwide rate. Texas also has a special exemption for homeowners over age 65.

Different states offer different breaks for older people on different taxes. They include:

Income taxes. There still are a few states left that have no state income tax at all. In addition to Florida and Texas, they are Alaska, Nevada, South Dakota, Washington, and Wyoming. The states of Connecticut, New Hampshire, and Tennessee limit the taxation to such things as capital gains and dividends.

Also, many states that do have income taxes exempt parts of certain kinds of retirement income. Arkansas, for example, exempts the first $6,000 a year from government retirement annuities; New Jersey exempts up to $10,000 a year from private or public pension plans; Illinois doesn't tax income from qualified pension plans, Keogh plans, or IRAs.

Sales tax. Alaska, Delaware, Montana, New Hampshire, and Oregon don't have a general sales tax. Wyoming pays rebates on its sales tax to residents 65 or older. Many states offer special exemptions from their sales tax to benefit older people. North Carolina, for example, exempts prescription medicine, hearing aids, prescription eyeglasses, orthopedic appliances, and false teeth.

Property tax. Most states offer some kind of tax break for older homeowners. Usually they are one of two kinds. Like Florida and Texas, about 20 states have "homestead" exemptions, which simply exclude part of a home's value from taxation. At least 29 states and the District of Columbia have "circuit breakers," which give rebates or tax credits to hold property taxes below a certain percentage of income.

In Kentucky and a few other states, the homeowner exemption for older residents is adjusted for inflation. Kentucky revises its rate every two years in line with changes in the Consumer Price Index.

California lets homeowners 62 or older put off paying property taxes indefinitely. Actually, the state pays the tax for them and puts a lien on the property; interest is charged each year on the amount postponed. But the amount isn't payable until the home is sold or the owner dies, in which case that person's estate or heirs would pay. A similar tax deferral plan is available in Oregon. Several other states have variations of tax deferral plans. Check your locality.

Renter taxes. Some states also offer tax breaks to older renters. New Jersey's general tax credit of $65 a year is boosted an additional $100 for renters over age 65. In Illinois, a renter 65 or older may claim 30 percent of his or her annual rent as a deductible property tax.

In short, tax breaks for older residents are an important item to check in evaluating an area for retirement. Table 2·7 shows at a glance how each state ranks in terms of tax benefits for older people. But you'll need to check more closely—most states exempt some retirement income, but precisely which kinds of income are exempted are severely limited in some states. Property-tax concessions sometimes are limited to lower-income retirees.

For more complete details, get a copy of *Your Retirement State Tax Guide*. Revised annually, it is available at no charge from the American Association of Retired Persons, 215 Long Beach Blvd., Long Beach, CA 90801.

Peek Before You Plunge

"We shopped for the area to which we would retire from Ohio in 1973, having looked all over the country for 10 years during our summer and winter vacation periods. We wanted to be away from snow; we wanted to live where the seasons change, however."

So wrote Alice Lloyd Grant about their search for the perfect retirement home. They found it in a new subdivision on Lake Palestine in Bullard, Texas.

"We retired in 1973 and moved immediately, although we kept our house in Cincinnati as a hedge in case we didn't like Texas," Mrs. Grant said. "We are extremely happy in our housing situation. Our neighbors are nice, our setting is as beautiful as something in House & Garden, and we have plenty of space for living and entertaining. My husband enjoys riding his 10-horsepower tractor-mower so much that he not only keeps our yard nice, but happily mows the vacant lots across the street."

Before you decide to move somewhere away from your current home, you should do more than calculate the pros and cons on paper.

Table 2·7

	Income tax rate[a] (in percent)	Special treatment retiree income	Property tax concession	Rent concession	Medicine exempt from sales tax
Alabama	2–5	yes	yes	no	yes
Alaska	none	yes	yes	no	no
Arizona	2–8	yes	yes	yes	no
Arkansas	1–7	yes	yes	no	no
California	1–11	yes	yes	yes	yes
Colorado	2.5–8+	yes	yes	yes	yes
Connecticut	none[a]	—	yes	yes	yes
Delaware	1.4–13.5	yes	yes	no	no tax
District of Columbia	2–11	no	yes	yes	yes
Florida	none	—	yes	no	yes
Georgia	1–6	yes	yes	no	no
Hawaii	2.25–11	yes	yes	no	no
Idaho	2–7.5	yes	yes	no	yes
Illinois	2.5	yes	yes	yes	no
Indiana	1.9	yes	yes	no	yes
Iowa	0.5–13	yes	yes	yes	yes
Kansas	2–9	yes	yes	yes	yes
Kentucky	2–6	yes	yes	no	yes
Louisiana	2–6	yes	yes[b]	no	yes
Maine	1–9.2	yes	yes	yes	yes
Maryland	2–5	yes	yes	yes	yes
Massachusetts	5.375	yes	yes	no	yes
Michigan	5.1	yes	yes	no	no
Minnesota	1.6–16	yes	yes	yes	yes
Mississippi	3–4	yes	yes	no	no
Missouri	1.5–6	yes	yes	yes	no
Montana	2–11	yes	yes	yes	no tax
Nebraska	17% of federal tax	yes	yes	no	yes
Nevada	none	—	yes	yes	yes
New Hampshire	none[a]	no	yes	yes	no tax
New Jersey	2–2.5	yes	yes	yes	yes
New Mexico	0.5–6	yes	no	no	no
New York	2–14	yes	yes	no	yes
North Carolina	3–7	yes	yes	no	yes
North Dakota	1–7.5	yes	yes	yes	yes

(continued)

You need to get a firsthand look. One way is to do like the Grants did—look during vacation trips. Find out about the cost, availability, and location of housing, check shopping and cultural facilities, see if a city is growing too fast or is the right size for you, and just get a "feel" for the place to see whether you would be comfortable living there.

Table 2·7 (continued)

	Income tax rate[a] (in percent)	Special treatment retiree income	Property tax concession	Rent concession	Medicine exempt from sales tax
Ohio	0.5–3.5	yes	yes	no	yes
Oklahoma	0.5–6	yes	yes	no	yes
Oregon	4.2–10.8	yes	yes	yes	no tax
Pennsylvania	2.2	yes	yes	yes	yes
Rhode Island	21.9% of federal tax	no	yes	yes	yes
South Carolina	2–7	yes	yes	no	yes
South Dakota	none	—	yes	no	yes
Tennessee	none[a]	no	yes	no	yes
Texas	none	—	yes	no	yes
Utah	2.75–7.75	yes	yes	yes	no
Vermont	24% of federal tax	yes	yes	yes	no
Virginia	2.–5.75	yes	yes	no	no
Washington	none	—	yes	no	yes
West Virginia	2.1–9.6	yes	yes	yes	yes
Wisconsin	3.4–10	yes	yes[b]	yes[b]	yes
Wyoming	none	—	no	no	yes

a. Taxes capital gains, dividends, or other income.
b. Applies to all ages.
Source: "Your Retirement State Tax Guide," American Association of Retired Persons.

Like the Grants, you might consider moving on a trial basis to a possible retirement area before selling everything back home. Some even suggest moving there a few years before you actually retire.

"I moved to this warmer, dry climate in Phoenix, Arizona, from Wisconsin. I was looking for a place where I could work a few years prior to retirement," wrote Lilo Koehl of Phoenix. "This was done in order that I would be established, know the community and the people, also to give me time to leave should this not work out."

William Heinrich, a retiree in Lakeland, Florida, who hankers to move farther north, suggested another way to find out about a community:

"I send for information from various chambers of commerce and buy newspapers from towns I think I would like. I have learned quite a lot this way: how much things cost, rate of crime, history of the town, weather, rainfall, even who the politicians are. I wouldn't even consider moving to another town without first seeing a local paper and scanning the classified section."

Investigate before "taking the plunge," emphasized Bethune Gibson of West Sedona, Arizona. "A little intelligent reading would eliminate much of the problem; but for some reason, people who have managed their lives well up to the point of retiring seem to suddenly go bonkers and lose their senses entirely.

"They buy land in the middle of empty space, never asking where the water, power, and roads are coming from and when. This is a no-no.

"Questions to ask include: roads, access to shopping (food, gasoline, and so on), crime rate; taxes; water supply; medical services; climate—see yearly records of local weather bureau; vegetation—for hay fever victims this can be important; bugs, snakes, and the like, if these are important to you."

What to Evaluate

In evaluating a home to move to from your current home, here are some of the important points to check.

Where. No doubt about it—heading the list is where you'll be living. A Florida man agrees.

"First is location," wrote R. Earl Kipp, a retiree in Orlando, Florida. And he is right. "The home of older persons should be where they can walk to banks, shopping, post office, and medical services," Mr. Kipp added.

Medical facilities. A survey by *Multi-Housing News* showed that, unlike any other population group, persons in the 55 to 64 age bracket and older consider health-related concerns to be even more crucial than cost in choosing a residence.

"Access to shopping, hospitals, health and personal care, as well as mass transportation, becomes increasingly important as age takes its toll on elderly mobility," the survey said.

Check local health agencies for special services for older people. Public health departments in many communities will send nurses, therapists, and other medical personnel on house calls to treat older people who are ill.

Transportation. Related to location is the availability of public transportation to take you where you want to go—shopping, health-care facilties, church, the theater, wrestling matches, or wherever.

"One of the biggest problems older people have with housing is the lack of public transportation," wrote Ada Stanbro of Norwalk, Iowa.

Older people "are now independent, can come and go when and where they want, whenever they please! They look at new housing with longing—but would be a prisoner in their beautiful new apartments if they moved into them."

"Independence and walkability is so much greater than beautiful apartments," said Mrs. Stanbro, who is in her 80s. "Those homes built are all out too far to be handy to our town shopping. Can't use your new apartments or cottages because of distance."

Looking for Leisure? Check These Points

Leisure activities. Find out what's cooking in terms of sports, social activities, cultural programs, and educational facilities that appeal to your interests.

"Arnold and I retired to Santa Fe, New Mexico. We enjoy the hiking opportunities with the Sierra Club and the cultural life of Santa Fe," wrote Carolyn Keskulla. The Keskullas live in a "passive solar house on 6½ acres with a lovely view of the mountains."

Remember, your retirement years are active years, both physically and intellectually. In addition to the availability of golf courses and tennis courts, check the libraries, the museums, and the local colleges. Many colleges now offer special courses for older people. Or check local volunteer programs, such as the Foster Grandparents Program for volunteer work that will keep you active and vital.

Just don't let yourself be dazzled by the recreational facilities offered by some housing developments aimed at older people.

"It is my belief that recreational facilities, while nice, are emphasized disproportionately to the necessities that would make the residents more comfortable," said one Washington, D.C., woman. "The ads I see in newspapers emphasize tennis courts, party rooms, and other active pursuits. I believe many people would like benches under a tree so that they could meet their friends outside and chat."

Special benefits. Look for special services and price discounts for older residents. Things like free or cut-rate bus service, movies, dinners, and prescriptions. These benefits can save you money.

"We let the swimming pool go in order to get free bus service every day, since we have no car," said Betty White, in explaining one reason she chose a retirement community in Whiting, New Jersey.

Check the local office on aging to find out about benefits.

Crime. Unfortunately, crime must be a major concern of older people in seeking a retirement area. Check with the local police department to find out the local crime situation and which areas are safer than others. A major attraction of many retirement communities is that older people can find the security that they are looking for.

One reason that Belle M. Sicurella chose her retirement community in Cranbury, New Jersey, "was the personal safety factor, due to the security here. For instance, some of the women here, including me, have the courage to go to the movies at night, alone, without fear of being attacked or mugged. I would never have dared to do that where I lived previously."

Climate. Check the local weather bureau for information on average temperatures and humidity the year round. Just visiting a sunny spot for vacation isn't enough to get a true picture of what the climate may be for other parts of the year.

"The yearly climate records are important because most people have not lived in their prospective location for that long a period," counseled Bethune Gibson of West Sedona, Arizona. "Too many people who winter in Florida are in for a bad shock when they move there and find the horrors of summer are not to their liking."

Even in the Sunbelt, the sun doesn't shine everywhere all the time.

"We hope this will prevent someone from making the mistake we made five years ago when we retired" to Grove, Oklahoma, from California, wrote Mrs. H. W. Thomas. "We did not realize that as you grow older and activities are limited, the best morale builder is a walk in the warm sunshine."

Spring and fall are gorgeous in Grove, Mrs. Thomas said. "But July and August are too hot and humid to be outside," and "the winter is too cold for the older person to enjoy being outside. Five good months do not offset seven bad ones. Much as we hate the upheaval of moving, we are going to look for another area."

One way to check the climate in a city—and energy use—is to count the number of heating degree days and annual cooling hours. The heating degree days indicate how many hours in a year you will need heat for your home—the higher the number, the higher your heating needs. The annual cooling days indicate how often you might need air conditioning.

Consider, for example, Table 2-8. In this comparison, the best place—for energy-saving—is San Juan. You don't need heat at all, and air conditioning is required at about the same level as that in Fargo, North Dakota.

Table 2·8

City	Heating degree days	Annual cooling hours
Fairbanks, Alaska	14,290	190
Fargo, North Dakota	9,250	560
Phoenix, Arizona	1,680	2,010
Miami, Florida	200	3,250
San Juan, Puerto Rico	0	630

A table showing the heating degree days and annual cooling hours for cities across the United States is included at the end of this chapter. Look for Table 2·11.

Family and Friends

A vital factor in your decision to stay where you are or to retire elsewhere may be the nearness of family and friends. You should consider that if you move it might be difficult for your relatives and friends to visit you and for you to visit them.

"It's especially hard to make a whole new group of friends," said Leo E. Baldwin, housing coordinator for the American Association of Retired Persons. A resident of Sun City, Arizona, also noted that "people who have been wrapped up with their grandchildren back home seldom adjust well to remote retirement havens."

"The best place to retire," said Dr. Robert Butler, formerly of the National Institute on Aging, "is the neighborhood where you spent your life. When you move from your home, you tear apart the social fabric of your life. Friends, relatives, children, and good medical facilities are far more important than the blue skies and warm weather."

But there are other factors.

"Whether to stay or move is a very hard question for many. Who wants to say good-bye to old friends and a neighborhood which brought many pleasures?" said Whiting, New Jersey's Carl F. Hyder. "But as retirement approached, many of my friends moved away, and the neighborhood changed, in many ways for the worse." So Mr. Hyder picked his home in Crestwood Village on the basis of "visiting friends who had already moved into same."

And, in fact, many retirees move to be closer to their families.

"One of the various phenomena that occurs with aging is the hard-to-accept fact that your life-long friends and business associates are aging, too, moving closer to family or even dying off," wrote Dorothea M. Strang. "Visiting and dinner parties tend to become more tiring and burdensome.

"So after two years of utter boredom, we decided to move and chose Reston, Virginia—where our daughter and her family live—over Sun City, Florida," Mrs. Strang said. "Already the family-related activities involved with three young grandchildren are a welcome diversion along with occasional babysitting, birthdays, holidays, and so on."

Many older Americans, though, do live away from their relatives. We surveyed retirees who wrote us letters and found that 67 percent of the respondents did not have relatives living in the immediate area. More than four-fifths of the retirees had no trouble getting around to places they wanted to go, and 84 percent had no friend or relative to help them get there.

Some of these same retirees say they would have preferred to stay in their previous home areas if more retirement housing had been available.

"Why aren't contractors building more retirement communities in parts of the country other than the so-called Sunbelt? Many retirees would like to remain in their native cities or states, but are unable to do so because of the lack of such retirement communities close to families, lifelong friends, family doctors, churches, and shopping facilities," wrote Mr. and Mrs. Richard G. Hayn of Hemet, California.

"Why drain the Midwest and East of a good source of human resources and good revenue?" the Hayns said. "We're natives of Cleveland, Ohio, and feel those areas would be good marketplaces for contractors to build retirement homes, not just apartments, near a fair-sized city for our rapidly growing age group of the population."

New Friends—Younger or Older?

Will there be people compatible with your interests where you retire? Meeting and enjoying new friends can be an enjoyable part of retirement living. Different people have different ideas, though, about living mainly near other retirees and away from kids, or mixing with younger people.

"We think it is important to be in an area with a goodly number of retirees if you move away from your present neighborhood," said Helen and John Downie, who moved from Syracuse, New York, to Asheville, North Carolina. "We would miss our old friends very much if we hadn't found a wonderful church," they added.

Others prefer to live mainly amid younger people.

"It's better that you live in a mixed community where you can see, communicate, and be annoyed with youth. It all helps to keep the mind young," said Nola E. Walsh of Cottonwood, Arizona. "I'm 70 and for the past five years have avoided people my age like the plague!"

Many retirees enjoy the company of a mixture of people of all ages, but want to avoid being surrounded by others in a community-living arrangement.

"I want to have my own house where I can be by myself," said Minnie Coleman, a retiree who lives alone in a single-family house in Johnstown, Ohio. But, she added, "some companionship would be nice, too."

Our survey of homeowners of all ages shows that people in the middle ages of 45 to 54 start thinking they would like to retire in "adults only" areas. But the majority of those nearing retirement age and especially those past 65 say they prefer living in family developments.

Table 2·9 shows the results of our "preferences" survey.

Table 2·9 Preferences for living in various types of developments

Type of development	\multicolumn{7}{c	}{Age of head of household}
	Under 25	25–29	30–34	35–44	45–54	55–64	Over 65
Adults only (no one under 18)	0.0%	11.7%	20.8%	35.7%	46.7%	41.7%	16.7%
Pre-retired/ retired	0.0	4.2	0.0	7.1	10.0	33.3	33.3
Developments for families	100.0	84.1	79.2	57.2	43.3	25.0	50.0
Total	100.0%	100.0%	100.0%	100.0%	100.0%	100.0%	100.0%

Source: Authors' survey.

The Choice Is Yours

Finally, remember that more important than costs, climate, and recreation is that your retirement living will be best where you will be comfortable and content. And if you are a couple, there is an important point to remember:

"The first priority is that it has to be right for both. If it's good for him and not for her, it won't work," advised Carl Kneip of Livonia, Michigan. He and his wife, Bobbi, are testing the winter life of Florida in a condominium.

Pets, Too

And if there are some furry or feathered creatures who will be retiring with you, don't forget them in your plans. Pets are important to many older people, who should make sure animals will be welcomed in a new home in a retirement, rental, or condominium community.

"My husband and I would like to move to California. But we own an Airedale and a standard poodle," wrote Mrs. Otto G. Boegner of Hyde Park, Massachusetts. "The problem is that it seems to be impossible to get anything when you own dogs. What kind of person would just give dogs away? Why not provide dog lovers with the same options others have? Many older people are lonely, and pets are of a tremendous benefit for depressed, sickly, and lonely people."

To help you make sure that not only will the welcome mat be out for your pets but also for you in a prospective retirement settling place, Table 2·10 contains a checklist to help you in your search for the place where the living will be easiest for you.

Table 2·10 Checklist

Item	Very high	High	Moderate	Low	Very low	Available yes/no
Housing:						
Prices	___	___	___	___	___	___
Rents	___	___	___	___	___	___
Cost per square foot	___	___	___	___	___	___
Utilities:						
Heat	___	___	___	___	___	___
Air conditioning	___	___	___	___	___	___
Electric	___	___	___	___	___	___
Garbage	___	___	___	___	___	___
Water	___	___	___	___	___	___
Food:						
In house	___	___	___	___	___	___
Restaurants	___	___	___	___	___	___
Transportation:						
Gasoline	___	___	___	___	___	___
Car repairs	___	___	___	___	___	___
Bus service	___	___	___	___	___	___
Other public transportation	___	___	___	___	___	___
Medical:						
Private	___	___	___	___	___	___
Public	___	___	___	___	___	___
Services	___	___	___	___	___	___
Taxes:						
Sales	___	___	___	___	___	___
Property	___	___	___	___	___	___
Condo costs:						
Condo fees	___	___	___	___	___	___
Maintenance fees:						
Exterior	___	___	___	___	___	___
Roof	___	___	___	___	___	___
Gutters	___	___	___	___	___	___
Paint	___	___	___	___	___	___
Walls	___	___	___	___	___	___
Elevators	___	___	___	___	___	___
Walks	___	___	___	___	___	___
Water system	___	___	___	___	___	___
Outside improvements	___	___	___	___	___	___
Common areas inside:						
Appliances	___	___	___	___	___	___
Light	___	___	___	___	___	___
Climate:						
Cold (number of seasons with snow)	___	___	___	___	___	___
Tropical	___	___	___	___	___	___
Subtropical	___	___	___	___	___	___
Moderate	___	___	___	___	___	___
Pets allowed	___	___	___	___	___	___

(continued)

Table 2·10 (continued)

	High	Moderate	Low
Degrees:			
Mean temperature:			
Summer	___	___	___
Winter	___	___	___
Heating degree days	___	___	___
Cooling annual hours	___	___	___
Sunshine-days	___	___	___
Rainfall	___	___	___
Humidity	___	___	___
Wind (breeze)	___	___	___
Dust	___	___	___
Tornado	___	___	___
Hurricanes	___	___	___
Pollen	___	___	___
Air quality	___	___	___
Air visibility	___	___	___

	On premises	Nearby	Not available
Recreational:			
Tennis	___	___	___
Golf	___	___	___
Swimming	___	___	___
Shuffleboard	___	___	___
Bicycling (paths)	___	___	___
Walking	___	___	___
Jacuzzi	___	___	___
Athletic studio	___	___	___
Others	___	___	___
Clubs–hobbies:			
Literary	___	___	___
Ceramics	___	___	___
Photo	___	___	___
Reading (library)	___	___	___
Music	___	___	___
Lecture	___	___	___
Luncheons	___	___	___
Dancing	___	___	___
Entertainment	___	___	___
Other clubs	___	___	___

	Very high	High	Moderate	Low	Very low
Crowding:					
Population growth	___	___	___	___	___
Densities	___	___	___	___	___
Transportation	___	___	___	___	___
Immigration	___	___	___	___	___
Prospect for growth, 10 years	___	___	___	___	___

(continued)

Table 2·10 (continued)

	On premises	Close by	Far away	Not available
Theaters and entertainment:				
Movies	___	___	___	___
Live entertainment	___	___	___	___
Opera	___	___	___	___
Popular music	___	___	___	___
Symphony	___	___	___	___
Others	___	___	___	___
Sports:				
Races	___	___	___	___
Sea-swimming	___	___	___	___
Lakes	___	___	___	___
Boating	___	___	___	___
Football (local club)	___	___	___	___
Golf	___	___	___	___
Others	___	___	___	___
Restaurants				
How far?	___	___	___	___
Cost?	___	___	___	___
Quality?	___	___	___	___
Kind of food and restaurants	___	___	___	___
Shops:				
Food (grocery)	___	___	___	___
Delicatessen	___	___	___	___
Wine-liquor	___	___	___	___
Department stores	___	___	___	___
Beauty shops	___	___	___	___
Barber	___	___	___	___
Service stations	___	___	___	___
Dressmaking	___	___	___	___
Drycleaning	___	___	___	___
Bank (savings and loan)	___	___	___	___
Others	___	___	___	___

	Excellent	High	Moderate	Low	Not good
Rents:					
Comparative cost	___	___	___	___	___
Lease how long?	___	___	___	___	___
Danger of conversions	___	___	___	___	___
Utilities included in cost?	___	___	___	___	___
How frequently raise rents?	___	___	___	___	___
Private or government, semi-government?	___	___	___	___	___
Type?					
Low-rise	___	___	___	___	___
High-rise	___	___	___	___	___
Single	___	___	___	___	___
Double	___	___	___	___	___

(continued)

Table 2·10 (continued)

	Excellent	High	Moderate	Low	Not good
Rents: *(continued)*					
What is in rental complex:					
Mixture of population	___	___	___	___	___
Age limit	___	___	___	___	___
Laundry—common or separate	___	___	___	___	___
Services	___	___	___	___	___
Pets allowed	___	___	___	___	___

	Excellent	Good	Not good
Transportation:			
Own a car	___	___	___
Garage—one or two	___	___	___
Garage—covered	___	___	___
Parking only	___	___	___
Good access to unit	___	___	___
Close enough for unloading	___	___	___
Public:			
Cost	___	___	___
Availability	___	___	___
Kind	___	___	___
How far	___	___	___
How reliable	___	___	___

	On premises	Close by	Far away	Not available
Hospital and medical services:				
On premises—kind	___	___	___	___
Clinic	___	___	___	___
House visits	___	___	___	___
Cost	___	___	___	___
Hospitals:				
How far	___	___	___	___
What cost	___	___	___	___
Reputation	___	___	___	___
Ophthalmologist	___	___	___	___
Nursing service	___	___	___	___
Maid service	___	___	___	___
Special shoe store	___	___	___	___
Vet	___	___	___	___

(continued)

Table 2·10 (continued)

	Excellent	*Good*	*Not good*
Employment opportunities:			
Part-time	——	——	——
Full-time	——	——	——
Kind:			
Clerical	——	——	——
Managerial	——	——	——
Manual	——	——	——
Governmental	——	——	——
Others	——	——	——
Type of industry jobs available:			
Public	——	——	——
Business	——	——	——
Industry	——	——	——
Utilities	——	——	——
Pay scale	——	——	——
How far?	——	——	——
Work hours	——	——	——
How to get there?	——	——	——
Friends and relatives:			
How far?	——	——	——
Can you bring them in (sleep, visit)	——	——	——
Cost of visit	——	——	——
Cost of you visiting them	——	——	——
Miles	——	——	——
Emergency visits and costs	——	——	——
Pets	——	——	——

Table 2·11 Degree days and cooling hours for cities (If your city is not listed here, consult your local weather service or select the nearest city with similar climatic conditions.)

Location	Heating degree days	Annual cooling hours
Alabama		
Birmingham	2,710	1,430
Huntsville	3,190	1,290
Mobile	1,620	1,690
Montgomery	2,250	1,610
Alaska		
Anchorage	10,860	40
Fairbanks	14,290	190
Arizona		
Flagstaff	7,290	540
Phoenix	1,680	2,010
Tucson	1,700	1,790
Arkansas		
Fayetteville	3,840	1,320
Little Rock	3,170	1,440
Pine Bluff	2,590	1,490
California		
Bakersfield	2,150	1,420
Fresno	2,610	1,180
Los Angeles	1,960	530
Redding	4,000	800
Sacramento	2,700	850
Santa Ana	1,670	660
San Bernardino	1,890	1,450
San Diego	1,500	620
San Francisco	3,040	180
San Jose	2,410	400
Stockton	2,760	960
Colorado		
Boulder	5,540	700
Colorado Springs	6,410	660
Denver	6,150	750
Grand Junction	5,660	970
Connecticut		
Hartford	6,170	630
New Haven	5,890	780
New London	5,920	690
Stamford	5,460	690
Waterbury	5,930	640
Delaware		
Wilmington	4,930	860
District of Columbia	4,240	1,808

(continued)

Table 2·11 (continued)

Location	Heating degree days	Annual cooling hours
Florida		
Fort Myers	430	3,180
Gainesville	730	2,120
Jacksonville	1,230	2,040
Lakeland	660	2,370
Miami	200	3,250
Orlando	720	2,340
Tallahassee	1,520	1,720
Tampa	700	2,420
West Palm Beach	270	2,940
Georgia		
Atlanta	2,990	1,320
Augusta	2,400	1,480
Columbus	2,380	1,540
Savannah	1,820	1,600
Valdosta	1,520	1,760
Hawaii		
Hilo	0	2,850
Honolulu	0	3,950
Idaho		
Boise	5,830	680
Coeur D'Alene	6,660	480
Idaho Falls	7,890	480
Pocatello	7,030	640
Illinois		
Carbondale	4,080	1,210
Evanston	6,640	700
Peoria	6,070	820
Rockford	6,840	690
Springfield	5,530	1,010
South suburban Chicago	6,160	790
Indiana		
Fort Wayne	6,220	780
Indianapolis	5,630	870
South Bend	6,460	720
Terre Haute	5,360	930
Iowa		
Cedar Rapids	6,600	750
Davenport	6,090	820
Des Moines	6,610	810
Fort Dodge	7,070	740
Mason City	7,790	660
Sioux City	6,960	800
Kansas		
Salina	4,980	1,010
Topeka	5,210	1,030
Wichita	4,640	1,090

(continued)

Table 2·11 (continued)

Location	Heating degree days	Annual cooling hours
Kentucky		
Lexington	4,760	1,000
Louisville	4,610	1,150
Owensboro	4,200	1,130
Paducah	3,650	1,250
Louisiana		
Baton Rouge	1,610	1,900
Shreveport	2,160	1,640
New Orleans	1,400	2,090
Maine		
Bangor	8,220	360
Portland	7,570	390
Maryland		
Baltimore	4,680	970
Cumberland	5,070	730
Frederick	5,030	990
Salisbury	4,220	970
Massachusetts		
Boston	5,630	660
Hyannis	5,400	490
Pittsfield	7,580	570
Springfield	5,840	650
Worcester	6,970	540
Michigan		
Detroit	6,290	710
Flint	7,200	580
Grand Rapids	6,890	640
Kalamazoo	6,660	680
Lansing	6,940	610
Traverse City	7,700	530
Minnesota		
Duluth	9,890	310
Minneapolis	8,250	640
Mississippi		
Greenville	2,580	1,600
Jackson	2,260	1,620
Meridian	2,340	1,610
Vicksburg	2,040	1,700
Missouri		
Jefferson City	4,620	1,020
Kansas City	4,750	1,180
Saint Joseph	5,440	1,080
Saint Louis	4,880	1,140

(continued)

Table 2·11 (continued)

Location	Heating degree days	Annual cooling hours
Montana		
Billings	7,150	580
Butte	9,730	530
Helena	8,180	500
Missoula	8,000	440
Nebraska		
Grand Island	6,440	820
Lincoln	6,050	820
North Platte	6,680	750
Omaha	6,290	860
Nevada		
Las Vegas	2,610	1,760
Reno	6,150	700
New Hampshire		
Concord	7,380	610
Manchester	7,100	610
New Jersey		
Atlantic City	4,850	830
New Brunswick	5,400	820
Newark	4,900	840
Paterson	5,360	790
Summit	5,010	790
Trenton	4,980	770
New Mexico		
Albuquerque	4,350	1,120
Santa Fe	6,120	720
New York		
Albany	6,900	600
Binghampton	7,340	460
Buffalo	6,960	610
Elmira	6,410	530
Hicksville	5,550	770
New York	4,900	850
Plattsburgh	7,900	500
Poughkeepsie	5,820	720
Riverhead	5,620	770
Rochester	6,760	590
Schenectady	6,780	600
Syracuse	6,720	630
Utica	7,200	620
White Plains	5,800	660
North Carolina		
Asheville	4,130	1,050
Charlotte	3,200	1,250
Fayetteville	3,080	1,280
Florence	2,480	1,450
Greensboro	3,810	1,090
Raleigh	3,440	1,180

(continued)

Table 2·11 (continued)

Location	Heating degree days	Annual cooling hours
North Dakota		
Bismarck	8,960	550
Fargo	9,250	560
Grand Forks	9,930	500
Ohio		
Akron	6,140	670
Bowling Green	4,280	1,060
Cincinnati	4,830	970
Cleveland	6,200	740
Columbus	5,670	890
Dayton	5,620	940
Springfield	5,280	920
Toledo	6,430	690
Youngstown	6,370	630
Oklahoma		
Oklahoma City	3,700	1,240
Tulsa	3,730	1,310
Oregon		
Pendleton	5,190	620
Portland	4,700	340
Pennsylvania		
Allentown	5,820	740
Erie	6,540	680
Greensburg	5,800	710
Harrisburg	5,280	800
Philadelphia	4,980	920
Pittsburgh	5,950	720
Scranton	6,160	630
York	5,450	800
Puerto Rico		
San Juan	0	630
Rhode Island		
Providence	5,950	600
South Carolina		
Charleston	2,070	1,530
Columbia	2,520	1,460
Spartanburg	3,070	1,230
South Dakota		
Rapid City	7,370	660
Sioux Falls	7,840	730
Tennessee		
Chattanooga	3,380	1,220
Knoxville	3,510	1,210
Memphis	3,210	1,430
Nashville	3,610	1,210

(continued)

Table 2·11 (continued)

Location	Heating degree days	Annual cooling hours
Texas		
Amarillo	4,140	1,130
Austin	1,720	1,860
Corpus Christi	930	2,530
Dallas	2,320	1,820
El Paso	2,680	1,620
Fort Worth	2,390	1,700
Houston	1,410	2,060
Lubbock	3,570	1,270
McAllen	600	2,810
San Antonio	1,560	1,980
Texarkana	2,530	1,520
Wichita Falls	2,900	1,570
Waco	2,040	1,780
Utah		
Ogden	5,850	760
Salt Lake City	5,990	820
Vermont		
Burlington	8,030	520
Rutland	7,440	580
Virginia		
Fredericksburg	4,240	1,090
Norfolk	3,440	1,150
Richmond	3,910	1,090
Roanoke	4,150	990
Washington		
Seattle	5,190	200
Spokane	6,770	490
Yakima	5,950	580
West Virginia		
Charleston	4,510	1,010
Huntington	4,340	960
Morgantown	5,100	680
Wisconsin		
Eau Claire	7,970	510
Green Bay	8,100	470
La Crosse	7,530	610
Madison	7,720	640
Milwaukee	7,470	570
Wyoming		
Casper	7,510	640
Cheyenne	7,370	510

Source: National Association of Home Builders, *Thermal Performance Guidelines: One and Two Family Dwellings*, pp. 20–22.

Cashing In Your Housing Assets

You can't eat equity.
Stephen R. McConnell
Andrus Gerontology Center,
University of Southern California

Your biggest retirement asset is probably your home. That is if you are among the 65 percent of Americans who own their homes—or the more than 75 percent of older people who are homeowners.

"So I own a big house. What can I do with it?" asked a Seattle woman.

Plenty. Maybe you can't "eat equity," but you can eat well and live well by taking advantage of the increased equity in your home. Equity is the difference between what you owe on your mortgage and what you could sell your home for. The homes of many older people have doubled, tripled, or jumped even more in value over the years. And the mortgage is often paid off, or nearly paid off.

You then have two options: You can stay where you are, or you can move. If you just sit on your assets, the increased value of your home remains untapped. You may be sitting on a golden nest egg that can be used for your retirement needs or invested to produce more retirement income. Increasingly, there are ways you can tap these resources even if you stay. And there are powerful new incentives to cash in your equity gains by selling out and moving to a smaller and less-expensive home.

Here are some ways you can cash in on your housing assets.

The Great $125,000 Tax Break

Having reached retirement age, Charlotte and Robert Jones decide to sell their four-bedroom home in a Los Angeles suburb and move to a smaller home. Until 1978, they would have had to pay a big federal tax on their profit because their home had greatly increased in value since they bought it in 1950 for only $20,000.

But thanks to the Tax Acts of 1978 and 1981, their profit is tax free. The law allows a one-time exemption from taxation for up to a $125,000 gain on the sale of a primary residence by homeowners 55 years or older. The Joneses sell their home for $185,000. They use part of their $165,000 profit to buy a condominium for $60,000, and they invest the remaining $105,000.

Table 3·1 shows how it works.

Table 3·1

Sale price of old home	$185,000
Tax basis (original cost)	20,000
Gain	165,000
Price of new home	60,000
Taxable gain under old law (sale price of old home minus price of new home)	125,000
Exclusion	125,000
Taxable gain	0

Of the Joneses' actual economic gain of $165,000, permanently exempt from taxation is $125,000, and $40,000 is deferred because it is being reinvested in another home within 24 months. If they were not to purchase another home within 24 months, the extra $40,000 profit would be subject to a capital gains tax.

Selling and Renting

Instead of sinking your profit into another home when you sell, you could rent and keep all of your gain up to $125,000.

Table 3·2 shows how the $125,000 tax break looks for someone who doesn't purchase another home.

Table 3·2

Sale price of old home	$120,000
Tax basis (cost)	50,000
Gain	70,000
Exclusion	70,000
Taxable gain	0

The Rules in a Nutshell

The $125,000 tax break is the answer to the often-asked question, "What good does the inflated value of my house do me, since I just have to put it in another house if I sell?" When you reach age 55, you can buy a smaller or less expensive home, or rent, and take the rest of your money and run.

Here are the basic rules:

1. You or your spouse must be 55 years old or older. The tax break applies even if only one spouse is 55 or more and the other is younger.

2. Taxes are exempt on up to a $125,000 gain from the sale of your home—or from the cumulative gains of homes you have sold over your lifetime.

3. The home must be your principal residence—vacation homes and investment properties don't qualify. And you must have lived in the home for three of the five years preceding the sale. The three years don't have to be consecutive, though. You must be able to show you have lived in your home for at least 36 months out of 60. That is, you must own it and use it for a full 1,095 days (365 days a year × 3).

4. You and your spouse are considered as one and can use the exemption only once in your lifetimes—neither of you can ever use the tax exemption again, even if you subsequently are divorced or one spouse dies.

5. Individual owners of a home who aren't husband and wife can each take exemptions on their own gains.

6. You must claim the exemption; it isn't automatic. To do so, use IRS form 2119, "Sale or Exchange of Personal Residence," which is shown in Figure 3·1.

Figure 3-1

Form **2119**	Sale or Exchange of Principal Residence	OMB No. 1545-0072
Department of the Treasury Internal Revenue Service (O)	► See instructions on back. ► Attach to Form 1040 for year of sale (see Instruction C).	**1982** 24

Do not include expenses that you deduct as moving expenses.

Name(s) as shown on Form 1040: **Tom and Joan White**
Your social security number: **444 44 4444**

1. (a) Date former residence sold ► **9-12-83**   Yes / No
   (b) Enter the face amount of any mortgage, note (for example second trust), or other financial instrument on which you will receive periodic payments of principal or interest from this sale ►
   (c) Have you ever postponed any gain on the sale or exchange of a principal residence? . . . . **No ✓**
   (d) If you were on active duty in the U.S. Armed Forces or outside the U.S. after the date of sale of former residence, enter dates. From _____ to _____
2. (a) If you bought or built a new residence, enter date you occupied it; Otherwise enter "none". ►
   (b) Did you use both the old and new properties as your principal residence? . . . . **Yes ✓**
   (c) Are any rooms in either residence rented out or used for business for which a deduction is allowed? . . . . **No ✓**
   (If "Yes" do not include gain in line 7 from the rented or business part; instead include in income on Form 4797.)

Part I   Gain and Adjusted Sales Price

3. Selling price of residence. (Do not include selling price of personal property items.) **3**   130,000 00
4. Commissions and other expenses of sale not deducted as moving expenses **4**   10,000 00
5. Amount realized (subtract line 4 from line 3) **5**   120,000 00
6. Basis of residence sold **6**   50,000 00
7. Gain on sale (subtract line 6 from line 5). (If line 6 is more than line 5, enter zero and do not complete the rest of form.) If you bought another principal residence during the replacement period or if you elect the one time exclusion in Part III, continue with this form. Otherwise, enter the gain on Schedule D (Form 1040), line 2a or 9a* **7**   70,000 00
   If you haven't replaced your residence, do you plan to do so within the replacement period? ☐ Yes ☐ No
   (If "Yes" see instruction C.)
8. Fixing-up expenses (see instructions for time limits.) . . . . **8**   -0-
9. Adjusted sales price (subtract line 8 from line 5) **9**   120,000 00

Part II   Gain to be Postponed and Adjusted Basis of New Residence

10. Cost of new residence **10**
11. Gain taxable this year (Subtract line 10 from line 9. Do not enter more than line 7.) If line 10 is more than line 9, enter zero. Enter any taxable gain on Schedule D (Form 1040), line 2a or 9a. *If you were 55 or over on the date of sale, see Part III **11**
12. Gain to be postponed (subtract line 11 from line 7) **12**
13. Adjusted basis of new residence (subtract line 12 from line 10) **13**

Part III   55 or over Exclusion, Gain to be Reported, and Adjusted Basis of New Residence

14. (a) Were you 55 or over on date of sale? . . . . **Yes ✓**
    (b) Was your spouse 55 or over on date of sale? . . . . **Yes ✓**
    (If you answered "No" to 14(a) and 14(b), do not complete the rest of form.)
    (c) If you answered "Yes" to 14(a) or 14(b) did you or your spouse own and use the property sold as your principal residence for a total of at least 3 years (except for short temporary absences) of the 5-year period before the sale? . . . . **Yes ✓**
    (d) If you answered "Yes" to 14(c), do you elect to take the once in a lifetime exclusion of the gain on the sale? . . **Yes ✓**
    (If "Yes," complete the rest of Part III. If "No," return to Part II, line 12.)
    (e) At time of sale, was the residence owned by: ☐ you,   ☐ your spouse,   ☒ both of you?
    (f) Social security number of spouse, at time of sale, if different from number on Form 1040 ►
    (Enter "none" if you were not married at time of sale.)
15. Enter the smaller of line 7 or $125,000 ($62,500, if married filing separate return) **15**   70,000 00
16. Part of gain included (subtract line 15 from line 7) . . . . **16**   -0-
17. Cost of new residence. If you did not buy a new principal residence, enter "None." Then enter the gain from line 16 on Schedule D (Form 1040), line 9a,* and do not complete the rest of Form 2119 . . . **17**   None
18. Gain taxable this year. (Subtract the sum of lines 15 and 17 from line 9. The result cannot be more than line 16.) If line 17 plus line 15 is more than line 9, enter zero. Enter any taxable gain on Schedule D (Form 1040), line 9a* **18**
19. Gain to be postponed (subtract line 18 from line 16) **19**
20. Adjusted basis of new residence (subtract line 19 from line 17) **20**

*Caution: If you completed Form 6252 for the residence in 1(a), do not enter your taxable gain from Form 2119 on Schedule D.

For Paperwork Reduction Act Notice, see back of form.   Form **2119** (1982)

Tax-break Tactics

The rules can be used to your advantage by doing some planning. Here are some points to consider:

Don't think it's too late. If you are past 55 and you sold your home in recent years without taking the $125,000 exemption, it may not be too late. The IRS allows you to claim the exemption within three years after filing your return for the year the sale occurred, or within two years of the time the tax for that year was paid, whichever is later.

Plan ahead. As part of your housing plan, make sure you stay put in a home you own for three of the five years before you sell the home after reaching age 55.

Wait until your birthday. Don't sell until you actually reach your 55th birthday. To qualify, the property must change hands on or after the day you turn 55.

Don't use the exclusion hastily. Remember, you can use this big tax break only once in your lifetime. So don't waste it on a relatively small home-sale profit. You may need the tax break later. And remember if you sell your home and buy another, you can postpone all or part of your gain anyway.

If you decide that you made a mistake in taking the exemption, you may have time to change your mind. You can revoke your decision within the same time periods set for changing your tax return to claim the exemption.

Beware of the "tainted" spouse. If you marry, before saying "I do," ask "Did you ever?"—Did you ever sell a home using the $125,000 tax break? Divorced people—widows and widowers—who, with their previous spouses, jointly used the exemption, are "tainted" for life in the eyes of the IRS. They can't use the exemption again, and as long as you are married to that person, you, too, will lose the right to the tax break even though you have never claimed the exemption.

One alternative, from a strictly financial viewpoint, is to live in "sin"—it could save you a bundle of taxes someday. But there is another possible strategy: If the nontainted partner is over 55 and has never used the exemption, he or she can sell their current home before the wedding bells ring and take advantage of the $125,000 tax break.

Double your financial pleasure. Single people over age 55 who plan to marry and who have never taken the $125,000 exemption can each sell their own homes and each can claim the exclusion before they tie the knot. That way, the newlyweds can give themselves a wedding present of a total $250,000 tax break.

Split now, sell later. If you get divorced after age 55, wait until the divorce papers are final before selling your jointly owned home. You may increase your tax benefits. For purposes of the $125,000 exemption, "you determine your marital status as of the date of sale or exchange of your home," said the IRS, which added with undeniable logic: "If you are divorced by the date of the sale or exchange, you are not considered married."

Capital Gains

But what if you don't qualify for the $125,000 tax break or don't want to use the one-time exemption right now? There are other ways to save on taxes and get most of your assets out of your old home when you sell.

One is simply to wait until you retire to sell. In the first full year after retirement, your income probably will drop and put you in a lower tax bracket. Then the gain from the sale of your home will be taxed at a lower rate than if you sold while earning your preretirement income.

What will help, too, is that when you sell a home owned for more than one year, the gain is considered a capital gain rather than ordinary income. That means the tax is lower. The capital gains rate is 40 percent of the gain, and the top tax rate on capital gains is 20 percent.

Here's an example of how the capital gains tax works. You sell for $100,000 the home you bought years ago for $25,000. Your gain on the sale is $75,000. The capital gains rate is 40 percent, meaning that you pay taxes on 40 percent of $75,000 or $30,000. And, as mentioned, if you are retired the tax bite will be less because you will be in a lower bracket.

You can reduce the taxation more if you reinvest part of your gain in another home. Table 3·3 shows the same example, but this time using part of your gain to buy a $50,000 home.

In this case, 40 percent of the $50,000 capital gain, or $20,000, is

Table 3·3

Sale price	$100,000
Tax basis (cost)	25,000
Gain	75,000
Price of new home	50,000
Taxable gain (sale price minus price of new home)	50,000
Postponed gain	25,000

taxed. Taxes on the remaining $25,000 are deferred. And, in this example, of course, if you bought a home costing $100,000 or more, all of the tax would be deferred.

Many people buy and sell more than one home during a lifetime. It is important to remember that in determining gains and taxes from selling a home, you must keep track of all of the homes you have owned over a lifetime, not just the one you are selling now.

And do be sure to consult your tax lawyer or accountant before selling your home.

You can obtain further information by ordering the following two free booklets from the IRS Forms Distribution Center in your state: "Tax Information for Homeowners" (Publication 530), and "Tax Benefits for Older Americans" (Publication 554).

Turning Equity into Income

There are other ways besides a traditional home sale to get the equity out of your old homestead. With an installment sale, you can turn your old home into a perpetual income machine.

Installment sale basically means that you act as the mortgage lender and your buyer pays for the house in monthly payments to you, including interest charges. This can be especially advantageous if you already own a retirement home or if you can buy one using the down payment and other funds that you have.

Another advantage is that during times when mortgage rates are high, financing is scarce and homes are hard to sell, you can provide a tempting "creative financing" package that will attract buyers.

While Edward and Suzette Blanke were searching fruitlessly for financing to buy a home during a time of scarce mortgage money, another family was trying fruitlessly to sell a four-bedroom home in Kirkwood, Missouri, an affluent St. Louis suburb.[1]

"We had a tremendous number of people look at our place, but they just couldn't come up with the financing," said Stuart Purvines, a retired executive, who, with his wife Norma, had already refurbished a retirement home. Asked by real estate people whether he would carry part of the financing, Mr. Purvines at first rejected the idea. "But later," he said, "it occurred to me: I'm going to reinvest the money anyway. Why not?"

An enterprising agent brought the two families together and meshed their individual needs in a typical example of creative financing.

The Purvines still had a $14,600 balance on their mortgage, which the Blankes assumed, or took over, at 5½ percent. The buyers made a $20,000 down payment patched together from several sources. The rest of the $64,200 purchase price came from a $29,600 second deed of trust on the house, at 12.8 percent (more about a second deed of trust later on this page and page 62).

Mr. Purvines, who could afford to grant the loan because he already had his retirement home, called the 12.8 percent "an adequate yield."

Installment Law Changes

Such installment sales were made easier by a new installment law passed by Congress in 1980. Previously, to qualify for installment tax treatment, the seller had to receive less than 30 percent of the price of the house in the year of the sale. In addition, there had to be at least two payments for a sale to qualify for deferred reporting, and the seller had to request the special tax treatment.

Now you can receive any percentage of the sale price in the year you sell your house. And a sale is eligible for installment reporting even if the purchase price is paid in a lump sum—if the payment occurs after the year of the sale (the interest you collect meantime is taxable, though). And the IRS automatically treats the sale as an installment sale unless the seller chooses otherwise.

There are various types of installment sales, which we'll discuss next, and if one or two of them seem good for your needs, be sure to discuss them with a reputable real estate broker, attorney, or CPA. Or all three.

Different Installment Methods

Take "back" a mortgage. This simply means that, instead of finding a lending institution to lend money to the people who buy your home, you become the lender. How?

If you own your home free and clear, you can grant the buyer a first mortgage loan, perhaps at an interest rate slightly below the going market rate. There is some risk if the seller doesn't keep up his or her payments, but if the purchaser defaults you can take your house back. The appreciation in value probably will more than cover any legal costs.

Second deed of trust. If you still have a mortgage on your home, you can do like Mr. Purvines of St. Louis—have the buyer assume your remaining mortgage and then take back a second mortgage.

This kind of combination is usually necessary on an older mortgage because the buyer would have to come up with a huge down payment to assume the first mortgage. And you should be aware that lenders frown on letting buyers take over an existing, low-interest mortgage. Some mortgages have what is called a "due on sale" clause calling for repayment of the entire loan if the house is sold, or requiring the new owner to pay an increased interest rate.

Under federal legislation passed in 1982, banks, savings and loan associations, and other lenders can enforce due-on-sale clauses despite state laws that permit assumptions without any increase in mortgage rates. The only exception is for loans by state-chartered institutions and national banks made in states that specifically allow assumptions, but only if the loans were originated between the date that the state restricted due-on-sale clauses and the date that the federal law was passed. Such loans will remain assumable for three years.

Many older mortgages don't have such restrictions, however, and FHA and VA loans are always assumable. As a result, assumptions plus second deeds are often feasible when the seller has owned his home for a long time. Before you get too far, find out what your mortgage agreement says, what your original lender thinks, and what the relevant laws are in your state.

Wrap-around mortgages. Many experts say that the best seller-financing arrangement is one that packages—or "wraps"—old and new financing together.

You may need some expert help to put together a wrap-around loan. Like straight assumptions, wrap-arounds may run into due-on-sale restrictions. But they are worth looking into if you plan an installment sale.

Take back and take a break. Take back a mortgage and use your $125,000 tax break, too. Sid Herlick is 63, and his wife is 61. They sell their home and take the $125,000 tax exemption. But instead of selling outright, they take back a $110,000 mortgage at 12 percent that gives them a steady additional income. They make sure the loan can be renegotiated after several years in case interest rates increase.

Lease-purchase option. This isn't exactly an installment-sales technique, but it can help you get the most out of your home if you try to sell during a slow selling period. A prospective buyer leases your home with an option to purchase, usually within 12 to 18 months. A purchase agreement is signed, with all terms of the sale outlined except the effective date and the selling price. (Or if you include a price, you should set the price at what you think the house will sell for when the option expires.) The buyer pays the seller "option money," which is usually applied to the down payment; part of the monthly rent also can go toward the down payment.

The buyer is able to move in with relatively little cash until he can obtain financing. You, the seller, are not stuck with an empty, unsold house. You get the option money immediately, and you retain the tax benefits of ownership until the lease option is exercised. Then, if you wish, you can offer the buyer, who has been able to build financially toward purchase, installment financing.

Renting Your Home

Instead of selling your home when you move, you might want to consider renting it instead.

The advantages of renting are that you generate permanent rental income and tax write-offs while maintaining ownership of the house, which likely will further increase in value. Thus, you can get income from the house now and, if you wish, sell it later when it will be worth even more. Renting can be especially important as part of your retirement planning.

If you include a cost-of-living adjustment in your rental contract, your rental income can keep up with inflation. If you decide to sell some day, you can profit from the increased appreciation of the house. The only complication then would be that the more depreciation you claim on your rental house to reduce taxes now, the more you'll have to pay the IRS piper when you sell.

Another complication is inherent in renting—you must look after and keep up the property. That can get more difficult as you get older, although you can hire management firms for a fee of 6 percent to 10 percent of the rental amount.

And, of course, to rent your old home you have to get another home without the cash that you would get from selling your home. Moreover, the importance of tax breaks from renting may depend on what tax bracket you are in.

Renting, Moving, Then Returning

Let's say you may want to return to the house where you live now, but for the next few years you decide to live elsewhere. Instead of selling your house, you can rent it. After all, you'll never be able to buy that house for less than you paid for it. And it can provide you rental income and tax deductions until you can return to it.

If you decide to sell after age 55, you can take advantage of the $125,000 tax break by using the house as your primary residence for three of the five years before you sell. Remember, though, that the depreciation you claim for the rental property will reduce the cost basis of your home—and expand the gain—when you sell.

Obviously, you should talk to a tax advisor before deciding whether to sell or to rent the house. But putting the house up for rent shouldn't be overlooked.

Owning Versus Renting after Retirement

Once you reach retirement age, one choice is to simply stay in the home that you already own. Your old home can provide a relatively low-cost roof over your head, especially if the mortgage is paid off. And about 72 percent of people over age 65 currently own their homes. That means your principal costs are upkeep and property taxes, which often can be reduced by using special tax breaks for older homeowners.

Even if you still have a mortgage, it likely will be at a relatively low-interest rate and payments are likely to be far less than for most other folks.

"I live in a house that my husband and I purchased when the four children were still small," said Lois J. Long of La Puente, California. "Now widowed, I continue to live here because I love the house, it is in a quiet neighborhood, and payments are now $90 a month, compared to $600 that a friend of mine is paying."

The disadvantage of staying in a home that has greatly increased in value over the years is that you may not be making the best use of your assets. A bigger house than you need also could become a costly albatross around your neck if fuel and maintenance costs as well as taxes shoot up sharply. If you sell, you can take advantage of the up to $125,000 tax break and perhaps put your profit to a better use.

Owning Versus Renting

If you sell, your option is between renting your new home or buying one. One advantage of renting is that you can take all of your profit from your home-sale and invest it to generate retirement income. Some apartment managers report that older renters have moved in after selling their homes and reinvesting their proceeds in Treasury certificates or other high-yield money-market instruments. The high interest rates paid by such investments enable the older renters to supplement their pension benefits and Social Security income.

Renters don't tie up their money in a house.

"After a lifetime of homeownership, I am a renter," said Sonja Braun of Oakland, California. "This came about because, as a widow, I wanted no concerns of maintenance and also wanted freedom to travel. In addition, the interest earned on my remaining capital supplements my Social Security to provide an adequate standard of living. If my capital were invested in a house, I would have a much lower disposable income."

But every silver lining has a cloud. The risk of renting for retirees is that you have less control over your housing costs than with owning. Mainly, rents can, and usually do, go up. In fact, many housing experts predict that rents will shoot up—and perhaps double—during the balance of the 1980s because of a growing shortage of rent housing nationwide.

Renters also may face the trauma of having their apartment buildings converted to condominiums or cooperatives, forcing them to buy anyway or to find some other place to rent.

Owning and Investing

The wisest move for many older people is to sell the old homestead to cash in their profits from the increased value and then *buy down* to a cheaper but more practical, smaller home.

If you pay cash for your home, or make a big enough down payment to keep the payments comfortable, you will have more control over your basic housing costs than if you rent. And you're still likely to have a sizable chunk of your profit left to invest for retirement income.

"Four years ago, I was left a widow and decided I could and should live a less expensive lifestyle," said Mrs. G. M. Rose of Venice, Florida. "I purchased a condominium in a 20-unit building just 2½ blocks from the beach. I was able to realize a profit from the sale of my villa. With wise investments, I am able to enjoy my two-bedroom condominium and still take vacations."

Homeownership offers another important advantage over renting: You can't sell rent receipts, but you can always sell a house if you need the money. Well-located houses are expected to continue to rise in value.

Price appreciation may not seem important to an older person. But remember that the home you buy when you first retire may not be the last home you will need. You may move a couple of times before you find the right place for your retirement years. Or with people living longer these days, you may need to move elsewhere as you advance in years.

"Many of our residents are of an advanced age—65 to 90—and when the spouse of one of them dies, the other usually sells and moves to a semi-care facility," wrote George Goody, who lives in Oceana, an over-40 condominium adult-community in Oceanside, California. "The substantial rise in market values of their properties has served to facilitate his/her ability to pay for these personal services."

Our surveys and others show that the majority of older people prefer to own their own homes. The choice is yours. In considering costs, the rule of thumb is that you shouldn't pay more than 30 percent of your income for housing. But that rule varies with each individual. You should figure out what you expect your retirement income will be and then figure your estimated costs to determine how much you can afford to pay for housing.

Table 3·4 is a guide published by the National Association of Home Builders to help you determine what you can afford.

Table 3·4   What can you spend for monthly housing?

1. Your average monthly income: Take-home pay
   (gross pay less taxes) .... $ _____
   Rents, dividends, interest .... _____
   Other stable income sources .... _____
      Net average monthly income (add) (1): .... $ _____
2. Your average monthly nonhousing expenses:
   Food, household supplies .... $ _____
   Clothing .... _____
   Medical costs and insurance .... _____
   Life and casualty insurance .... _____
   Automobile and insurance .... _____
   Education .... _____
   Commuting .... _____
   Installment payments/interest charges .... _____
   Recreation, hobbies (adjust realistically) .... _____
   Telephone .... _____
   Contributions, dues, fees, etc. .... _____
   Personal (cleaning, barber, etc.) .... _____
   Savings/investment program (adjust realistically) .... _____
   Other miscellaneous expenses .... _____
      Total average monthly nonhousing expenses: (add) (2) $ _____
3. Your monthly income available for housing:
   Net average monthly income (total 1) .... $ _____
   Subtract monthly nonhousing expenses (total 2) ..... _____
   Average monthly income available for housing
      expenses (3) .... $ _____

(continued)

Table 3·4 (continued)

4. Average monthly housing expenses:
   Condominium association fee .... $ _____
   Mortgage repayment, principal and interest .... _____
   Personal property and liability insurance (if not included
      in mortgage loan repayment) .... _____
   Unit property taxes (if not included in mortgage loan
      repayment) .... _____
   Utilities (heat, electricity/gas/oil/water) .... _____
   Other monthly housing expenses (decorating,
      appliances, etc.) .... _____
         Average monthly housing expenses (add) .... $ _____

How much down payment can you afford?

5. Available funds:
   Equity in present home/lot .... $ _____
   Savings, savings certificates .... _____
   Investments/mutual funds, (current value) .... _____
   Insurance (cash surrender value) .... _____
   Other available funds (such as a personal loan) .... _____
      Total available funds (add) .... _____
      Subtract amount you must keep in reserve .... _____
      Adjusted total available funds (a) .... $ _____

6. Expected cash expenses:
   Cash costs for closing and settlement .... $ _____
   Furniture, furnishings, (if any) .... _____
   Moving expenses .... _____
      Other expected expenses .... _____
         Total expected expenses (add) (b) .... $ _____

Now subtract total (b) (your expected expenses from
total (a) (your available funds) to get amount you can
afford to spend for your down payment (c): .... $ _____

Subtract the down payment from the sales price of the
home you wish to buy, and you will know how much of
a mortgage you will need to finance.

Should You Pay Cash?

If you decide to buy a home when you retire, another question arises: Should you pay cash or get another mortgage?

Many older home buyers pay cash. In the case of new-home buyers, 45 percent of those 65 years old or older purchase for cash, and an additional 12.5 percent buy with 55 percent to 99 percent down, according to a National Association of Home Builders' Profile of New Home Buyers. This is in startling contrast to younger people 25 years of age or less; nearly 70 percent of those buyers put less than 10 percent down.

One reason that older people often pay cash is that they have the money, after selling a previous home that sharply increased in value over the years. And many retirement advisers recommend that retirees pay cash for their homes so they can control most of their housing costs. What's more, many older people simply prefer to own their homes free and clear. It's called peace of mind.

If a mortgage-free retirement living means peace of mind to you, then by all means put up the cash, if you can, to buy your home. But paying cash is not always best—for several reasons.

For one reason, you are tying up a large hunk of cash in your home. A good part of that money could be put to work producing investment income. Second, if you pay cash for your home, you may not be left with much easily accessible money for emergencies, hospital bills, or other needs. Third, you could even use some of the cash for your personal enjoyment.

"What should I wait for? Until I'm 90?" asked a retired railroad worker living in a Whiting, New Jersey, retirement community.

Some retirees are discovering that, despite their doubts about debt, sometimes it may be better to take on another mortgage and put their profits from the old home to work. That's what Kathryn and Wilber White of Cape Coral, Florida, did.

"My husband and I took early retirement for health reasons, built a three-bedroom home, and moved to Florida. We sold our home up north and intended to pay off the new one immediately," Mrs. White wrote. But *"a Christian financial adviser warned us that was not a good practice, [because] if you were ever in a lawsuit they could take your whole life savings invested in your home.*

"Instead, he invested the majority of our funds, and we enjoy a monthly income check so that life is much easier for us," Mrs. White said. *"We appreciate that advice, tho it went against the grain of my training. I wanted our home 'paid for.'"*

As Mrs. White noted, going back into debt when you go into retirement means breaking the old lessons. But, if done prudently, it can help fulfill the dreams of some older Americans.

"Maybe at 58 or 59, I should not have taken on a $55,000 debt, seeing we had our house in town almost paid for. But I wanted to raise some beef, and this 28-acre farm will do the trick, I hope," wrote Tom Griffin of Tomah, Wisconsin.

Mortgages for Older People

Some folks think that older people—just because they are older—can't get long-term mortgages. Hogwash! Older people can qualify for mortgages just like anyone else if they meet the financial requirements. It's true that retirees likely will have lower incomes than younger mortgage borrowers. But they are likely to have more assets, fewer debts and an ability to make a bigger down payment to hold down the monthly payment.

The key question is, How much can you afford in monthly payments on your retirement income? As indicated, lenders generally say that home buyers can afford to pay up to 30 percent of their income for housing payments. Older people could get close to the 30 percent limit since generally they have fewer financial needs.

If you want a mortgage, shop around for one. Be forewarned that these days you'll find there are all kinds of new mortgages with interest rates that can be raised—or lowered—during the life of the mortgage. Generally, older buyers are better off with old-fashioned, fixed-rate mortgages so they will be certain of their mortgage costs. The interest cost on a changeable-rate mortgage could be increased by a larger amount than someone on a retirement income could afford to pay. You can always refinance your loan if mortgage rates drop sharply. If you want to gamble that a changeable rate will decline, make sure you get a mortgage with a lid on increases. Remember, you can still get fixed-rate FHA and VA loans.

The interest charged on a mortgage has a big impact on your monthly payments. As one woman told a retirement-housing conference conducted by the Federal National Mortgage Association: "Our prayers keep us in better health, but even God can't pay these high mortgage rates." If you decide to look into taking on a mortgage on the home in which you plan to live in retirement, see Table 3·5 to help you figure your monthly payment for principal and interest. To estimate your total cost, tack on the estimated costs for taxes and insurance.

The table goes up to a 17 percent mortgage rate. When it gets that high, you ought to think about holding off buying until you can get a lower rate.

Unlocking Your Assets

Even if you stay in your current home during your retirement, there are ways you can get the equity out of your house.

Table 3·5 — Monthly payment table per $1,000

Annual interest rate (in percent)	Duration of loan in years		
	20	25	30
8½	$ 8.683	$ 8.058	$ 7.692
9	9.000	8.400	8.050
10	9.813	9.087	8.780
10½	9.990	9.450	9.150
11	10.322	9.801	9.523
11½	10.664	10.165	9.903
12	11.011	10.532	10.286
12½	11.361	10.904	10.673
13	11.716	11.278	11.062
14	12.435	12.038	11.849
15	13.168	12.808	12.640
16	13.913	13.589	13.270
17	14.668	14.378	14.060

Example: Monthly payment of principal and interest on a $50,000 mortgage for 30 years at 12 percent:

$10.286 × 50 = $514.30 monthly.

You can refinance your home. Refinancing means getting a whole new mortgage. For example, say you have only a $10,000 remaining mortgage at 6 percent and payments of $144 a month in principal and interest. But your home is now worth $100,000. That means you are sitting on an equity of $90,000. You could get a big chunk of that equity by refinancing.

Let's say that you took out a new $40,000 mortgage. After paying off the $10,000 old mortgage, that would leave you $30,000 in cash. If you previously didn't have a mortgage any longer, you would get the entire $40,000 in cash.

The catch, of course, is that you have to pay the money back. You will end up with a bigger mortgage than you have now and it no doubt will have a higher interest rate—they don't make 6 percent mortgages anymore.

For instance, a $40,000 mortgage at 12 percent would mean your payment for principal and interest would be about $421 a month, compared with the previous $144. And you also will have to pay certain closing costs. So you must figure what payments you can afford before figuring how much to refinance. And whether the benefits from getting the cash justify going deeper into hock.

Frankly, for most older people, it doesn't make much sense to trade in a small, low-interest mortgage for a big, high-interest one just before you head into retirement and your mortgage is almost paid off.

The exceptions may be some people who plan to sell their homes anyway when they retire and pay off the mortgage from the sale's profits. For example, some older people who are at the peak of their earnings and could use more tax deductions could refinance with a new mortgage, invest the cash for now, and then use some of it to buy another home when they retire. Or you could refinance to get money to start constructing a retirement home.

Second mortgage. Another way to get part of the equity out of your home is to take out a second mortgage. The second mortgage, sometimes called an equity mortgage, is just what it sounds like—a mortgage in addition to a first mortgage that you are already paying on.

One advantage of a second mortgage is that you can keep your low-interest first mortgage. You pay the current higher interest rate only on the new debt. Also, second mortgages are for shorter periods, say, 5 to 10 years. They can be used to obtain cash for fixing up your home to get it into shape for retirement, if you plan to stay in your house.

Lenders like second mortgages because these are secured by property—your home. And the borrower thus can often get a lower interest rate than might be available on other kinds of consumer loans. You can also use the equity in your home as collateral for obtaining a personal loan instead of a mortgage.

The point to remember is that you will be making *two* payments—one on the first mortgage and a second on the second mortgage. Add them up to learn if you can afford them both. Also, shop for the best interest rate, and make sure you deal with a reputable lender. Find out the annual percentage rate (APR), which lenders must supply, to compare true rates.

Reverse Equity Loans

Both second mortgages and refinancing are less-than-perfect ways for retirees—who are moving into the years of shrunken incomes—to cash in on the assets in their homes. But better ways to unfreeze these frozen assets are on the housing horizon.

After all those years of paying to a lender for your house, there is now a way to have the lender pay you. It is called a reverse annuity mortgage. In effect, with this mortgage you borrow against the value of your home. It is designed for retirees who owe little or nothing on their homes.

Orlin and Goldie Folwick, both in their 80s, took out a reverse mortgage on their $125,000 Minneapolis home to get money to travel.

Their $40,000 reverse mortgage, at a fixed 11¾ percent interest rate, will give them $500 a month for 5½ years, minus about $70 for average monthly interest charges.[2]

"With that extra half a G-note, a few more goodies will show up in our living," said Mr. Folwick, a retired newspaper reporter. *"By the end of five years, we can remortgage or sell the home, because by then I'll probably be looking for one of those cozy places where all you do is get up, stretch, and go back to bed."*

From the American Association of Retired Persons' "Fact Sheet on Home Equity Conversion:" "Home equity conversion" or "reverse equity plans" are designed to allow homeowners to convert the asset represented by the value of their home (equity) into cash, without being forced to leave their home. Under these plans, a home is either mortgaged or sold to an individual or institutional investor, but is occupied by the homeowner until death or a negotiated future date. By these plans, older homeowners can increase their monthly cash resources, drawing on the equity in their homes.

It is estimated that homeownership among all older Americans represents assets in excess of $600 billion. The amount available to the individual depends upon the current value of the home, the life expectancy, the terms of the contract, and the type of equity conversion plan used. It is important to distinguish between the vehicles for converting home equity which are coming on the market, and to secure appropriate counseling and legal services.

"Reverse mortgage plans," or RAMs, allow a homeowner, by pledging the home as collateral, to borrow 60 to 80 percent of the appraised value of the equity for a specified period of time at a given rate of interest. Funds are received periodically for the duration of the lending period, after which the homeowner is responsible for repaying the loan. If the home has appreciated, the owner may be able to renegotiate the loan or the house may have to be sold to settle the obligation. In most cases the interest charged is compounded and, therefore, the total cost of interest may exceed the amount of cash received by the homeowner.

A "shared appreciation reverse mortgage" varies from the plan just described by providing a specified cash payment each month for as long as the owner remains an occupant of the home. The maximum amount of a payment, which constitutes a cumulative loan, is calculated by the life expectancy of the occupant(s), the current market value of the property, and the projected compounded interest. This maximum "draw" would represent 100 percent pledge of appreciation. Homeowners could, however, reduce the payment to, for example, 50 percent, and retain a claim on 50 percent of appreciation between the starting date of the transaction and the date of settlement. In either situation the house is accepted as settlement of the obligation upon vacancy and the appreciation distributed according to the contract. For people who live in the home beyond their life expectancy, the benefits can be substantial. For those who vacate before the term established by life expectancy, benefits would be drastically reduced.

Another arrangement is the "sales-leaseback." This involves an investor or investment group purchasing the older seller's home. As part of the sale agreement, the buyer gives the seller a lease establishing the right of the seller to remain in the home, either for life or until the lease is terminated by the seller. The seller receives payment for the home over the period of life expectancy, usually through a down payment and an interest-bearing installment note satisfied by monthly payments.

The seller/leasor must pay rent to the buyer/leasee. The net between the payments on the note and the rental fee constitutes the increase in the seller/renter's income—plus the fact that the buyer assumes the payment of real estate taxes, major maintenance and casualty insurance.

To provide the same level of income to the seller for life, it is strongly recommended that the buyer pay for a single premium annuity to which the seller is beneficiary, with the payments to start upon satisfaction of the note.

The lease should provide that rent increases be related to future income resources such as cost of living increases in Social Security benefits.

Generally, the investor is attracted to this arrangement because of tax benefits and the potential appreciation of the property plus the probability that the purchase price will be less than the appraised value due to the conditions listed above.

In addition to specific residency privileges and increased income, the seller may also benefit from the one time capital gains exemption upon the sale of the home.

"Deferred payment loans" differ from reverse mortgages in that the loan(s) are usually for some specific purpose such as payment of real estate taxes, home repairs or remodeling, or major personal expenses. The loan is secured by a lien which must be satisfied to clear title for sale of the property.

Questions Still Remain

Home equity conversion plans are complex and new to the legal profession, financial institutions, and the public. A number of questions including eligibility for programs such as Supplemental Security Income, food stamps, and Medicaid remain unanswered. No single plan can serve the best interests of all older homeowners. It is important that anyone considering the use of their assets in this manner secure adequate counsel. Nonetheless, homeownership represents an asset which, if used wisely, can greatly benefit many older individuals.

A primary source for more information is the National Center for Home Equity Conversion, 110 East Main, Madison, WI 53703. Also, a 21-page federal booklet, "Turning Home Equity into Income for Older Homeowners," is available for $3.50 from the Superintendent of Documents, U.S. Government Printing Office, Dept. 33, Washington DC 20402.

Buy Now, Move Later

The important thing about this retirement bit is to do a little research before leaping.
Bethune Gibson
West Sedona, Arizona

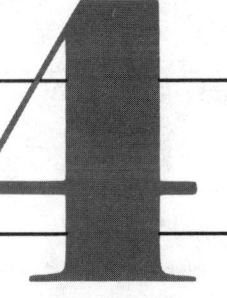

4

Retirement still seemed far away for Czechoslovakia-born Brano Lajda, but in 1970 he decided to buy what he had always dreamed of for his later years—a house in the Caribbean. In the summer of 1980, he retired, rented his Washington, D.C., townhouse and left the whirlwind life of the nation's capital to begin enjoying the warm climate of St. Thomas, Virgin Islands.

Sound far-fetched? Not at all. It all depends on starting a retirement plan, and sticking with it.

Mr. Lajda was two jumps ahead of the game. First, his initial investment in his Washington condo was only $12,000. By the time he retired, it was worth $100,000 and still climbing. Second, his retirement home in St. Thomas cost about $31,000 in 1970. If he had waited until he retired to buy, the same home would have cost more than $70,000.

Buying a home now that you may want to move to later makes sense for a lot of people. If you are not yet retired, you can start paying for the second home while you have the pre-retirement income to afford two houses. If you are moving into a higher tax bracket, a second home can provide additional tax deductions. And if you are retired and have the appropriate funds, buying a second home may be a practical action on your part. Even if you decide not to move to the second home, you can likely sell it for a profit. Or you can buy income property—a house, an apartment, a duplex, or even an apartment building—to generate income and tax write-offs now and to help provide retirement money or housing later.

Now Is Less Expensive

Vacation or other second homes are growing in popularity in the United States. There were as many as 4 million second homes in the United States in 1983, and an estimated 150,000 new second homes are built each year, on average.

The main advantage of buying a second (or third, or more) home now is that the particular home you buy will be less costly than it will be later. And that will mean less strain on your income later.

Plan for Your Needs

When buying a home that you may move to later, you should consider how the house will fit your needs, including your economic, physical, and psychological requirements.

"At age 50, I found a seven-room Victorian house. It was an appropriate background for heirloom furnishings and seemed to offer many advantages for retirement years," wrote Delight Millspaugh of Croton-on-Hudson, New York. *"Chosen for charm, but also with the future in mind, my location enables me to walk to essential places in the village. The yard is level for easy care.*

"As an older house in a high-tax area, it has a lower assessment," Mr. Millspaugh said. *"Hot-water oil heat promised steady warmth. High ceilings save the smallish rooms from feeling cramped; bay windows add a sense of charm.*

"My house has a view of the majestic Hudson River," he added. *"I recognized the ground level as a potential rental area—office space or housing for a homemaker if the need arrives for such service.*

"Housing is vitally important to emotional and physical health at any age, but to an older person his home may be his whole world," Mr. Millspaugh said. *"It must be comfortable; capable of providing beauty, warmth, space for friends, pets, and hobbies, and possibly sick-room equipment."*

If you know what you want, you can save in the long-run by buying now in the area where you plan to move. Even if you haven't made up your mind yet, there are ways to get started with real estate investments that can make it easier to fulfill your housing goals later.

Buying a Vacation Home

One way to get started is to buy a place where you can play now and where you perhaps can consider moving to tomorrow.

"After checking a number of recreational developments in Maryland and Virginia, we bought a lot at Lake Caroline, Virginia. Two years later we built a 900-square-foot pre-cut cedar log house—not as a retirement home but as an all-season weekend retreat," wrote Philip and Marianne Ryan, who lived in the Washington, D.C., suburb of Arlington, Virginia.

"At age 68, we decided to try living full-time at our 'get-away house' in the country," the Ryans said. *"We rented our nonmortgaged home in Arlington so as to be able to re-establish living there if this proved unsatisfactory. We escape winter months by taking our VW campmobile to Florida for January and February, thus reducing heating costs for our cabin.*

"Our investment in the house, garage, and lots totaled approximately $32,700. Real estate taxes, home insurance, water fees, and homeowners' association fees run about $600 annually," the Ryans said.

For some, a vacation home—when investigated as thoroughly as the Ryans did—can wind up as a permanent home. It may be a house on a lot, a condominium on a beach, or a ski lodge on the slopes. Second homes are popular in the Sunbelt where the climate guarantees sunny weather. For outdoor enthusiasts, there's no place like a home in the mountains.

With retirement, such vacation activities can be extended year-round.

"Every day is a vacation day," proclaimed John and Julie Donnelly, a retired couple who own a condominium at Mammoth Lakes, California, in the Sierra Nevada mountains.

"Since we like to visit other national forests, we have an 18-foot trailer, self-contained, and a four-wheel-drive Blazer to pull it," the Donnellys wrote. *"So when we leave for an extended period, we like our condo arrangement and have a worry-free time because the manager is close by to keep out unwanted guests. Also, we are able to rent it out during the ski season, which helps us since we live on a pension and Social Security."*

For those like the Donnellys who enjoy visiting our national forests, a helpful hint: People 62 years of age or older can get a Golden Age

Passport for free lifetime entrance to fee-charging federal recreation areas. These passports are available at any National Park Service office or any area of the National Park system where fees are charged.

Second Thoughts on Second Homes

Moving into a vacation home sounds beautiful, and it can be for many. But before getting caught up in the idea of year-round vacation living, there are some points to consider:

Don't buy a vacation home mainly as an investment. It is true that some vacation homes have escalated sharply in value and yours may, too. But generally speaking, vacation homes don't appreciate as much as some other real estate purchases. If you are buying a vacation home mainly for your own use and enjoyment, though, who can tell you that it is not a good investment?

Location is important. While you may not be buying a vacation home mainly as an investment, you can't overlook its potential resale value in case you decide to sell some day. Thus, at the sea, beachfront property is most likely to increase in value. It also will be easiest to rent for top dollar. A vacation home should offer privacy, but it shouldn't be too far from shopping and recreational facilities.

Measure the commuting distance. If you plan to use your vacation home regularly, don't buy one too far away from where you live. For most people, a commute of 2½ to 4 hours is about the limit. Also, the home will be harder to rent if it is too far from a large community. Distance is less of a factor if your vacation home is for use only once or twice a year and in a popular vacation area, such as Florida.

Make sure the vacation home can be used year-round or can be adapted to year-round use. Check the upkeep for heating or cooling. Energy bills are going up fast.

Visit your potential vacation home during the off-season. The area may seem like a bustling, enjoyable place during vacation. But what about when the tourists are gone? And what are the year-round services, such as hospitals and doctors, for residents?

Second Coming

One reason for the increased popularity of vacation or second homes is that financing has become more available. When mortgage money is hard to get, loans for second homes are squeezed hard. But otherwise, long-term financing is increasingly offered. At Sea Colony, a condominium village in Bethany Beach, Delaware, a popular vacation spot at the Atlantic Ocean, "there have been no foreclosures ever," said Carl Freeman, the developer. "For that reason, we can offer today a 30-year mortgage as compared to a maximum 20 years in 1971 when we broke ground."

The ocean beaches are becoming more attractive all year round. For instance, the 1,200 unit Sea Colony has become "more of a pre-retirement community than just a vacation home," said Pat J. Rhodes, general manager.

"What we provide are all-year-round amenities," he said. "Christmas for us at Sea Colony is a very busy period. People stay nine or ten months instead of just the summer."

With a second home, of course, you have the cost of carrying another mortgage. But you can reduce part of that by renting out the vacation home part of the year and by taking advantage of tax breaks.

Vacation Homes and Taxes

People who own vacation homes and rent them out part time can enjoy their property even more because of tax deductions.

If you own a beach house or other vacation home and rent it out for fewer than 15 days a year, you don't have to pay taxes on any of the income. If you use the second house strictly as an income-producing investment, you must report all of the income. But you can write off all your maintenance and depreciation, and you can even operate the property at a loss. You cannot report a tax loss, however, if you use the property yourself for more than 14 days or 10 percent of the total rental period, whichever is greater.

Most vacation homeowners, of course, use their second homes for both fun and income. To do this, you must separate personal expenses into those applicable to rental and those for personal use.

Let's say your beach house is used for a total of 70 days a year. You vacation there for 14 days and rent it out for 56 days, earning a rental income of $2,400. It costs $1,400 to maintain the property. As a result, $\frac{14}{70}$ of the maintenance costs, or $280, would be personal, and $\frac{56}{70}$, or $1,120, would be business expense and thus tax-deductible. Depreciation is figured the same way.

Before you begin deducting those expenses, however, you must subtract from rental income the real estate taxes and the mortgage interest allocable to rental use. Once you have done that, taking the maintenance and depreciation deductions as well could leave you with a loss.

If you use your property more than the maximum time allowed, you may not be able to use all of your deductions because you cannot report a loss on your property. (Any part of your real estate taxes or mortgage interest that isn't claimed can, of course, be claimed as a personal deduction.) So to get maximum tax benefits, you must make sure that your use of the property doesn't exceed the limit of 14 days or 10 percent of the rental period. That way, you can claim all of the deductions and the loss.

Some interpretations of the IRS tax rules on second homes are controversial and complex, so it is best to check with an accountant. But tax experts say most vacation homeowners who rent find they can report a taxable loss in the first years of ownership, partly because of the accelerated depreciation schedule for rental properties.

The beauty is that by the time you move into your vacation home permanently, much of the mortgage may be paid off. If you don't use the $125,000 tax exclusion on your former home, you still may be able to use it on your retirement home should you eventually decide to sell. Just make it your primary residence for at least three years before you sell.

Selling Your Vacation Home

What happens if you want to sell the house? Presuming that you own it for at least one year, any appreciation in value would be subject to capital-gains taxes. It is not a primary residence, and thus the gain cannot be rolled over into another house. Nor does that property qualify for the once-in-a-lifetime $125,000 exclusion for homeowners over 55. And if the house has been partly or fully rented, any depreciation that has been taken over the years has to be figured in.

Buy Land and Build

Another way to buy now and move later is to purchase some land and build the home that you want for your retirement years. For a Saline, Michigan couple who are avid golfers, it means a home on a golf course within a chip shot of the 17th fairway.

"We purchased a lot on the Oregon coast, and [a few years later] proceeded to build our future retirement home there," wrote Mrs. J. Trommershausser. *"It is on the 17th fairway in a beautiful setting. This house has been rented year round to the same family for several years.*

"At present we are living in a 3-bedroom, 2½ bath contemporary ranch ... on the 17th fairway of a rather new golf course and country club," said Mrs. Trommershausser, whose husband is a retired Air Force colonel now employed in industry. *"We both golf."*

By building ahead, when building costs and interest rates were less, the Trommershaussers saved money and are generating rental income from their retirement home until they move there. As costly as construction is now, it is still cheaper to build now than it will be several years from now.

Another advantage of having your own retirement home built is that you design a home that fits your specific needs.

"After my husband [Clarence] retired from General Motors as a repair machinist, he wanted to build us a new home, instead of repairing an older one, as we had all our married life. So at age 64, we started," wrote E. Eleanor Vredevoogd of Swartz Creek, Michigan. *"I drew the plans, the students at the high school made the blueprints, and we started—with the help of my husband's brother, our son, and several grandsons and one granddaughter.*

"Our home was designed just for older folks, and it is serving its purpose very well," she said. *"The only change we had to do was to enlarge one little part of the hallway. My husband had a stroke and is now in a wheelchair."*

Construction Financing

If you want to buy land and build a new house, you may be able to use the equity in your current home to get started. If you are nearing retirement and the mortgage on your current house is paid off or nearly paid off, you might consider refinancing your present home, suggested Benny Kass, a Washington, D.C., real estate lawyer and housing columnist:

> Let's assume that your house is worth $75,000. You can easily borrow up to $50,000 by obtaining a mortgage from a bank or savings and loan association. Using the refinancing technique, you will have adequate funds to plan the construction of your new home.
>
> While you are talking with the potential refinance lender, you might also discuss a construction loan at the same time. It may very well be that your income level will permit you to obtain a construction loan without having to refinance. After all, your land is valuable, and many lenders will take this into consideration in determining your assets.
>
> Discuss with the mortgage lender the possibility of obtaining a construction loan, which will become a permanent mortgage on the house when it is completed. Under this approach, the mortgage lender will be a participant with you in the building of your house. Periodic payments will be made to the builder, after the lender has inspected the job and is satisfied that the work is going smoothly.
>
> Finally, it may very well be that you can refinance your present home

and at the same time obtain a construction loan for your new home. The major determining factor here will be your present income and your ability to pay two mortgages.

Of course, after your retirement home is built, you can sell your old home and pay off the refinanced mortgage.

For sheer imagination and creativity, few can match the four women, all in their 70s, who formed the legal partnership to design and build their house on a lake in Southern Pines, North Carolina. As Ruth Pauley explained, she and her friends pooled their investments, got the biggest mortgage they could, and began enjoying together the dream house they had built.

"We luckily found an excellent builder," Mrs. Pauley noted. "The house is built to last by a local builder with many years' experience. We suggest that people [who move to a new area to build] hunt for a local builder who knows the local resources and has permanent working arrangements with subcontractors."

Land-buying Pitfalls

Buying land and building now could save you money in the long run. But it also could buy you a lot of trouble if you don't investigate carefully.

When buying land to build a home, you need to consider the costs, the likely appreciation, and your personal needs. Professionals use a couple rules of thumb:

1. The cost of the finished lot (a lot that is ready for construction) shouldn't be more than 25 percent of the cost of the house you plan to build—except in unusually high-cost areas. The lower the share of the finished lot to the price of the house, the better value the house is.

2. As an investment, the value of land should appreciate at least 15 to 20 percent a year or it is not worth buying—or keeping.

There is, of course, great variation among states, cities, and counties in the cost of land; there is also great variation in land cost between blocks within a city.

One way of checking on land cost is to go to the county court house and research current sales. The other is to ask Realtors to give you the most current information on sales of land.

Table 4·1 illustrates the great variety of land cost. It shows land cost by states from 1976 to 1981 with the annual rate of change between those years.

Table 4·1 Average Square-Foot Cost of Finished Residential Lot 1976–1981

STATE	1976	1977	1978	1979	1980	1981	Annual Percent Change
Alabama	$0.48	$0.47	$0.48	$0.55	$0.55	$0.54	2.5%
Alaska	—	—	2.27	2.27	3.00	3.15	12.9
Arizona	0.27	0.25	0.91	1.15	1.28	1.20	68.8
Arkansas	0.46	1.13	0.75	0.71	0.85	0.92	20.0
California	1.57	1.78	2.07	2.96	3.68	3.95	30.3
Colorado	0.95	1.09	1.25	1.44	1.70	1.94	20.8
Connecticut	0.44	0.45	0.49	0.63	0.64	0.78	15.5
Delaware	0.40	0.42	0.77	0.45	0.45	0.55	7.5
Wash., D.C.	—	—	—	9.43	11.39	12.08	14.0
Florida	0.95	0.96	1.02	1.13	1.18	1.21	5.5
Georgia	0.45	0.47	0.47	0.52	0.57	0.59	6.2
Hawaii	—	—	—	—	10.59	7.74	—
Idaho	0.50	0.67	0.89	1.07	1.16	1.18	27.2
Illinois	1.09	1.11	1.42	1.57	1.82	1.76	12.3
Indiana	0.50	0.52	0.58	0.69	0.74	0.76	10.4
Iowa	0.75	0.69	0.90	0.97	1.00	0.49	6.4
Kansas	0.75	0.93	0.96	1.08	1.14	1.20	12.0
Kentucky	0.87	0.79	0.70	0.78	0.89	0.95	1.8
Louisiana	0.61	0.65	0.95	1.21	1.34	1.27	21.6
Maine	0.16	0.12	0.14	0.17	0.19	0.22	7.5
Maryland	1.07	0.95	0.96	1.16	1.48	1.41	6.4
Massachusetts	0.35	0.40	0.49	0.48	0.49	0.50	8.6
Michigan	0.72	0.65	0.73	0.95	0.96	0.70	−0.6
Minnesota	0.48	0.51	0.71	0.87	0.99	1.02	12.2
Mississippi	0.41	0.47	0.63	0.70	0.74	0.70	14.1
Missouri	0.79	0.83	0.85	0.89	1.01	1.06	6.8
Montana	0.78	0.84	0.74	1.06	1.04	1.18	10.3
Nebraska	0.69	0.71	0.83	0.96	1.13	1.07	11.0
Nevada	0.55	0.89	1.03	0.76	1.82	2.03	53.8
New Hampshire	0.25	0.25	0.49	0.51	0.60	0.63	30.4
New Jersey	0.79	0.84	0.87	0.98	1.11	1.24	11.4
New Mexico	0.72	0.86	0.96	1.00	1.13	1.34	17.2
New York	0.73	0.86	0.57	0.70	0.79	0.89	4.4
N. Carolina	0.34	0.44	0.44	0.48	0.47	0.44	5.9
N. Dakota	0.42	0.45	0.48	0.53	0.86	0.51	4.3
Ohio	0.65	0.84	0.95	1.14	1.18	1.15	15.4
Oklahoma	0.59	0.63	0.80	0.92	1.00	1.13	18.3
Oregon	0.77	1.02	1.28	1.56	1.75	1.89	29.1
Pennsylvania	0.46	0.59	0.61	0.73	0.78	0.94	10.9
Rhode Island	—	0.32	0.36	0.40	0.42	0.29	−2.4
S. Carolina	0.38	0.71	0.63	0.65	0.62	0.65	14.2
S. Dakota	0.63	0.66	0.53	0.49	0.63	0.60	−4.8
Tennessee	0.62	0.63	0.49	0.59	0.79	0.57	−1.6
Texas	0.69	0.91	0.91	0.96	1.18	1.36	19.4
Utah	0.87	0.94	1.18	1.39	1.45	1.35	10.0

(continued)

Table 4·1 (continued)

STATE	1976	1977	1978	1979	1980	1981	Annual Percent Change
Vermont	$0.40	$0.41	$0.55	$0.44	$0.70	$0.53	6.5%
Virginia	0.87	0.80	0.97	1.19	1.42	1.26	9.0
Washington	0.62	0.70	0.89	1.01	1.25	1.50	28.3
W. Virginia	0.50	0.55	0.64	0.73	0.67	0.71	8.4
Wisconsin	0.57	0.62	0.78	0.88	0.92	0.92	22.8
Wyoming	—	1.00	NA	NA	1.80	1.75	18.8
U.S. Total	0.77	0.80	0.87	0.95	1.05	1.11	8.8

A total of 13 states had average annual increases of 20 percent and more; 17 states and Washington, D.C. had increases of between 10 and 20 percent, and 4 states showed a decline.

The most expensive finished lots were found in the District of Columbia ($12.08 per square foot); the least expensive lots were found in Alabama ($ .54 per square foot).

An update of this information is available from the Economics Department, National Association of Home Builders, 15th Street and M Street, N.W., Washington, DC 20005.

Land Buyers Beware

If you plan to buy an undeveloped lot for a homesite in a planned community, check into it carefully. The records of consumer-protection agencies are crammed with woeful tales of people who bought land sight unseen from fast-talking salespeople, only to discover their future homesites were in swamps with the promised swimming pools and golf courses nowhere to be found.

In May, 1981, the Federal Trade Commission (FTC) ordered Horizon Corporation to refund $14.5 million to about 40,000 customers who bought undeveloped land in the southwest based on what the FTC said were "false and misleading claims." An FTC law judge had ruled that the land "has little value as an investment and little use as a homesite." Horizon agreed to the settlement, but did not admit to the charges.

In another case an FTC law judge ruled that Amrep Corporation misled potential customers and used high-pressure sales tactics at dinner parties to sell undeveloped land sight unseen at three to five times its value. The case involved the sale of land in Florida, Missouri, and New Mexico. Amrep contended that the FTC charges were "contrary to the record and replete with error." In 1982 the FTC obtained an agreement with General Development Corporation, which is based in Miami, Florida and was not part of any FTC investigation. General Development Corporation would buy some of the Florida property from Amrep and provide property owners with the option of selling their lots to General Development or exchanging them for other lots.

"The sale of land by interstate operators has now rocketed to a volume of $4 billion a year—with mounting numbers of you buying undeveloped lots for future retirement homes, second-home locations, recreational, or campside use," wrote Sylvia Porter, the consumer columnist.

"If you are among those Americans, you may find you've made a good deal with an honest and reliable developer—and you also may not," Mrs. Porter said. "There is simply no denying that this field has long been blotched by a racketeering fringe of unscrupulous operators whose promotions hurt the vast majority of honest developers as well as you, the victim."

Protecting Yourself When Buying Land

There are ways you can check a developer and his or her proposed land sales before buying. For one, if the company is selling 50 or more undeveloped lots in interstate commerce, it must file a statement of record with the Department of Housing and Urban Development in Washington, D.C. The company also must provide prospective buyers a Property Report containing detailed information about the property. If you have a complaint about such land purchases, you can write HUD and its Office of Interstate Land Sales Registration (OILSR) at 451 7th Street, N.W., Washington, DC 20410.

Many land sellers, however, aren't registered with HUD. Check with the real estate or land-sales offices in your state for information on such sellers. But remember, the checking of the reports filed by the companies is only one step in a prudent land purchase.

Land-buying Tips

"Thousands of lot buyers have lost all their savings because they didn't take time to find out about the risks built into the subdivided land business," said Joanna Underwood, Director of INFORM, Inc., a nonprofit New York group that has investigated numerous land-sales operations. Some of the tips INFORM provides in "The Insider's Guide to Owning Land in Subdivisions," are condensed here:

Step 1: Visit and inspect the lot you're considering buying.

You can't spot the potential dangers unless you see your land. The lot may be half a mile or more from the central area or "core" a development often builds to make the subdivision attractive. The core may have a fancy entrance drive, a plush "welcome center," a swimming pool, golf course, several new homes, and even a store. Don't be fooled by the window dressing; the rest of the development may never resemble this sample.

Don't let the developer show you a lot "just like" the one you've picked out on his plan. Your lot may be two miles away and still under water, waiting to be dredged out of the swamp.

Step 2: Ask the developer's salesperson to show you a federal Property Report, or if it is not available, a state Property Report.

The Property Report must disclose many, but not all, of the vital facts—good and bad—about the land being offered. For example, a Property Report may state that improvements are "planned" or "proposed," but may not indicate whether the developer has the long-term financial ability to provide them.

Read the Property Report carefully. However, since you probably won't understand all its legal details, you should talk to a lawyer or real estate broker and find out exactly what the report means. Be sure your questions are answered so that *you* really understand the answers.

Step 3: Beware of the installment contract.

Many people buy lots on the installment plan, and what they sign—the installment contract—is a peculiar beast. It is not a deed, it does *not* give you ownership of the land and, depending on its conditions, the contract may or may not give you the right to use the land.

You will need answers to specific questions: What happens to your installment payments? Are they placed in a separate (escrow) account to pay for the lot, or are they simply used to pay for the developer's current operating expenses or even to buy more subdivision acreage? What happens to your contract if the developer sells out or goes bankrupt? You'd be wise to hire a lawyer to go over the installment contract with you, point by point, to make sure your rights are protected.

Step 4: Check the resale value of the lot.

Don't believe the salesperson who says your lot is a "sure thing." Relatively few subdivision lots have ever been resold at a profit. All too often they can't be resold at all.

To check on a lot's value, ask the Board of Realtors in a city near the subdivision for the names of real estate agents who might know the lot's potential resale value. If the agent can show you lots almost the same as yours, at lower prices, and with the same "basic services," you would be foolish to buy through a developer.

Step 5: Check the "basic services" the developer has promised to build for you.

The value of your lot will depend largely on the availability of six "basic services." These are: a central water supply, central sewage disposal, paved roads, a drainage system, garbage collection, and electricity. These services make a piece of raw land usable as a "homesite." They also give the land its future resale value.

You do not have a right to improvements the developer has said he intends to provide unless the developer's promises are written into the contract. All six of these services should be checked out carefully.

Step 6: Check the natural hazards to your lot.

Don't assume that developers don't sell lots that are prone to floods, earthquakes, and landslides. Check for these hazards.

Flooding: A common danger in the Southwest and Florida. You can find out about the risks of flooding in a subdivision by looking at the flood maps on file at the town hall near the subdivision or by calling the local office of the National Flood Insurance Program.

Earthquakes and landslides: Most common on the West Coast, but they occur in many other areas as well. The U.S. Geological Survey can tell you whether the lot in a specific subdivision is subject to earthquakes or landslides.

The slope of your lot: A steeply sloping lot may be beautiful, but it's often more difficult and expensive to build on. A slope of more than 25 percent—a one-foot drop in every four feet on the horizontal—should be avoided.

Too little open space: As a rule of thumb, good planners reserve 25 percent of the land—not counting the space for roads—for parks, recreational and other open space purposes.

Step 7: Look for hidden costs.

When you buy a lot, don't assume you're paying a fixed amount to own the land and that there will be no additional charges. Before you sign a contract, check carefully to be sure you're not obligated to pay hidden costs which have not been explained to you. Pay careful attention to:

The finance charge: Most installment plan purchases now include an annual charge on the unpaid balance of the cost of the lot. You're actually lending the developer money, interest free, for all those years until you make the last payment.

Taxes: These may add another load of hidden costs to your property.

Maintenance charges for basic services: These also may be passed on to you.

Basic service costs: These may be called "special assessments" or "betterment fees," or "standby" utility charges. Whatever they're called, they can add up fast.

Special services district costs: Instead of installing and paying for basic services himself, the subdivider can pass on to you the cost of constructing, operating, and maintaining these services. Developers can do this by setting up, under state laws, a local authority to finance improvement. This is sometimes called a "special services district," "irrigation district," or "improvement district." To protect your interests, get written information on any "special service district" in your area.

A suggested "Step 8" is that you invest $2.50 in INFORM's *The Insider's Guide to Owning Land in Subdivisions*. The 38-page guide is loaded with detailed information that could protect you in a land purchase. Write INFORM, 381 Park Avenue South, New York, NY 10016.

You also can get for $2.50 a 20-page government booklet, "Buying Lots from Developers" from the U.S. Consumer Information Center in Pueblo, Colorado. (See page 250 for instructions on ordering.)

Income Properties

Another way to invest in real estate is to become a landlord.

"At age 49, I bought a large old house in an old neighborhood which some former owner had made into three apartments," said Nancy Brums of Fayetteville, North Carolina. "At age 56, I renovated it and moved into one of the apartments. The house cost $11,000 and the renovation about $12,000.

"For a relatively small investment, I live in a 1,500-square-foot gracious, spacious apartment," she said. "I have a tidy income to supplement my Social Security. And the house only increases in value. I can recommend this course to anyone who has reason to believe they have a reasonably healthy 20 years of life ahead."

You can buy a house, apartment, or apartment-house that you can rent out now and sell—or move to—later. The advantages are that it will probably provide some income and a tax shelter now, and you can probably sell it for a profit later. Or it will provide a cost-free roof over your head and you can generate retirement income later. Meanwhile, the renters and Uncle Sam can help you pay for it.

If you have the urge to be a landlord, an income property can be a good long-term investment and even a lot of fun if you do it right. As a starter, what follows are a few professional tips from Frank Calcara, an active developer and owner of many properties in the Washington, D.C. area.

Rental Property Rules

Don't pay too high a price. That seems obvious enough. But what is "too high" a price for a rental property? A rule of thumb that professionals use is that the price of the house shouldn't exceed 150 times the monthly rental income. Thus, if a property can be rented for $400 a month, $400 × 150 or $60,000 is the maximum you should pay for the property.

"Of course, you should pay less, if possible," Mr. Calcara said. "But 150 times is the absolute tops." And, of course, you should personally investigate the location of the property to make sure it is in an area where values are likely to appreciate.

Don't put too much money into the purchase. Make as small a down payment as possible, but no more than 20 percent. "Never pay cash," Mr. Calcara advised. You don't want to tie up your money, and you need to have reserves for expenses.

Row houses and townhouses that aren't in condominium developments often are the best investments. Such units generally are cheaper to buy, and maintain, than single-family houses. Thus, your rental income will cover a larger share of your expenses. Units in condo developments should be approached warily because the landlord—that's you—hasn't any control over the condo association's management and fees.

Make sure your expenses don't exceed more than 50 percent of your "cash flow." The cash flow is your net monthly rent that is paid to you. Your expenses should not be more than your cash flow plus 50 percent. For example, if you are getting $400 a month rent, your expenses shouldn't exceed $600, giving you a "negative cash flow" of $200. The expenses include your mortgage payment, taxes, insurance, maintenance, and an adjustment for a possible vacancy. For maintenance, generally allow for 1 percent of the sales price annually. Figure on the house being vacant, with no rental income, for one month a year, on average.

With this negative cash flow, you obviously would have to dip into your pocket to pay expenses. And obviously a positive cash flow would be better. If you are retired and renting your old house, which presumably has a small or no mortgage, your rental income should cover your expenses. But as an investment, a negative cash flow is acceptable as long as it doesn't exceed the 50 percent limit and you can afford the extra expense. Eventually, the rent can be increased so that the rental income will cover expenses.

A key factor in your expenses will be the mortgage rate you pay when you buy the house. With a $60,000 mortgage at 9 percent, the payment for principal and interest is $483 a month. But at 12 percent, the payment jumps to $617 and at 15 percent to $758.

One alternative if you decide to move from your current home and buy another one: Instead of selling your old home, rent it. It will be easier for the rental income to cover the mortgage payments and costs on your current home than if you buy a second home with a higher price tag and mortgage rate.

Never let a tenant occupy the house without a lease. Generally, don't make the lease for longer than one year, unless you include a provision that allows you to raise the rent each year if you wish. Spell out what are the tenant's responsibilities (to pay the rent on time, take care of minor maintenance problems, cut the grass, and so on) and what are the landlord's responsibilities (maintain the exterior, replace worn-out equipment, such as the furnace).

Manage the property yourself if you only have one or two. If you use a management company, your best bet may be to hire a small real estate company that also manages rental properties. The company will have the incentive of knowing that if you ever decide to sell, you may give it first crack. You generally pay about 6 percent of the monthly rent for such management services. Don't give the company authority to spend more than $50 or $100 for ordinary repairs without contacting you first.

Divine Guidance

Father Nicola, a teacher at Georgetown Preparatory School in Rockville, Maryland, is counting on more than prayer for his retirement. Following the advice that the Lord helps those who help themselves, he has invested in real estate.

"You see, I have to take care of myself. Without a pension, I had to plan ahead," Father Nicola said.

He did. In 1971, he bought a two-bedroom, two-bath condo in Clearwater, Florida. He put down $16,000 for this $48,000 house.

"I just figured it out," he said. "My house appreciated at a compound rate of 16.7 percent and is now worth $175,000. My rent income in 1980 was $11,200.

"In 1979, I also bought a house in Petoskey, Michigan, for $47,500. It is being rented for $600 a month for nine months a year—in summer and in winter for skiing. I borrowed $50,000 from my mother for this one."

Meanwhile, "I live in [a] retirement community with my mother, and this house is a part of [my] retirement plan," Father Nicola said. He enclosed the "Florida room" (a covered porch) and converted it into a chapel, "so I can invite my friends there for a Mass."

In addition, "with three other priests, we bought a condominium in Florida for $103,000," he said. "We will be renting it until we are ready to retire there."

Father Nicola is a 6-foot 3-inch former high school and college football player. He also has played on golf courses around the world.

"I'm looking toward retirement so all of us will have plenty of time to play golf during the day and then play cards," he said, adding with a devilish smile: *"We are a very involved bunch of bridge players."*

Thinking Big

If you can afford it, you don't have to stop at owning just one rental property. Some people as part of their investment plan buy several properties, hold them for price appreciation, and then sell one a year during their retirement.

This is what nationally syndicated housing columnist Robert J. Bruss calls the "One Property A Year Plan." If you want to think big, you can buy a whole apartment building. The only difference is that the numbers—sale's price, rental income, expenses, and tax deductions—are larger.

When you do sell, you can reap the increased appreciation of the income property to generate retirement income. Since the profits from an income property can't be deferred for tax purposes by reinvesting in another home, your best bet may be to sell on an installment basis.

Duplex Doings

For the many first-time investors who put their money into residences for rent, John T. Reed, editor of a real estate newsletter, suggested that to provide a margin of safety against possible market downturns, the investors should try to buy properties that have positive cash flows.

For such investors, Mr. Reed added, duplexes, which are houses divided into living quarters for two families, often are better buys than single-family homes "because the relation between price and income is more sensible." Where a duplex might be priced at 8 times its rental income, he said, a single-family house might have a multiple of as much as 15.

In fact, you might consider a duplex as a place that you might want to buy to live in yourself when you retire.

"Has anyone given thought to two-bedroom, side-by-side duplexes?" asked Stanley Cousins of Detroit, Michigan. *"If the elderly owned such housing and rented the other side to younger people, this would provide almost free housing to the owner and break up a cluster of retirement housing."*

Yes, Mr. Cousins, many older people have thought of duplexes, whether they are side-by-side or up-and-down. The duplex can be an ideal arrangement for them.

"Since 1969, I have been very well satisfied with our duplex house," wrote Jean S. Trimble of Lincoln, Virginia. "The arrangement gives us a home. The income from renters gives us money and other necessities. For 10 years, the depreciation on the rental side also gave us a tax shelter. That has expired, but we can still deduct expenses for insurance, repairs, and one half of the real estate taxes for the rental side.

"We have been fortunate to have congenial tenants on the rental side," Mrs. Trimble added. "The tenants take over the lawn mowing, unless they want to pay more rent. They also are helpful in many ways. We feel more secure to have people in the other side, especially when we take a trip."

Bethune Gibson, the West Sedona, Arizona, retiree who owns a duplex, agreed that such housing can provide both income and companionship.

"My tenants are young and we consider ourselves a family. Tenants are, in fact, a good feature for a person living alone. This couple checks up on me to be sure I am OK, does odd chores for me, and minds the pets and plants when I am away. I do the same for them."

A duplex also can be a solution for people who are friends and want to live near each other, yet have their privacy.

"In 1971, a friend of long-standing and I purchased a duplex jointly. At that time I was 53 years old (a widow) and she was 48 (divorced). We were both renting at the time," said Mrs. Gwen Waddington of Seaside, California.

"We each have our own two-bedroom, living-room, bath and kitchen facilities, each with two separate entrances," she said. "We have individual garages and a joint patio. We reserve the patio ahead if we are going to entertain. If we are only sunbathing or having lunch alone, the other is always welcomed to join, because we are friends.
"We have made a point of not intruding on each other. In fact, we seldom see each other; if the week has gone by and we have not been together, we try to have Saturday morning coffee and bring each other up to date on the activities.

"We share taxes, upkeep, garbage-and-sewer bills, which come jointly," Mrs. Waddington said. "We have wills made out in order that our heirs will not usurp our plan that we shall each have a home as long as we live.

"We are very ecstatic about our arrangement," she said. "It has been very harmonious, and we are paying $128 a month mortgage [each], including taxes and insurance. Duplexes in our area are renting from $295 to $350 for similar accommodations. Need I say more? Except that I have since retired and can still live."

Need we say more about the advantages of a duplex? Except that if you decide to sell it after age 55 you can count half of your gain toward your once-in-a-lifetime $125,000 tax break.

Landlord Lessons

If you own rental property, your experience as a landlord—or landlady—may even help you be more savvy about selling and buying another home.

"I owned and lived in the upstairs of a duplex in a high-tax area for 30 years. I looked for a small house for two years. I must own a place to move before selling," wrote Gladys Whitfield of Louisville, Kentucky. "What I look for—a neighborhood where the owners took pride in their houses; well-kept neat houses and lawns—I found.

"The house is a five-room Victorian 'restored' cottage. A hardly-any-upkeep house, it is covered with white aluminum siding, double-insulated doors and windows. I bought it from an estate, and I got a very low price for I made them an offer.

"When I was ready to sell my duplex," Mrs. Whitfield continued, "I called three Realtors, to look it over and give me a written estimate on it. I selected the one that would get me the most and held him to it. I had all kinds of up and down people trying to chisel me. I paid no attention to anyone."

Indeed, this ex-landlady knows what she wants, and she isn't about to slow down.

"I have lived here and I am well satisfied," she said. "I get in my car every day and go someplace."

Housing Options- A Home Of Your Own 5

We prefer to own our own homes.
Eva L. Sturrock
a retiree in Skokie, Illinois

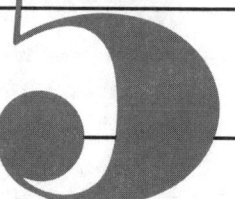

"I am very content in my present home, bought in 1956. It is a modest size in a modest neighborhood, but I'm not modest in saying how satisfied I am with my living conditions."

That letter from Mrs. C. H. Thuemmel of Flushing, Michigan, reflects two fundamental housing preferences of many older people: They want a smaller home that requires minimum upkeep, and they want a home that they own.

Our surveys and others show that the great majority of older people prefer to own their homes rather than rent.

"I am 80 years old, and I am still living in my own home," said Grace Kelso of Clovis, New Mexico. "I feel that a lot of older people would be happier living in their own home. So many many have to sell their lovely home and move to one room in a retirement home."

If you decide that homeownership is what you want in retirement, you have several options: You can stay in the home you already own, you can move to a smaller single-family home, you can move to a condominium or cooperative, or you can move into a mobile home.

Look Before You Leap

To stay or to go can be a difficult decision. Richard Bergere, a retiree and a "holdout" in his Victorian home in Flushing, New York, advised older people to "look before you leap."

"Many an older homeowner, frustrated by social and economic change, thinks that selling the 'old homestead' would solve their immediate problems," Mr. Bergere said. "One cannot project psychological factors onto a house. In other words, 'moving' won't solve your innate problem and oft-time moving will intensify the problem. So instead, stay put and evaluate your home," as follows:

Are you too old to make a new life in the Sunbelt?
Do you really want a homogeneous group of oldsters to live with?
Are you near conveniences like libraries, museums and movies, concerts, stores?
With age in relation to your psychological and physical needs, might it be better for you to "stay put?"

"In summary," Mr. Bergere said, "don't sell; evaluate your needs. Move to another place only on a trial basis and try to reach a conclusion to the question: 'Will I be better off selling?'"

To Go . . . or To Stay

Here are some other factors you should consider, according to the American Association of Retired Persons.

Some reasons for staying put[1]

1. Expenses of your present home are not a strain on your budget, and you can meet them in the future. Or, if you rent, you don't expect the rent you are paying for your present apartment to increase very much.
2. You will avoid the trouble and expense of moving.
3. You will remain among established friends and neighbors where you are familiar with the social life, services, and standards.
4. Your home fits your needs. You enjoy it and can afford it.
5. You like the climate.
6. Your present community offers adequate facilities, including medical facilities, and services.
7. Your children live nearby.
8. The neighborhood isn't likely to deteriorate.

Some reasons for moving

1. Your house has become "too big," too expensive, or otherwise unsuited to retirement life.
2. Too much of your capital is tied up in your home and could provide needed income if invested.

3. Your neighborhood has become unsuitable. If deteriorating, it may cause your home to lose value and upset your way of life. If improving too rapidly, rising taxes and cost of services may become a burden.
4. You dislike the climate or believe it is bad for your health.
5. Your community offers few opportunities for the social, cultural, and physical activities you like.
6. Health facilities and special services for older people are few, expensive, or poorly managed.
7. Your children and friends have moved away.

The final decision is yours. Weigh the advantages and the costs of staying against the advantages and costs of moving. You may decide to stay right where you are. Or you may decide that it's time to say good-bye to your big old house and move to a new and smaller home.

Single-family Houses

Surveys show that most Americans' dream idea of a home-of-their-own is a detached, single-family house. The same is true for older people. The difference for many older people is that the dream may not be as large as it was when you were younger and raising a family.

"Twenty-six years ago we bought a three-story, frame house with a double garage. Now our children are grown and off on their own. The house is too big now for me to take care of it," wrote Jeanne Smyczynski of Youngstown, Ohio. "I have osteoarthritis in both knees and find it difficult to go up and down the stairs and to the cellar to do the wash. We would not buy this type of house again," Mrs. Smyczynski said.

Similarly, that big yard that was such a pleasure when the kids were small can become a grassy headache. Lucille B. Abel of Ben Lomand, California, still loves the three-bedroom, single-level house that she and her late husband built in 1963.

"The only thing I get discouraged about is the yard," said Mrs. Abel, who is in her late 60s. "It is a little over one third of an acre and is becoming a problem to keep up. I have planted too much, and there are gophers and dogs who dig holes, so altogether I never get caught up."

Thinking Small

The advice that many older homeowners give to those following them into retirement is that when it comes to a house, think small.

"It is my opinion that most older people do not need the type of houses that are being built today. All they need is a small compact house," wrote O. L. King, who retired on his 67th birthday and bought a house in LaVerne, California.

"The house measures 850 square feet and sits on a lot 60 feet by 160 feet," Mr. King said. *"The two-bedroom house is about 60 years old and near shopping areas. I am satisfied with my housing situation."*

Actually, an 850-square-foot house isn't considered small in most parts of the world. The median size of all homes in Russia is less than 500 square feet. Most homes in other countries aren't much bigger. But for Americans, an 850-square-foot house is about one-half of the median size of new homes built in 1983.

Many older people advocate living in a small, one-level house that doesn't require climbing steps, with two or possibly three bedrooms instead of four bedrooms, and a small yard. They want to own their homes, but they complain that the compact, well-designed houses they desire are hard to find.

Most don't want houses that are too tiny, however.

"We find that when two people spend 24 hours, 7 days a week together each of us must have space to pursue our own interests," said Joseph Stasick of Albuquerque, New Mexico. *"My place is a small workshop in the garage, while my wife has turned a small bedroom into a hobby room. A second bedroom is for grandchildren and other relatives and friends when visiting. We occupy together a large master-bedroom with a three-quarter bath."*

And others warn that when you do scale down your living space, don't forget that some of your favorite furnishings might not fit.

"We bought a smaller, two-bedroom house to cut heating costs," said Mrs. H. W. Thomas of Grove, Oklahoma. *"However, we didn't realize the furniture pieces we bought were too large for a home with smaller rooms. They were out of proportion and impossible to use."*

Detecting Defects

Shop carefully. You want to avoid the kinds of problems that one retired woman, Mrs. Marjorie Rovillo, and her husband in Amhurst, New York, ran into. They made the mistake of buying a house that, despite an FHA inspection, turned out to have a bad foundation, a bad roof, and obsolete wiring.

"We learned a lot and fast," she wrote. *"Had we checked the code, we would have known we had to rewire the house. Had we

known about roofs, we wouldn't have had the city on our neck to replace the boards and put on a new single-layer roof. We still haven't finished digging the tons of dirt out from under the house. And I don't even want to talk about the obsolete kitchen and bathroom or the fireplaces and furnaces," the woman said.

"Needless to say, both my husband and I have taken courses in real estate," she added. "I'd advise it for every home buyer."

What To Look For

Educating yourself on what makes a good home-buy is a good idea, especially if it's been many years since you purchased a house. The last thing you need during retirement is a home that will add to your worries—and your costs—rather than easing them.

When shopping for a house, here are some key things to look out for:

Construction: How well the house is built is a vital consideration. You probably won't be able to tell yourself. So before you agree to buy a house, it's worth paying $100 or so to hire a professional home inspector. Write it into the sales contract that the purchase is subject to a favorable inspection report. Consider getting an inspection even if you are buying a new home and it doesn't have a warranty—new houses can have defects, too.

Potential repair problems. If you are buying an older home, find out the age of key parts of the house and determine how soon they may need replacing. How old is the roof, the furnace, the wiring, and the plumbing? If they will need replacing in a few years, the cost will eat into your retirement income. For guides on the basic housing structure, and how long parts of a house should last, check Chapter 8 of this book.

Location. You've heard it before and it's true—the three most important features of a house are location, location, and location. Since your house is also an investment, you need to make sure that it is located in an area that isn't on the decline. At the same time, as an older home buyer, you want to avoid an area where values are zooming skyward; that means your property taxes could zoom up, too.

For older buyers, other location factors are important as well. Walk or drive around the area to see how close the house is to transportation, shopping, churches, theaters, recreation areas, and doctors and medical facilities. As one Arkansas City, Kansas, retiree discovered, such considerations can make a big difference.

"In preparing for retirement, I purchased a middle-to-lower price home, which when the needed improvements had been added, makes

an investment of about $25,000," the man wrote. "Although my home is adequate for two people, and utilities are not excessive, it has the following faults:

"I am still too far out from the business district; therefore a car is needed even for the shortest trips to the grocery store, etc. There is no surface transportation, and a car is an expensive addition to one on retirement. So my location is not the best."

As a heart patient, the construction of the house posed other problems, he added.

"The house demands frequent painting and minor repairs. I suggest a more durable siding and even metal-framed windows."

Watch Those Fuel Bills

Check fuel bills and property taxes. These can be the most uncontrollable costs for retirees. Ask to see copies of utility and tax bills. Check the energy-saving features of the house. Are there storm windows? Or will you have to add them? How well is the house insulated? Does it have gas heat or costlier electric heat?

Space. Inspect the interior of the house with retirement living in mind. A big family room may look great, but it may require a lot of upkeep and you might not use it much anyway. Make sure the storage space is adequate for your life-long belongings. See if there are too many stairs to climb. The most important room to many retirees, and to many homeowners of any age, is the kitchen. Check for modern appliances and practical work space.

Remember, the kind of house you preferred in your pre-retirement days may not fit retirement needs.

"We bought our house in 1971. It is a 7-room, 2½ bath, 2-car garage, 1/2 basement split level. I fell in love with it and I still love it," said a West Caldwell, New Jersey, woman. "But the different levels and stairs I must climb really get to me. No matter how I plan, I find I am constantly up and down stairs. And what makes it worse is that I have arthritis and a spinal curvature the last few years.

"I feel we made a mistake with a second full bathroom, as it is too much work," she added. "There should have been one large bath and shower with the 3 bedrooms. I also would have liked a 'Great Room.' We don't need a basement, as it is not used."

Think ahead. "Don't move into a place and assume you always will be as mobile as you are now. Get one level and a house that is as barrier-free as possible," suggested Barry Robinson, communication counsel for the American Association of Retired Persons. Check Chapter 7, on housing design, for more tips on what to look out for.

Use your bargaining power. If you have a big profit from selling a house that has greatly jumped in value over the years, you may be able to make a bigger down payment than usual or even pay cash for your retirement home. That makes you a better-than-average prospect. Use your leverage to negotiate a good price on the home you buy. You may be able to get a bargain price or lower mortgage rate, especially with seller financing, when the housing market is slow and younger buyers are having a difficult time qualifying for financing.

A Check List

There is so much more to look for when buying a house that an entire book could be written on the subject. In fact, the authors of this book have written just such a home-buying book. It is called *The Complete Book of Home Buying*. Published by Dow Jones-Irwin (hardcover) and Bantam Books (paperback), it contains over 350 pages of specific advice about buying (and selling) houses, condominiums, and mobile homes. The book covers everything from "used houses versus new houses" and "What Makes a House a Good Investment," to "House-hunting Hints," and "protecting yourself with a warranty plan."

If that sounds like a plug for the book, it is. But many reviewers agree that you will find it useful when shopping for a house, especially if it has been several years since you purchased a home. To help you get started, two of the tables from the other book are presented here; they show checkpoints for outside and inside a house (Tables 5·1 and 5·2).

The point is that buying the house where you plan to live later may be your most important housing purchase of your life, and you need all the expert advice you can get. Talk to other older people who have bought homes—they can probably give the best advice of all. Frank Zito, a retiree in Bridgewater, New Jersey, for example, offered these specific home-buying tips:

1. Hire a lawyer who is competent in real estate transactions.
2. Make certain that all water and sewer installations and assessments have been paid by the previous owners.
3. Check with the city or township's planning board to ascertain if new shopping centers [and so on], are being planned for your immediate area. Property devaluation may occur.
4. Park near the home you are going to buy during the middle of the night. This will enable you to discover if you will be kept awake at night by excessive traffic noise from nearby highways [and other disturbances].

Table 5·1 Checkpoints for outside the home

Make your own personal observations, but also consult your builder, local government, real estate agent, and friends. As you explore various homes and neighborhoods, use these checkpoints to compare them and see whether the housing environment matches up with your wants and needs.

	Home 1	Home 2	Home 3
Shopping Are there adequate facilities close by?			
Churches Are they available and convenient?			
Community Is the community well-planned?			
Neighbors Are they likely to be compatible with your tastes and lifestyle?			
Police and fire protection Are they adequate for the area?			
Schools Are the schools your children will attend located to suit you?			
Hospital Is there a hospital or medical center nearby?			
Hazards Are there hazards such as gas or oil tanks and streams that might overflow at a considerable distance?			
Recreation Are there suitable facilities within walking distance for young and old alike?			
Trash and garbage disposal Are the arrangements adequate and frequent enough?			
Traffic Are streets likely to be busy or quiet? Does the speed limit suit you?			
Car parking Are there adequate car parking spaces and garage facilities for your needs?			
Transportation Is public transportation adequate and handy?			
Lay of the land Is land well-drained? And do you like the "micro-climate"? For example, in a valley you may have a great deal of fog; on a hill, it may be windy!			

(continued)

Table 5·1 (continued)

	Home 1	Home 2	Home 3
Landscaping Has proper landscaping been done to prevent erosion?			
Water Is there a reliable and drinkable source of water with adequate pressure to fit present and future community needs?			
Sewerage Is the sanitary sewerage disposal system reliable and adequate, and does it meet present and anticipated future community needs?			
Privacy Are lots or units arranged to suit your family lifestyle?			
Nuisances Are there nearby sources of excessive noise, smoke, soot, dust, or odors that will degrade your housing environment or endanger members of your household?			
Assessments Are there special assessments covering a portion of the lot, street, or community development costs which will mean added monthly charges to you for a specified number of years?			

Table 5·2 Checkpoints for inside the home

What you should look for inside the house depends on what you personally need and want, so it's a good idea to compile your own list of features to check. Here are some questions to start you off, but you should add checkpoints according to your personal concerns. Rate the houses you're comparing as good, fair, or poor.

	Good	Fair	Poor
Is the roof leakproof?			
Do walls seem sound and smooth, floors firm and level, carpentry well-fitted and joined?			
Is the basement clean and dry?			
Is lighting good, in daylight and at night?			

(continued)

Table 5·2 (continued)

	Good	Fair	Poor
Are rooms large enough to take your furniture and is there sufficient wall space for arranging furniture?	___	___	___
Is the floor plan well-laid-out with separate areas for living, working, and sleeping?	___	___	___
Do bedrooms and baths provide quiet and privacy away from the living area?	___	___	___
Can you get from entry doors to other parts of the house without crossing the living room?	___	___	___
Does the kitchen suit you: does it allow for good light and ventilation and are there enough outlets for plugging in all your kitchen appliances?	___	___	___
Are there ample cabinets and counter work space for your family needs?	___	___	___
Have all interior wall, ceiling, and floor surfaces been properly finished?	___	___	___
Is there adequate and convenient closet room and storage space for linens and equipments?	___	___	___
Do doors, windows, and drawers work easily and safely?	___	___	___
Does plumbing work well and quietly, with adequate water pressure and free-flowing drains?	___	___	___
Is heating, cooling, and ventilating equipment satisfactory, convenient?	___	___	___
Are there enough electrical outlets well arranged and sufficient amperage for your electrical equipment?	___	___	___
Are bathrooms and lavatories conveniently located?	___	___	___
Are wall spaces usable for attractive furniture arrangement, and not too chopped up by windows and doors?	___	___	___
Are the rooms located to take advantage of sun and shade?	___	___	___
Are the views from the windows to your liking?	___	___	___
Are the temperature controls located in safe and convenient places?	___	___	___
If there are stairs, are there landings and adequate handrails?	___	___	___
Does the home have full roof gutters and an adequate number of downspouts and splash blocks?	___	___	___

Going Condo

If even a small house seems like too much bother, there are alternatives. Many older people are turning to condominium apartments and townhouses, which offer the advantages of homeownership without the upkeep.

"We have been living here in northeastern Pennsylvania since 1973, so we knew at that time that we did not need acres of land to care for or to keep snow-free. We also did not need a large house. We solved our living problem in a very satisfactory way," wrote Jacquelin Craig of Laflin, Pennsylvania.

"We own our small townhouse, but pay dues to an owners association for lawn care and snow removal," Mrs. Craig said. *"Since my husband, David, enjoys gardening, the trees and flowers and bushes are our responsibility. The house is small, but there is an adequate basement with the space for me to do the laundry and for him to have an office. There are three bedrooms, so we have room for a guest and for a TV room. Because we live in a townhouse, we have neighbors on either side, so we are neither lonely nor isolated,"* she said.

With the condominium concept, you buy a housing unit that is all your own. But you also buy part ownership of the development's "common elements," which can include everything from the hallways to the swimming pool. You and the other owners run the development (or hire a management firm) and pay somebody to cut the grass and maintain the grounds. For this, you pay a maintenance fee in addition to the cost of your unit.

Condo housing comes in all shapes and sizes. There are high-rise apartment buildings, low-rise garden apartments, townhouses that are like row houses and even attached houses. Some are as big as a house inside, but, generally, condo units are smaller than single-family houses. In 1982, the average living space in a newly built condominium was 1,250 square feet, compared with 1,710 square feet in a new single-family house.

Big and Little Developments

The primary buyers of condominium housing are young singles and "empty nesters" over age 45 who don't need large homes and who don't want to bother with the upkeep of big houses and yards. Many developments, especially in the Sunbelt, are aimed specifically at those who are retirees.

One of Florida's three Century Village developments in Deerfield Beach north of Miami, considered to be one of the largest retirement condominium projects in the United States, has a population of 15,500. It boasts a huge clubhouse that is used each night by 3,000 to 4,000 residents, a 1,600-seat theater that would put many Broadway houses to shame, and a social staff so large that one employee refers to Century Village as a "sleep-away camp for senior citizens."

The emphasis on culture and educational activities there is aimed at attracting former city dwellers, and most of the Century Village residents are from New York. The spartan-but-pleasant apartments in two-story and four-story buildings cost $29,000 to $45,000 for one bedroom and $45,000 to $70,000 for two bedrooms.

But there are plenty of smaller condo developments, some with buildings of three or four apartments arranged in clusters.

"To me, the cluster-home type of condominium is an ideal setup for people who want to own their own home, a single residence, and yet be relieved of the outside maintenance and the lawn area," wrote Mrs. Robert Montgomery of Venice, Florida. *"It is very easy to meet your neighbors in this situation. Most of the residents here are retirees, and we help each other in times of emergencies."*

Condo Advantages

Condominium living offers various advantages for homeowners of all ages, but especially for retirees. They include:

Cost. There's no limit to the price you can pay for a luxury condo penthouse on New York's Park Avenue, on the Atlantic Ocean in Palm Beach, Florida, or many other places. But condominium housing generally is somewhat cheaper than single-family homes because the condos are smaller, have joint walls, and need less land. In 1983, the median price of new condominiums was $67,000, compared with $76,000 for new houses. And condos converted from rental apartments are even less costly. As a result, a converted condo can be an affordable alternative for older people who want their own home but without the hassle of a big house.

"After retiring at age 65 and working part-time as a free-lance writer, "the care of my house got me down. I could no longer afford cleaning help and to do it myself was rough on the joints," said Margaret Barnetson of Broadview Heights, Ohio. "I sold my house and bought a small condominium and haven't been sorry up to the present time. My suite is on the ground floor, has two bedrooms, one of which I use as a work room, a bath-and-a-half, an adequate kitchen for one person."

Maintenance-free living. Well, you still have to vacuum the floor yourself. But you don't have to worry about mowing the lawn, fixing the roof, and repairing the swimming pool and other parts of the development. At Willow Creek, Colorado, a Writer Corporation development near Denver, Dick and Juanita Frank, after their children had moved out, bought a townhouse less than half the size of their sprawling 3,500-square-foot ranch house.

"We upgraded ourselves," said Mr. Frank. "We released ourselves from weekend chores."

Recreation facilities. With a condo development, facilities like a swimming pool and a clubhouse usually come built-in. If you want, you can find about as many services as you want.

When Lester and Mary Ruth Olson retired and moved from New Jersey to McAllen, Texas, they bought a condominium at a village adjacent to the LaPasada Hotel.

"We have the advantages of the hotel swimming pool, switchboard, and they also take in our mail," Mrs. Olsen said. "If you are ill, they will deliver meals to your apartment. Also maid service (but of course, extra charges), elevator service, and covered garage is included. You can't beat it, we believe.

"The condominium is located in the center of town. We selected an efficiency apartment furnished," she added. "We are happy we did."

Condo Shopping—What To Look For and Watch Out For

Condos are an increasingly popular housing alternative and now account for about 15 percent of all new homes built each year.

But condo living isn't for everyone. In a condo project, your neighbors are close by. While you own your own home, what you do to the exterior must be approved by other owners. Indeed, how the development is run is determined by a majority of the owners—if most want tennis courts and lighting for the courts, they can vote to raise the assessment fee and you must pay, even though you don't play tennis. Keeping the project running smoothly requires the cooperation of many residents.

Nevertheless, studies indicate that most condo owners are happy with their arrangement. If you decide to go condo, here's what to look out for:

Location. As with any housing buy, location is a prime consideration. Is the condo development near to needed facilities and transportation? Are values increasing so that it is a good investment. Check with real estate agents to find out the resale value of units.

Construction. Poor construction quality was the No. 1 complaint of condominium owners surveyed by the U.S. Department of Housing and Urban Development. Poor soundproofing was the deficiency most often cited. Before you buy, have the unit inspected by someone who knows condos. Make sure the inspection includes the common areas and facilities, because you share responsibility for those, too.

"Some condominiums may be trouble-free, but others can be dreadfully disappointing," warned one couple from Connecticut. *They bought a condo on Long Island, and "unfortunately, the flaws were not apparent. Two years ago we had a 'special assessment' of over $400 to pay for a new pool. The original one lifted right out of the ground during a heavy rainfall and the developer disclaimed responsibility."*

In addition, *"all of the buildings need new roofs,"* they said. *"They leak so badly that many of the units have suffered severe interior damage. The cost of replacing the roofs and correcting the many other construction defects would be so prohibitive we have had to make do with patch jobs here and there."*

If you plan to buy an apartment that has been converted to a condominium from a rental unit in an older building, check closely. The exterior refurbishing may look great, but what about the building's innards—the plumbing and heating systems, for example? Before you buy, make sure to check the engineering report that should be provided by the seller on the condition of the entire building.

Maintenance fees. Find out what monthly fee you will have to pay for maintenance and other upkeep costs, including management of the project. In new projects, watch out for "low balling," where the developer may keep the fee artificially low to attract buyers. Once the developer leaves the project in the hands of the owners, the fee must be raised sharply to meet actual costs.

Budgets. Check the project's operating budget to see if fees seem realistic. Also, make sure the owners association has an adequate reserve for emergency expenses and repairs. Experts say that the reserve should be equal to 1 to 3 percent of the property's replacement value.

Recreation facilities. Don't be swayed by fancy clubhouses, swimming pools, tennis courts, and other amenities. You may not really need them, and they add to your monthly fee. Talk to some of the residents and find out if the project offers the activities you want—or if the owner-residents are likely to push for costly additions that won't interest you, but for which you will have to help pay.

"Our association fees were used for an elaborate clubhouse, with a paid social director, pools, tennis courts, professional manager, etc. But we didn't use these facilities," said one Michigan woman. She and her husband had purchased a condominium near Detroit. "I loved the condominium, but our association fee ran about $100 a month," she said. So they moved to a detached, single-family house."

Responsive management. If you plan to move into a condo project catering to older people, make sure the management is in tune with the residents' wishes.

One developer said that, in line with his high-priced consultant's advice, he installed a huge swimming pool at a Florida condo complex for older people. But few of the residents used the fancy pool. Puzzled by the lack of interest, the developer asked the residents why they didn't use the pool. Their answer: They didn't want to swim. What they wanted was to have more chairs around the pool so they could meet and chat with friends. And what they *really* wanted was a place to dance.

"I could have made the pool out of blue cardboard and put up a lot of chairs around it, and most people would have liked it better," the developer said. He vowed to stop listening to consultants and pay more attention to his customers. And he built a dance floor that is jammed every weekend.

Hidden costs. Make sure that the builder of the project hasn't retained ownership of the land or recreational facilities. In Florida, some developers leased the recreational facilities back to the condo owners for an additional monthly fee on contracts running up to 99 years. What's more, the contracts contained clauses allowing sharp annual increases to adjust for inflation. If the residents refused to pay the fees on these "recreational leases," the builder could foreclose on their condo units.

"The worst mistake we made was buying a condominium in a development of which the developer retained title and possession of the recreation facilities, so that we had to pay recreation rent which this developer tied to the Consumer Price Index for annual increases," said Herman and Helen Donn of Century Village in West Palm Beach, Florida. "This situation has now been corrected, but if we had the chance we would never buy a home in any development where we would have to pay ground rent to anyone other than our own condominium association. We believe a developer should relinquish control of the recreational facilities."

These "rec leases" are banned now. But be on guard for projects where previous escalation clauses are still in effect.

Protect your deposit. If you put down a deposit on a new condo, make sure the money is placed in a separate escrow account. Some condo builders have gone bankrupt and prospective buyers lost their down payments, which were mingled with the builders' other funds.

Check those condo regulations. Make certain you know the rules of the owners association before you buy. Otherwise, you may discover too late that in an "adults only" community, for example, your grandchildren may not be able to stay overnight. Or that your pets may not be allowed. Make sure there aren't restrictions against selling your unit without the approval of other owners.

Inspect those condo documents. Buying a condo is even more complex than buying a house, because you also buy an interest in the entire development. The legal documents are long and difficult to read. The basic documents are:

The master deed. This is the controlling condominium document and describes the size, location, equipment, and assessment provisions of the entire project.

The condominium sales contract. This is your purchase agreement to buy your unit.

The by-laws. These are the rules and regulations that you must abide by as a resident of the development.

All of these documents usually are written in legalese. You should have a lawyer who is familiar with condo purchases look the documents over before you put your name on the dotted line.

Additional Reading

If you want to know more about condominiums, several good publications are available:

1. *Questions and Answers about Condominiums,* published by the U.S. Department of Housing and Urban Development. This 53-page booklet is available free from the U.S. Consumer Information Center in Pueblo, Colorado. (See page 250 for instructions on ordering.)

2. *Condominium Buyers Guide,* published by the National Association of Home Builders, 15th and M Street, N.W., Washington, DC 20005.

3. *The Condominium Book,* by Lee Butcher, published by Dow Jones-Irwin, 1818 Ridge Road, Homewood, IL 60430.

Going Co-op

Another way to buy an apartment is to buy into a cooperative apartment building. About half a million people live in co-ops, mainly in the

Northeast and in a few large Midwest cities, such as Chicago and Detroit. Co-ops are especially popular in New York City, where units typically sell for over $100,000—and for $500,000 or more at some swank addresses. But co-ops also can be sold for more modest prices in retirement communities and in buildings catering to lower-income buyers.

The main difference between a co-op and a condominium is that with a co-op you don't own your individual apartment. Instead, you own a share of the entire cooperative, which gives you a right to occupy your unit.

As with a condo, you generally are responsible for two separate monthly payments. First, you must make payments on the mortgage —but principal and interest only—the mortgage that you got to buy your co-op share. You also pay a monthly fee, or "rent," to the co-op corporation to cover your share of the building mortgage, property taxes, and maintenance costs.

One advantage is that there are no individual settlement fees when you buy, because the cooperative already has a mortgage for the entire building. When you sell, you sell your stock, and it's not a deed transfer. That's quite different from buying a condo or a house, which requires shelling out dough for closing costs.

The cooperative is owned by the residents of the buildings. When you buy an apartment, you are issued a share of stock. It's like owning a share of General Motors, but with one very big difference. As a shareholder in a cooperative, you are not only an owner, you are also part of management. You have a vote in how the cooperative is run.

The co-op owners have the right to use all common facilities owned by the building. These might include a lounge, a swimming pool, a game room or other amenities. In a retirement community you would have the same right as other residents to such outdoor facilities as a golf course, a medical center, a bus service, or other services.

A co-op purchaser should make the same kind of inspections and checks about the building that a condo buyer should make about investing in a condo development. That is, to check the operating costs, whether reserves are adequate, the structural condition of the entire building, the common facilities owned by the co-op association, and whether the "rent" is likely to be increased. One thing to check in an older co-op building is whether the old mortgage may have to be refinanced at a higher interest rate, which would raise the "rent."

Co-op Problems

Co-ops have disadvantages. For one, they aren't readily available in many cities and, like other housing, co-op apartments that are on the market can be very expensive. In addition, financing can be difficult to obtain since the purchaser doesn't own the apartment itself. However, lending laws have been changed to make co-op financing more feasible, so that problem may be easing.

Another disadvantage can be the difficulty in selling a co-op unit when other co-op owners veto your sale if they don't like the purchaser. In New York City, co-op owners in top-dollar cooperatives have balked at proposed sales of units to show-business celebrities and others who they fear will generate too much public commotion. One New York City co-op turned down the sale of a luxury apartment to former President Richard Nixon on grounds that he and his Secret Service contingent would disrupt the lives of other residents.

Co-ops and Older People

The owner control of cooperatives, though, can offer special advantages for older people. The co-op can be structured to hold down housing costs for resident-members.

In many older cooperatives—and most cooperatives are older—the mortgage either is paid off or has a very low interest rate. As a result, the monthly fees need to be high enough only to cover a little more than basic operating costs, such as property taxes and maintenance. And to hold down the purchase price of the apartments, the by-laws may limit how much residents can sell their units for, or require them to sell the units back to the cooperative. This keeps the purchase price from shooting up, as it might on the open housing market.

These "limited equity" arrangements have been used for years in some places, sometimes with the aid of local housing agencies. In one Detroit co-op for example, owners were paying under $200 a month for apartments of the same size as those renting for twice as much in rental buildings.

In considering membership in a housing cooperative, the National Association of Housing Cooperatives recommends that you keep these points in mind:

Considerations for co-op membership

1. The cooperative association's board of directors must keep its members informed of all its actions. A regular communications system—frequent newsletter, information bulletin, special meetings, solicitation of members on opinions and priorities—strengthen the relationship between the board of directors and the members.

2. The cooperative association must maintain adequate financial reserves to protect the cooperative and its members' interests. These usually include a general operating reserve and a reserve for replacement of components

of buildings as they deteriorate. Such reserves reduce the possibility of members having to pay unexpected special charges in emergencies.

3. An annual audit conducted by professional accountants should be available to all members.

4. The co-op board must have the right to approve incoming members who take the places of those leaving the cooperative to protect the interests of the remaining members.

5. Sub-leasing should be permitted only for the short-term absence of a member, if allowed at all. To allow sub-leasing on any scale would be a return to absentee ownership.

Further information is available from the National Association of Housing Cooperatives, 2501 M Street, N.W., Washington, DC 20037.

Mobile Homes

One of the most economical ways to get rolling in retirement is to buy a mobile home.

"I am 66 years old. Ten years ago, I moved from a 15-room house into a 2-bedroom house trailer, and I am very glad I did," wrote Alberta Brown of Middlebury, Vermont.

"My family of six children had grown up and gone, and I didn't need all that big house to care for," Mrs. Brown said. "The time I saved keeping house was fantastic. The house trailer is cheaper to heat also.

"I parted with many things, especially antiques. But, after all, one tends to save too much, especially nick-nacks," she said. "My husband died four years ago, so I am alone in my home and I am very glad that I live in smaller quarters. I see the trailer home as a good idea for senior citizens."

The major advantage of mobile homes is that they are the least expensive housing around. The median price of even a new, double-wide mobile home is under $30,000, compared with a median of over $70,000 for single-family homes. Used mobile homes are even less costly and can be good buys.

What's more, you can forget about those tiny old tin cans on wheels of yesteryear. Today's mobile homes are big—the typical size is 14 feet wide by 69 feet long—and many are double-wides or manufactured houses that are much larger. Most "mobile" homes are never moved once they are set on a home site.

"I find it amazing that many persons still confuse mobile homes with motor homes and trailers," said Elsie H. Cesak of Calimesa, California. "I have an amusing mental picture of a startled traffic gaping at our 24 × 64-foot house blocking most of the freeway.

"Our double-wide home has two bedrooms, two baths, living room, with dining area and a family room. It has central gas heat and central refrigeration. Certainly it is satisfactory in space and comfort," she said.

Increasingly, mobile homes are made out of wood instead of metal. Often they are factory-built homes set on permanent subdivision lots. In fact, under the 1980 Housing Act they aren't even called mobile homes anymore—the government says that now they are to be called "manufactured houses."

These new-generation mobile homes—whoops, manufactured houses—look just like conventional houses. They are sold and financed with the land included. In Germantown, Maryland, multi-section homes, including land, were selling for $40,000 to $62,000. In Sarasota, Florida, an adult community of condominium manufactured houses ranged in price from $33,850 to $46,550, with 25-year mortgages. Such new condos, dealers say, are practically indistinguishable from regular site-built houses.

Nearly 8.5 million people live in about 4 million mobile homes* in the United States. And the popularity of such living is growing as the cost of conventional housing increases. The new mobile-homeowners have nearly wiped out the old negative images of trailer dwellers.

"People who own mobile homes are no longer 'tramps,' 'floaters,' etc. They are law-abiding people with limited incomes who wish to do something besides support a home," asserted Dorothy L. Harmening of East Moline, Illinois. "I live in a 10-foot by 50-foot, 2-bedroom mobile home and I personally would not live any other way," Mrs. Harmening said.

The places where mobile homes are parked also have changed dramatically. The seedy parks of yesteryear have rapidly been replaced by sparkling subdivisions with paved streets, green lawns, driveways, sidewalks, swimming pools, and other amenities. Many parks cater specifically to retirees.

"Mobile parks are a way of life, and for retired seniors offer advantages," said a widow from San Mateo, California. "They have their own individual dwelling without the large yard upkeep. They have the companionship and concern of neighbors who respond quickly in an emergency. And contrary to the belief of some, most senior citizens don't feel depressed being among others like themselves. Indeed, they appreciate having their own problems understood."

---

*Since our survey participants in their letters refer to these homes as *mobile homes* rather than *manufactured houses*, we also will refer to them generally as such.

The "Ideal Housing"—Mobile

Many older people find mobile homes an affordable way to combine homeownership and the fringe benefits of community living.

"The most ideal housing for the middle class retiree is the mobile home in a good park," said Erma C. Bordewisch of St. Petersburg, Florida. "My home is 24 feet by 64 feet with loads of closet space, 2 baths, 2 bedrooms, family room, large living room, dining room and sun room. I have everything a house has to offer, plus a screened porch.

"The advantage of the mobile home is that you have instant friends and social activities," Mrs. Bordewisch said. "The monthly fee includes lot rent, water, garbage pickup, use of all the clubhouse facilities, which include the pool room, card room, plus a large swimming pool, finished streets for biking, and being in an adult park frees one from vandalism, yet the grandchildren are permitted to visit anytime.

"My home is spacious, well-planned and a joy to live in," she added. "The mobile home always comes with carpeting and draperies throughout. The best of mobile homes cost about one-fifth the cost of a home with equal space. I am a very satisfied mobile-home dweller."

Mobile Home Concerns

Living in a mobile home offers lots of advantages, especially for retirees on limited budgets. But there are possible pitfalls, too. They include:

Lot fees. In addition to buying your mobile home, if you park it in a mobile-home park you must pay a monthly rent for the lot it sits on. These fees can range from $60 a month to over $600 a month in some luxury parks. And, like rent, these fees can—and usually do—go up.

"In July 1977, I sold my home of some years just outside of Boston, and moved to California to be near my only daughter. I bought a mobile home in a mobile-home park, upon which I paid $120 a month space rental plus my utilities," wrote Florence Munro of Morgan Hill, California. "Within a few months, my space rent was increased to $140 a month. [Soon thereafter] we were notified of a 15 percent increase. That brought space rent for a lot approximately 48 × 80 feet to $169. And the increase in gas and electricity brought our monthly payments up to $200 or more.

"We find it all so exorbitant," Mrs. Munro said. "One park has a long-term lease which residents sign and then the owners [of the park] agree to a reasonable increase. We are hoping that something similar can be worked out for all of us."

Construction problems. Construction quality has been a problem with some mobile homes. So have fires and a vulnerability to high winds (e.g., the wind blows the homes over) in some areas. But construction standards were upgraded by federal standards in 1976. Those rules also require builders to give at least a one-year warranty—though a continuing problem, according to the Federal Trade Commission, is that some builders either don't adequately honor the warranties or move too slowly to fix defects.

Owners report other problems:

"We thought we were getting a double-insulated mobile home, but it isn't. You can feel cold air coming in here and there," said Betty Smith of Whiting, New Jersey. *"Also, never pick one where the oil burner heater is not in its own enclosed closet,"* she advised. *"When that Coleman comes on at night, and there's no door to muffle it, you need ear plugs to sleep through the noise.*

"Aside from these two problems, we like it here," she added.

Park rules. The regulations set down by the mobile-home park may affect your mobile-home living. For instance, when your mobile home gets too old, you may have to move out.

When Mr. and Mrs. Melvin Dahlstrom retired—Mr. Dahlstrom had been a pastor for 54 years—and bought a $17,000 mobile home, they put it in a park in LaVerne, California.

"It is a beautiful park—with wide streets and a beautiful clubhouse and pool," Mrs. Dahlstrom said. *"But now there is a new rule that when your house is 18 to 20 years old, it can no longer remain on the grounds. My husband is 81 and I am 73. Within the next five years, we must decide what to do. The extreme expense of moving a house off the lot and where to move it is heart-breaking.*

"We feel safe in this retirement community," she added. *"Rules are not extreme—it's just that you feel so governed."*

Indeed, overall the Dahlstroms are happy with mobile-home living, after living on no more than $600 a month during Mr. Dahlstrom's 54-year ministry in such cities as Detroit, Seattle, and Pasadena.

"We never dreamed we could live so well on Social Security and a church pension," Mrs. Dahlstrom said.

Price appreciation—or the lack of it. Mobile homes historically have declined in value like cars instead of increased in value like houses. But that is changing, too. Many modern mobile homes hold their value or actually appreciate if they are located in modern, desirable parks.

"I agree that there are parks that aren't appealing. But the reason for the upsurge of mobile homes is not those parks and their tinny mobile homes that do run down," asserted Mrs. T. H. Biedenkopf of Saugus, California.

As part of their retirement the Biedenkopfs moved from their single-family house to a $50,000 wooden mobile home in a modern park.

"The first people who have sold their homes in the first park area here have lost no money on the sales. In fact, homes are now appreciating in value," Mrs. Biedenkopf said.

Financing problems. Instead of a 25-year mortgage, mobile-home buyers often get a 7- to 10-year loan at a relatively high interest rate. But that, too, is changing. Lenders are beginning to offer long-term loans at rates competitive with house-mortgage loans, especially for manufactured homes situated on permanent lots. Both the Federal Housing Administration and the Veterans Administration have active mobile-home loan programs available through private lenders.

Mobile-home financing should be more readily available because of the 1980 Housing Act that officially sanctioned the name "manufactured housing." Among other things, the law raised the maximum for FHA-insured loans for mobile homes; the maximum is $47,500 on a double-wide, and up to $90,000 on certain manufactured homes in high-cost areas. It also authorized the Federal National Mortgage Association (Fannie Mae), to create a secondary, or re-sale, market for mobile-home mortgages. This is important because it means lenders will be able to sell mobile-home mortgages to Fannie Mae, where the lenders will be more willing to make such loans.

Of course, because of their relatively low price, mobile homes can be purchased for cash by many retirees. That means the only housing outlays are for the rental fee, utilities, and taxes. It may be the least expensive way to have a home of your own.

"After 30 years of owning homes, my husband and I purchased a mobile home, 1,250 square feet. We are very happy with our decision," said Ray and Linda Bilohlavek of Rohnert Park, California. "Not only is it a joy for housekeeping, more cupboards than I've ever had, but the fringe benefits of a swimming pool, jacuzzi, and clubhouse are just a few of the positive items," Mrs. Bilohlavek said.

"Naturally, it would have been a different story if we hadn't been able to buy the mobile home outright," they said. "There is a monthly rent that does keep going up. At present, our bill, including gas and electricity, averages $165 monthly.

"We would say that if a couple has an income of $13,000 to $15,000, and own their mobile home, they could be very comfortable and happy as they become older," they said.

Design is important, too, in mobile homes. After buying her first mobile home, which is 14 feet wide by 60 feet long, Lucille B. Coopersmith, a registered nurse and a widow in her late 50s in Glendale, Arizona, offered this advice:

> First, know your own needs. Physical handicaps must be considered. I have arthritis in my elbows and hands. Therefore, most of the kitchen needs have to be at the level of my waist or below. Make a list of kitchen needs and be sure that what you request can be altered. I would have had more shelves placed in the appropriate cabinets to increase storage for dishes, pots, and pans.
> Faucets should be up and down to avoid having to use hands and more physical energy. Be sure the kitchen faucet is high enough to fill your coffee pot—most mobile homes have smaller sinks or tend to be shallow.
> There should be room for company and out-of-town guests. I have two baths and two bedrooms—each located at either end of the house for privacy.
> Money: determine outside needs for landscaping, etc.; add another $1,000 to $1,500 so no surprises come up.
> Go ground level to give you accessibility; it's also safer without steps. Check the vents, particularly floor types, to be sure your bed isn't going over one or your sofa [over one] in the living room.

And, for cat owners, said Mrs. Coopersmith, "be sure there is an adequate space for your kitty litter."

Because of their compact size and price, mobile—or manufactured—houses can be an economical and enjoyable housing alternative for many older people. For further information on mobile homes, write the Manufactured Housing Institute, 1745 Jefferson Davis Highway, Suite 511, Arlington, VA 22202.

12 Rules for Mobile Home Buying

Just be sure to shop carefully before choosing the mobile home and the park where you will put it. Here are 12 rules to follow:

1. Always have a space to put your mobile home *before* you purchase the home. Get a written guarantee from a mobile-home park that you choose in advance that there is a space reserved for you.

2. Check various brands of mobile homes before buying. Check local owners' groups for advice. Don't be dazzled by fancy interiors of floor models. Instead, check for sound construction.

The American Association of Retired Persons gives this advice: "Look for wood rather than plastic, for thick walls, floors, and roofs, and for heavy insulation (in a moderate climate, insulation should be at least three-and-a-half inches at the ceiling and two inches in the walls and floors). Ask about the capacity of the water heater. Is the wiring copper? It should be. Do the doors have reinforcements against warping? Are the windows well caulked?"

3. Check the warranties. Though federal law requires a one-year warranty, some makers offer warranties of up to five years, sometimes at an extra cost. Find out what is covered by the warranty and what isn't. Ask for, in writing, the correct procedure for making a warranty claim. Make sure you understand what will be covered by the dealer who sells you the home, by the manufacturers, and others, such as the company that made the appliances.

4. Check for extra costs. Find out if the sale price includes the cost of transporting the mobile home to a park and setting it up.

"William R. Palmer of Monmouth, New Jersey, added this caution: "My contention is that mobile home dealers and landlords still set up large mobile homes like travel trailers. They need to be treated more nearly like houses. A complete foundation isn't necessary, but a concrete slab is advisable to avoid even casual drainage of water under the home. And the slab should be laid over perimeter footings at no more than 10-foot intervals that go 6 inches below the frost line in undisturbed soil, or down to the hardpan in fill dirt.

"Aside from that, we love our mobile home," said Mr. Palmer.

5. Consider buying a mobile home from an owner who is in the park. If the home is already on a lot, you will save transportation and hook-up fees. But don't buy a mobile home just to get into a park. And beware of parks that require you to buy a mobile home from a particular dealer. The sale price probably will be higher than at other dealers.

6. Consider buying a used mobile home, especially one already in place in an attractive park. The price will be cheaper, and, again, you save money in moving and setting-up costs. Stick to models built since June 1976, when the U.S. Department of Housing and Urban Development began requiring mobile homes to meet certain quality and safety standards.

7. Consider paying cash if you can afford it. This will reduce your monthly costs. If you finance, shop around for the best terms. Look for 15-year loans insured by the FHA or, if you are a veteran, guaranteed by the VA. You can get longer-term loans for manufactured homes on permanent sites.

8. Check the taxes. Most states now charge personal-property or other special taxes on mobile homes. Homes on permanent lots may be charged regular property taxes.

9. Shop around for a modern, attractive mobile-home park. Drive around and look at the lots to make sure they aren't too close to each other. Check the streets, the kinds of homes that are parked in the community, the services, and the recreational facilities. Look around to see how far it is to stores, churches, theaters, and police and fire protection.

"The greatest mistake I made was failing to check on public transportation," said one 74-year-old mobile-home owner in Harbor City, California.

Also, talk to local real estate agents and find out if homes in the park are appreciating or depreciating.

"It is very important to really shop for the mobile park that fits your needs," said Mrs. Bilohlavek of Rohnert Park, California. "Because my husband is still employed, we did not want to live where everyone is retired. Because I've been a pre-school director all my working years, I wanted children around. We were fortunate to find a park with adults in one section and families in another."

10. Check all fees. Find out if the park has an entrance fee. Ask if it charges a fee to hook up a mobile home to utilities. Find out how much you pay each month to rent your lot and for other facilities. Remember, the fancier the amenities, the more you'll probably pay. Make sure you get at least a one-year lease so that you can't be evicted without adequate cause. And check the lease to make sure your fees can't be raised without proper notice.

11. Investigate the park rules. Make sure they won't restrict your lifestyle or your rights as a homeowner or home seller. Are there restrictions on having people visit or stay overnight, or on pets, or on certain activities? Are there minimum size and age requirements for mobile homes allowed in the park? Do older homes have to be moved out after they reach a certain age?

Talk to current residents and learn if they are satisfied with the park management.

"In choosing a mobile park, it would be wise to talk to some tenants in the park to find out if it is a happy place or not. Managers can be a pain," advised Margaret D. Seibel of Desert Hot Springs, in California.

12. Take safety precautions. Make sure your mobile home has a smoke detector. Check with the local fire department for other safety tips for mobile homes. If necessary, make sure your home is firmly anchored to protect against high winds.

Shop wisely and you, too, can find permanent retirement happiness in a mobile home, like one couple from Bradenton, Florida.

"My husband is 96 years old and I am close to 90. We retired in 1946 and purchased a mobile home and have lived in a mobile-home park ever since," the wife wrote. *"We are still happy and able to take care of each other in Florida."*

More Housing Options- Renting

Americans have been brainwashed into the idea that they must own a home.
Geraldine Beeman
retiree in Houston, Texas

For many older people, a pleasant apartment provides a comfortable and convenient lifestyle.

"After age 65, I gradually decreased my hours of employment and retired at the age of 75. I feel that I made a good choice of living quarters back in 1958—an apartment to rent within less than 10 minutes' walk to my place of employment—and will remain here as long as circumstances permit," said Grace M. Haire of Newport, Rhode Island.

"I am centrally located in a delightful city with a good climate and easy walking distance of a good shopping center. Bus service is close by, with free hours for older persons. What more could one ask?"

Advantages of Renting

If you don't have the money to buy a home, you have no choice but to rent. And renting can make sense for those who have the cash to purchase a home, or make a hefty down payment on one, but who don't want to tie up their money in a house. Instead, the money can be invested to generate income.

Renting also can offer these advantages:

Renting may be cheaper. Rents generally haven't gone up as fast—so far—as housing costs. And more than 100 communities have rent controls. With rising home prices and high mortgage rates, plus increasing property taxes, renting may be the cheapest way to go.

Renters have less maintenance. If something goes wrong with the furnace or the plumbing needs fixing, you just call the landlord. And you don't have to worry about mowing a lawn or shoveling snow.

"Older people do not need the worry of homeownership and many times can not afford to have the repair work done," said Houston's Miss Beeman.

Interior upkeep requires less work. With less space, generally, than a house, there is less to take care of in an apartment. Single older people especially don't need as much room, and apartments often are located near in-city conveniences.

"Before I retired, in order to eliminate transportation to and from the job, I took a studio-efficiency apartment near the job," said Carl P. Anderson of St. Petersburg, Florida. *"Best move I ever made.*

"For one person, there is no equal to the compact living a studio provides," he said. *"Even more so for one retiree, as it seems 'homey,' where a large place or a house would and does give an empty-home feeling leading to a depressed attitude for one having a tendency to be lonesome, which I may say I am not."*

Utilities. In a rental apartment, your utilities may be included in the rent—although landlords increasingly require tenants to pay their own utility costs.

Whether to rent or own depends largely on what kind of lifestyle you prefer as an individual. But as far as economics are concerned, sit down and figure out on paper what it would cost you to own a home and what it would cost you to rent a comparable apartment. In evaluating homeownership, you might want to consider the likely appreciation in the value of a house. You can balance that against what income you could generate now by investing the money that you would put into a house.

But before making your final decision, consider all the aspects of apartment living that you can, including the possibility of increasing costs.

Problems of Renting

The advantages of renting must be compared with the disadvantages. And the biggest worry of all for renters is that their rents can—and usually do—go up.

"My rent on a one-bedroom apartment goes up $30 per month per year; I would like, and need, a one-bedroom and den apartment. But I cannot manage the rent, $358 a month, on my income; my one-bedroom is $317," wrote one woman, who is single.

"In this regard, one wonders if one should spend one's savings on the difference," she said. "As a woman alone, it seems perhaps too late to get a small, inexpensive house, even though it would be welcomed for my pets and plants."

The outlook for rental housing in the United States can be summed up in one word—gloomy. Not enough new rental housing is being built to keep up with demand. Builders maintain that the cost of construction exceeds what they can get back in rents, especially in areas with rent controls. More rental apartments are being "lost" every year than are being built, because of conversions to ownership and demolition.

The result: Vacancy rates nationwide have dipped to what federal officials call a "dangerously low" level, averaging about 5 percent; in some cities, only 1 percent of rental apartments are vacant. This means that good apartments will be increasingly hard to find and that rents likely will shoot up.

Little relief is expected from the tight rental-market conditions soon. Between 1950 and 1980, the percentage of renter-occupied housing units fell from 45 percent to 34 percent, and it is expected to decline further by 1990 to 32 percent. Meanwhile, homeownership has increased greatly.

> The changing composition of the rental market is contributing to the supply woes. The market is leaning more heavily on multifamily units and less on single-family homes. As recently as 1960, nearly half of all rental units were in single-family homes. The current proportion is one-third and a further decline is expected.[1]
>
> The multifamily sector is called upon to perform a double duty; of providing a resource for the increasing number of renter households and of making room for the movement away from single units. These demands, coupled with a lagging construction volume, are creating an imbalance in the demand and supply of rental units.
>
> The low level of new rental construction expected in the 1980s does have some rather ominous implications. This is because in addition to insufficient levels of new units being built, rentals are being taken out of inventory due to conversion and demolition.
>
> What this indicates is that we will have a period of unprecedented demand for home-ownership types of housing, leaving a greater shortage of rentals. This in turn means that the available rental units will see a more rapid increase in rents than was the case in the 1970s. And as the market tightens, renters will lose their mobility.

More Rental Problems

Older people who move from their own homes to apartments also face other potential problems. They include:

Less privacy. People who are used to living in a house and doing as they please, sometimes find the adjustment to living in the same building with others to be difficult.

"What I don't like is the lack of privacy," said one Bellerose, New York, retiree. "Sound travels to my apartment from the floor below—loud TV and radio. The flush toilet noise, hammering noise from the adjoining apartment, and other noises are bothersome," he said.

Less room. Many moderate-priced apartments are much smaller than houses or even condominium units. While older people often want smaller housing quarters, a small apartment can be too much of a change.

"Almost five years ago, we sold our home, a beautiful one, because my husband had heart surgery and the children all said an apartment would be the best thing for us, because we wouldn't have the trouble of taking care of a home. It was the biggest mistake we have ever made," said a Lavalette, New Jersey, woman.

"We now live in a four-room apartment and feel cramped. We don't have the pleasure of having the children come as often and stay or have friends and relatives from out of town to come and visit," she lamented. "I feel stifled and have been extremely nervous and unhappy every minute of the days since we moved in."

Old buildings. Many existing apartment buildings are old and deteriorating. And nearly 46 percent of the apartments rented by people age 65 or older are in buildings constructed before 1940, according to the U.S. Census Bureau. You may have a hard time finding a good apartment in a modern or remodeled building at a price you can afford.

Removal. Renters, for various reasons, have to move more often than homeowners. Between 1970 and 1980, nearly 90 percent of all renters moved, compared with 56 percent of homeowners. The incidence of moves by renters 65 or older was about double the rate for homeowners that age, the Census Bureau reported.

To help you compare the costs of renting versus buying, you can write for a government book, "Rent or Buy." It is available for $3.50 from the U.S. Consumer Information Center in Pueblo, Colorado. (See page 250 for instructions on ordering.)

Finding an Apartment

Finding a good apartment can be difficult, but such places still exist. Be prepared to use some time and shoe leather to locate an apartment. Here's how to start:

Research. Investigate the rents and rental markets in the city where you plan to live. In a few cities, landlords have even cut rents for some apartments because of overbuilding. Those are the exceptions, but that's what happened in Houston in 1980 where the vacancy rate soared to over 11 percent, compared with the nationwide average of 5 percent or less.

Find out what rents are for different types of apartments, and don't overlook renting a small house. Don't rely on the classified ads in newspapers. Check real estate firms that manage rental units.

Scout the location. Where the rental unit is located will have a lot to do with how much the rent is. If it's too cheap, it may be in a bad neighborhood. You want something safe, convenient to transportation, shopping, and other activities that interest you. Check the crime rate for the neighborhood through the local police department.

The American Association of Retired Persons adds this advice:

> Keep looking until you find the right combination of pleasant, quiet quarters with a pleasant, nongreedy landlord. Try the older but well-kept sections of town. Explore the quiet side streets for duplexes or smaller and older, but well-kept, buildings. An old-fashioned flowerbed in front rather than modern gaudy advertising may be a good sign.

Visit the building before you rent. Get a first-hand look at the apartment you would rent and the building itself. Go at different times of the day to see if it is too crowded, too noisy, and if secure. Make sure the hallways are well lighted. If it has more than one floor, check the elevator.

Consider renting on an upper floor. A first-floor apartment may be too near a noisy entrance and also could be easier to burglarize. If a building is an elevator building or if you can cope with stairs, consider renting on a higher floor.

Eva M. Brown, who rents a second-floor apartment in Lakeland, Florida, noted: "I can have my windows open for good air, while all first-floor dwellers are boxed and shut in by venetian blinds because we all fear prowlers and peeping toms."

Check utility costs. Find out if tenants are charged individually for gas, electricity, and water, or if such costs are included in the rent.

One apartment renter even suggests that you find a "happy heater" in the building and rent the apartment over them. She noted that the woman in the apartment below "heats so well it keeps my floor warm. I find my heat bill is about half the size of hers."

Investigate the landlord. Find out who owns the building and what kind of reputation he or she has for dealing with tenants. Talk to other tenants and ask them if the owner and managers are responsive to tenant complaints and requests. Check with local housing agencies to learn if many complaints have been filed against the building owner.

Think small. Consider the advantages of a small apartment building over a larger one. The owners of smaller buildings tend to be more concerned about frequent tenant turnover than are owners of large buildings. The small-building landlord prefers renters who will stay a long time, pay their rent on time, and not damage the property —a perfect description of older renters. In order to keep such tenants, an owner may hold down rent increases.

Try to get interest for security deposit. When you rent, you will have to put up in advance a security deposit equal to one or two months' rent. This is to cover potential damage costs. According to advice columnist Ann Landers, in Illinois and some other states, owners of large buildings must pay interest on the security deposits.

Tax breaks. Check with local housing authorities to see if you are entitled to any tax breaks as an older renter. Some states offer special tax considerations for renters similar to tax breaks given to older homeowners.

Read first, then sign. Read your lease closely before signing. Consider having it checked by a lawyer. Make sure your rent can't be raised, and that you can't be evicted, arbitrarily. Look for any restrictions that limit your use of the apartment. If you have pets, find out if they are allowed. Include a provision that if the apartment building is converted to for-sale units you cannot be evicted until your lease is up.

Condo Conversions

Even after you find a suitable apartment, you may end up having to buy your home anyway—or be evicted and move again.

That's what happened to Geraldine Beeman, a Houston retiree who thinks people shouldn't have to own their homes.

"My income was quite adequate until I was forced, with many others, to purchase a converted condominium that I had rented as an apartment since 1964," Miss Beeman said. "None of us wanted the responsibility of maintaining separate houses, but we were forced back into this responsibility when the building was sold and converted into a condominium.

None of us wanted to leave our homes of 13 to 14 years, and many did not want to move back to separate homes. So we were caught," she said.

What happened to Miss Beeman has happened to rental tenants in many places. Across the country in the late 1970s, tenants were caught up in an almost frenzied trend by owners of apartment buildings to convert their rental apartments to condominiums. Many people suddenly found themselves facing the choice of moving out or coming up with thousands of dollars to buy their own apartments.

In the early 1980s, the pace of conversions slowed to a rate of about 40,000 a year from over 100,000 in 1978. But the conversion craze could return, and older renters especially should know how to protect themselves.

Guarding Against Conversion

The best way to protect yourself against your apartment being converted to condominium or cooperative ownership is to learn in advance what protections you have as a renter in the city where you live. Many states and localities have passed laws designed to block or slow condo conversions. For example, Marin County near San Francisco bans conversions whenever the rental vacancies in the county drop below 5 percent. Many places require that renters be given three to five months' advance notice before they must decide to buy or move; in New Jersey, tenants must be given at least three years' advance notice.

Some areas ban conversions unless a certain percentage of renters in a building agree to buy their apartments within a specified time. In New York State, for example, 35 percent of the renters must buy within 18 months of notification. In many cities, renters must be given first crack at buying the converted apartments, sometimes at discount prices. And some localities bar converters from evicting elderly tenants even if they choose not to buy. In New York, tenants over age 62 who have annual incomes under $30,000 and who have rented an apartment for two years or more can't be evicted in certain types of conversions.

Fighting Back

What can you do if your rental apartment is converted to condominium or cooperative ownership?

1. You can fight the conversion. If a certain percentage of tenants must approve a conversion, you can join the opposition. Or you can hire a lawyer to fight for your own apartment. Even if you can't stop the conversion, a strong tenant group can win some valuable concessions, such as sharp price reductions and an increase in the building's reserve fund. The first thing many tenant groups do is hire an engineer to inspect the building and an accountant to check the financial details. They then use these reports to start bargaining.

Converters are learning that dealing with tenants "can be very, very sensitive," said Jack P. Studnicky, whose New York firm manages the conversions of apartments. "Doing a condominium conversion is like making love to a porcupine," he said. The insensitive owner who barges in, starts evicting tenants and seeks a quick financial killing may be borrowing trouble, he said.

2. You and your fellow tenants can buy the building. That, in fact, has been the reaction in some cities to the flood of eviction notices—dubbed "mailbox roulette" in Chicago. In Washington, D.C., a local ordinance permits tenants to match any offer from an outside investor. The cost might be lower because it would eliminate the middleman's profits.

3. Rent from the new owner. Some converters who buy apartment buildings continue to rent some apartments. Or if the local market suddenly becomes flooded with conversions, they have a hard time selling their units and are forced to continue renting. Hang in there and find out if you can get one of the rental units. But make sure that the rental rate will not be increased to an amount more than you can afford.

4. Rent from an investor. Some buyers purchase converted apartments strictly as an investment. They don't want to live in the apartment and would be happy to find someone to rent to.

5. Consider buying your apartment. If you can afford it, a converted apartment can be a good buy and a good investment, especially if you can buy at a discount. And you can deduct real estate taxes and mortgage interest on your income tax.

If you buy your apartment, you can either continue to live in it permanently or sell it. Often newly converted units can be sold by their individual owners within a year or so for a generous profit.

But don't buy your apartment just because it's being converted to ownership. Make sure, since you are going to buy anyway, that you can't make a better purchase elsewhere. Be sure that the building is refurbished and is in good repair. Some condo conversions involve little more than taking down the For Rent signs and putting up For Sale signs.

6. If you have to move, get the converter to help pay some of your moving expenses. Some localities require such aid for older renters.

Even if your city doesn't have such a law, as an older tenant you may be able to wangle such help. Converters hate bad publicity—that they are throwing out older tenants with no help.

Conversion Concessions

Indeed, the best strategy for older tenants faced with the conversion of their apartments to condominiums or cooperatives is to take advantage of concessions that may be available for tenants like themselves.

Concessions by converters can pay off in good will, as one real estate firm found. International Developers, Inc. (IDI) plunged into the conversion market by purchasing Park Fairfax, a 132-acre garden apartment complex in the Virginia suburb of Washington, D.C.[2]

The project seemed a natural for conversion. In its 236 buildings and 1,600 apartment units were many longtime tenants. Once conversion began, however, the developers found that dozens of elderly residents couldn't afford to buy their apartments, yet were reluctant to move from their homes of 20 or 30 years.

"I felt terrible" when the conversion was announced, recalled 75-year-old Thelma Costikyan, who had lived at Park Fairfax with her husband, Simon, now 80, for 18 years. The Costikyans couldn't afford to buy and had no place to move.

But IDI president Giuseppe Cecchi found a way to help such tenants. All residents were offered discounts of $3,000 to $5,000 on purchases of their units, which were initially priced at $27,500 to $46,000. Additional discounts were offered to "founders," who had lived there 30 years or more, and to elderly tenants, such as the Costikyans, who are over 70 and had been residents at least 10 years.

The plan enabled the couple to buy their apartment for $34,500, about $11,000 less than the market price.

Seek a Subsidy

Another source of housing for older people are apartment complexes constructed by local, nonprofit organizations specifically for older renters. Much of this housing is built by churches, labor unions, or other groups using direct federal loans of up to 40 years. Section 202, administered by the U.S. Department of Housing and Urban Development, has become the most common way for the government to participate in the financing of low- and moderate-income housing for older people.

At Section 202 developments and others built by state and local housing agencies, or by private contractors, low-to-moderate income people can use federal subsidies to help pay their rents, such as what's called the Section 8 program. More information on federal subsidies can be obtained through your U.S. Department of Housing and Urban Development Area office.

Many older people are reluctant to accept subsidies. There is nothing wrong with seeking a subsidy to help yourself if that's what it takes to put a decent roof over your head. And you don't have to be absolutely poverty-stricken to qualify for housing subsidies. In addition to federal programs, at least 35 states and the District of Columbia have housing finance agencies that help provide housing. The problem is that housing subsidies are available only for a fraction of the people who need them, and waiting lists to get them are long.

Many older people have a concern that projects built by the government or nonprofit groups will be like the dreary public housing of yesteryear. In fact, most are modern, well designed, attractive complexes that make the housing indistinguishable from other apartments.

As with most large groups of tenants, not everyone will be happy, but surveys have disclosed that most find such low-cost housing enjoyable, with plenty of good activities and companionship. Listen to Rose Dolat, who with her husband in 1977 moved into Riverview Manor, a 64-unit "Senior Citizen" apartment house in Burlington, Wisconsin. The development was constructed by the local housing authority.

"We are situated in an ideal location—within the city limits. Along one side of the grounds a winding river flows by, so it looks like we're in the countryside," Mrs. Dolat said. *"There are ducks galore here, too. For those of us who do not drive, we have cab service, plus a bus service which is subsidized. We have a laundromat in our building. Also a beautiful lounge for get-togethers, plus a community room for our parties and special-occasion dinners."*

Getting on the Waiting List

For many older people on limited budgets, a well-managed, attractive subsidized apartment complex may be the best alternative. The good ones have long waiting lists, but there are ways to gain an advantage if you plan ahead. Also, keep an eye out for nongovernment developments that have more leeway than government projects in choosing tenants.

The first key is to get your name on the waiting list before the building is constructed. "If you wait until it's built, it's too late," said Tim Wintermute, former housing director for the National Council of Senior Citizens, Inc., a national advocacy group for older Americans. The council's Housing Management Corporation has developed or manages more than 15 projects for older people across the country.

Mr. Wintermute, now a housing consultant in Washington, D.C., suggested that people look for announcements in the newspaper that a nonprofit group plans to build housing for older persons, or to check with local housing agencies to see if any housing is planned. "When you see the announcement, get your name on the waiting list then," he advised, even though the housing may not be completed for another year or two.

If the development is nongovernmental, there are ways to move up on the list. The developers usually are "looking for someone who will fit their idea of a community," Mr. Wintermute said. They don't have to take applicants on a first-come, first-served basis. The National Council of Senior Citizens at its projects seeks to create an atmosphere of community involvement, with plenty of activities and services for a wide mix of older people in attractively designed low-rise and high-rise buildings.

Developers often seek a variety of ages among older people, singles, and couples, and incomes. In some areas with high median incomes you can have an income of $16,000 a year or more and still qualify for subsidized housing.

Once you get on a waiting list, keep in touch with the developer to let him or her know you still are interested. "Make yourself known. That can be a plus," Mr. Wintermute said.

When you are interviewed by representatives of the developer, show why you would be a valuable addition to the community that he wants to create. Don't gripe about your current landlord; take a positive approach. Talk about your interests and hobbies, or your volunteer work; talk about what you could bring to this new community. Sell yourself as a person.

The people who must pick prospective tenants for these new buildings "want someone who is pleasant," and able to get along well with others, Mr. Wintermute said. "That can be more important than your credit rating."

Living with Others

There is another housing option for older people—you can live with others and share expenses and companionship.

One way is for you and your friends to catch the entrepreneural spirit of the four women in North Carolina who pooled their money to build their own retirement home on a lake. But there also is a less elaborate option. It is called housesharing.

Housesharing simply means you share housing with another person who owns a house or an apartment. Or you share yours with them. In Seattle, Washington, for example, a program, Housesharing for Seniors, begun by the Stevens Neighborhood Housing Improvement Program, has been expanded to the entire city.

The program's staff interviews and matches people to share homes. In the program's first one and a half years, it placed 179 people in 84 matches. About 60 percent to 70 percent of the matches lasted over one year or were still in effect.

"The agreements between homeowners and tenants vary," the program's officials said. "Some tenants pay rent while others provide services such as cooking or yard work."

The program originally mated older tenants with older homeowners or renters. Now about 40 percent of the matches involve people of different ages. The program was developed in cooperation with the Gray Panthers. Stephen R. McConnell of the Andrus Gerontology Center at the University of Southern California said that, in the program, women in their 70s and 80s seem to prefer younger men as housemates over women "because they don't wash out their underwear and leave it hanging around."

Check the housing agencies in your city for local housesharing programs. For information about shared housing, write Shared Housing Resource Center, 6344 Greene Street, Philadelphia, PA 19144. (more about housesharing in Chapter 8)

A Wing for Mother

When it comes to living with others, the happiest arrangement may be to live with or near your children. Not in a way that imposes on their—or your—privacy, but in a way that combines independence and family togetherness.

"I live in a raised ranch house that was built by my son-in-law. The family has seven rooms, and he built a three-room apartment in

the lower level for me," wrote a Rhode Island widow. "It is custom-built for me, with counters and cabinets made for a short person. It is just beautiful," she said proudly.

"Now if more young people who are thinking of building or having a home built would include a small apartment for a retired relative, how much nicer than putting the person in a nursing home," she added. "I am a senior citizen and we all get along beautifully in this arrangement. I cook my own meals and have all the privacy I need. And the in-laws could very nicely contribute a sum as rent and the income would help the young people with expenses."

This woman has a good idea. Just remember, unless you as the renter are charged a fair-market rent for such an apartment, the relative or person you rent from can't claim rental "business" deductions, such as depreciation and improvement costs.

The beauty of an attached, but independent, home with the children is vividly described by Ruth M. Casto of Round Rock, Texas, who calls her home "A Wing for Mother":

"For lack of a better name, the architects call it a mother-in-law house. By any name it is a wonderful accommodation, and I predict that time will see more of these structures being built. Parents are living longer these days, and the family unit can remain intact through such houses, yet afford the complete privacy for all parties concerned.

"My private wing, jutting out from the big main house, has an entrance off the front courtyard. The door swings wide and discloses an oriental tile floor which meets with the wall-to-wall beige carpeting of a huge room. Three sections open off this main room. The first is a walk-through closet, which is my egress to the main house. The second is an open doorway revealing a dressing area. The third opening . . . reveals a compact kitchen.

"The French doors exit on a private patio where my wrought-iron chair and table and an ancient bonsai juniper tree offer outdoor hospitality.

"It provides all the advantages of living in a private house with none of the responsibilities for the senior citizen. Because this arrangement is so ideal, I am living with my children and yet I am living alone. We are so satisfied with this house plan that my son-in-law will build it again, should his company transfer him."

Designed For Mature Living

Now as to the houses. They are for the birds!
Geraldine Beeman
Houston, Texas

The verdict is in and it's nearly unanimous. The design of homes for older people is the Edsel of the housing industry.

"Why is it that builders do not talk to us about what we would like to have and what we need?" asked one retired railroad worker from Buffalo.

Older people bitterly complain that houses are too big, they can't reach the shelves in the kitchens, they can't easily get into the house because of steep steps, the stairs are dangerous, there isn't enough storage space, the doors aren't wide enough, the gauges on the stoves are unreadable—and a myriad of other problems.

When they go looking for a smaller home, they can't find any that meets their needs. Wrote Marion G. Rudnick of Cape Neddick, Maine:

"I have been looking at recently built apartments and condominiums. All have walled-in small living rooms, dining rooms, and kitchens; painted woodwork that has to be scrubbed, painted or papered walls that are expensive to maintain, no bookcases, no space to store firewood, washers and dryers down a flight of stairs into a cellar, inadequate closet and cabinet-drawer space, and some apartments located on a third floor with stairs to climb.

"I have stopped looking and am more than content with my own house."

Older people who use walkers or wheelchairs, or who are having a little harder time getting around than they used to, are especially upset about what they say is a lack of good planning and design. They all say, "There must be a better way."

"As to the architecture design, it might be well for the designers to try getting around in a wheelchair, reaching storage, trying to cook, bathe, and do laundry," said Isabelle Murray of Whiting, New Jersey.

Expert Advice

Indeed, it is the older people who know the problems and who can offer the best advice on what to watch out for in home design.

Lydia King Penny's home in Jacksonville, Florida, is her "pride and joy," but the 65-year-old widow said "there are so many things I know now since I have had the upkeep of the house for all these years."

Mrs. Penny's advice:

> First of all, I would have bought a brick house with very little wooden trim. This house has to be painted every three years and the wood trim more often.
> For older people, low houses are best, and they should be warned to keep off ladders. (I fell off a ladder trying to see a new roof I put on.)
> I long for the windows (that were covered during remodeling) again for this was where the cross-ventilation came through. This is a recommendation for older people to find a house that has cross-ventilation, for lots of them do not like air conditioning.
> I would have grab rails on the shower . . . .
> Just stick to as small a yard with as little in the way of shrubs and trees to care for as you can, and still let it look pretty.
> Insist on knowing how much insulation the house has.

You Can Dream, Too

Older people know what kind of house they want if they could find it. R. Earl Kipp of Orlando, Florida, offered this advice on what a house for a retiree should look like:

> The house needs to be large enough so the old man has a room where he can smoke his pipe, doze in an easy chair and play his favorite TV shows.
> In a far corner of the house, the lady of 55 years' companionship has her sleeping room and another room where she quilts, stores the memories of the grandchildren, and other hobbies that are sacred and dear to the aging.

It all needs to be on one floor. Some people prefer little or no yard, but we like a place where we can have some orange trees, roses, day lilies.

We don't need a lot of mechanical gadgets, such as dishwashers, as there aren't many dishes any more, and it is a bother to get servicemen to repair them.

"We see many older people who are forced to leave their homes because they are no longer able to live in them due to their design or location," said Aldro Lingard of Valparaiso, Florida. He retired at age 52 after 30 years in the U.S. Air Force. *"We do not want to do this. Our ideal house, therefore, should be designed for people suffering the normal infirmities of the elderly, including but not limited to the following features:*

Our living space, including the master bedroom, should all be on one floor. Spare bedrooms could be on another floor.

Design should accommodate a wheelchair.

There should be a supermarket and drugstore within walking distance for an elderly person.

There should be room for a modest vegetable garden, but lawn and garden maintenance requirements should be a minimum—in particular there should be *no* requirement to move a lawn mower from one level to another or wrestle with it on embankments or terraces.

More Than a House

The complaints of older people about housing designs are echoed in other studies. It was a leading gripe at a forum on Housing for the Retired, sponsored by the Federal National Mortgage Association (Fannie Mae). Participants "expressed hope that the housing industry would be shown the real need for small, single-family houses for many retirees of moderate income," Fannie Mae said.

But they want more than a roof and four walls—a view noted in a study of apartments for older people by the Massachusetts Institute of Technology's Department of Architecture. The MIT report stated:

For the older person, the living unit is a container for daily activities and a storehouse of experience and memories. An apartment unit which is insensitively designed affects the life of occupants by constraining the activities which they wish to conduct and by making it impossible either to retain valued furnishings or to create a setting for such objects consistent with a prior lifestyle.

Those issues do not always seem important to the designer since adaptation appears to be expected and acceptable. From a psychological and physical standpoint, however, the intimate environment of later life can have a profound effect on health and morale.

The MIT study was based on a survey of 53 public housing sites and 55 apartment units in Cambridge, Massachusetts, which were constructed specifically for older residents. The researchers found that because of design problems, the apartments didn't meet the needs of older people for privacy, furniture, space to entertain guests, to tend plants, to store belongings, and to enjoy their living.

The study concluded that "policy and practices in the design for the elderly should assure a reasonable mix of unit sizes and types. Our studies indicate that the efficiency model is an inappropriate residential model for most single elderly."

Many older people agree that apartments often aren't properly designed. A Herndon, Virginia, woman complains:

"The apartments we looked at were pathetic. Whoever designed a one-bedroom apartment for the elderly must be out of their mind. They are entirely too small. At this age we spend more time at home than any other time in our lives. So we need space to breathe."

Problems and Hopes

What MIT and others are saying is that older people have different needs and different lifestyles that should be taken into account when designing homes. The shortcomings cover all kinds of housing. Both the problems and the hopes for improvement were vividly expressed by Dorothea M. Strang of Reston, Virginia:

> A three-story townhouse is not exactly a housing solution for us. Though we haven't found the stairs to be a problem, hauling a lawn mower out of the lower-level family room around to the end of the row is a problem. No laundry tubs is a problem. Insufficient cupboard and storage space is a major problem.
>
> No clothes chute and no broom closet! Everything has to be hustled up or down to the basement. Oi!
>
> The whole layout is absolutely bare of any shelves for books or the 50 or so family heirlooms, mementos of Europe and South America, and the cherished family photos.
>
> What an inspired layout, suitable, I conclude, mostly for young people who have yet to acquire much in the way of tools, mementos, photos, books, clothes, cooking utensils, and bedding.
>
> I hold out for five rooms, plus a covered carport long enough for a tool or hobby area to the rear, a very thoughtfully planned kitchen with broom closet and separate cupboard for canned goods and outsized kettles, cornpoppers and cookie pans.

The laundry facilities could be along a rear hall.

The third room is a kind of office space for the male who still has to exist somehow not totally stripped of every interest. My husband (74) still plays the violin, pays the bills, figures the income tax, listens to chamber music, reads *The Wall Street Journal* and keeps a four-drawer filing cabinet pretty well stuffed.

Please remember that at 80 I expect to have to vacuum the place. Where should the Hoover be? Built in, maybe.

Please think of the placement for the TV. No living room seems to have the right place for it.

Desired Designs

Older people have constructive construction-criticism about almost every room in a house. The wisdom of many of the 1,400 people who wrote us can help future buyers learn what to watch out for in terms of design.

Here's what they said, starting with the basic housing design:

1. One level is enough.

"My husband and I (in our mid-60s) are in the process of searching for a new home. Most of the newer, energy-efficient construction we are interested in is built on at least two levels, and sometimes three or four," said Mrs. Gary Agler of Kalispell, Montana. *"Of course, this is happening because of the high cost of land. But many of these projects are built with the retired in mind, and stairs are a no-no. Try vacuuming a carpet and stairway when you are suffering from arthritis."*

2. Avoid unnecessary steps, inside and out.

"If steps there need be, make them safe!" pleaded a lady retiree from Tucson, Arizona. *"If steps must be used, why cannot they be broad, shallow and always have a rail to prevent accidents? Some of them are even made of imitation marble and other slippery things.*

"The real gripe," she added, *"is for stylish little step-ups and step-downs on the floors from room to room. They are positively dangerous for all people of all ages, and I cannot see they add anything to the beauty of a room."*

3. Check the floors.

"I do like my home, but there is one thing wrong with it," wrote Mike Tenzor of Ridge, New York. The developer built *"homes for older, retired people with concrete floors and no wood over the concrete. Just a plastic liner and rugs. That's it. To live on a concrete*

floor—didn't they think what it would take to heat these homes with electric heat?"

Other retirees agreed.

"Wooden floors (not concrete) would make more sense, particularly for those who are troubled with arthritis or rheumatism," said Tom Zappulla of Torrington, Connecticut.

What's more, *"Builders should not have just-waxed floors or throw rugs,"* said Dollie M. Isaman of Boonville, Indiana. Added Mrs. Penny of Jacksonville, Florida: *"It is better to have a carpeted floor; then there are no slippery floors to fall on."*

4. Design is important all around the house.

"Smaller rooms are more acceptable to older or slightly disabled people because they don't walk as much and [they] use portable types of furniture," said Mrs. Vina S. Oczytko of Arlington, Virginia. *"Smaller rooms can be cleaned quicker, too."*

But don't make the rooms too small, said Mrs. Isaman, who is in her 70s.

"The rooms should be large enough so they could get around without bumping into the furniture. The ceilings should be low enough so that the house isn't hard to heat. The electric receptacles should not be down at the baseboard. They should be up high enough for the people to reach without stooping over and getting lightheaded."

"Low windows, at least in the kitchen and living room, are a must, for we sit down more as we age," added Mrs. Marvin Meeker of Union, Ohio.

"Sliding glass doors are a no-no—too hard to keep clean," Mrs. Meeker continued. *"Rods in the closets about 2 inches lower so we can reach them, as our shoulders and arms hurt."*

Through the House, Critically

Inside the house, many design features are "no-nos." With our experienced advisers as our guides, here's a walk through a typical house with an eye open for the problems facing older people.

The tour starts with what most Americans would agree—and older Americans are no different—to be the most important room in the house—the kitchen.

Kitchen Complaints. Most kitchens, older people say, are poorly designed and too big for older people, who need compactness to save steps and adequate closets within easy reach.

In Dorothea Strang's Reston condominium, "the kitchen layout is especially discouraging to a confirmed home baker of pies and cakes. The vast expanse of white Congoleum that has to be coped with from the front door to the cupboard and all over the kitchen floor is a real muscle and bone-jarring challenge."

The biggest gripe older people have about the kitchen is the cabinets.

"Kitchen cabinets are out. They are too high to find anything without standing on a chair, then maybe falling off the chair or ladder," complained Virginia Potraty of Burlington, Wisconsin. "The bottom cabinets are out, too. One cannot get on her knees when older to find what one wants.

"Give me the old-style pantry shelves," she added. "They do not have to be high and one can see where things are."

Other older people had one thing to say to that suggestion—amen!

"The kitchen cabinets should be in reach so the elderly don't have to climb," said Mrs. Isaman of Boonville. "The younger generation thinks we can do like they do. They will find out, if they live long enough."

"No matter how well we may look or strong, or how well we keep in shape, our legs and heads are dizzy and not strong enough to reach up or climb like monkeys," added Marina Corte of Miramar, Florida. "Do these builders think we are all giants?"

The problem, declared the outspoken Miss Beeman of Houston, is that "women are forced into houses designed by men who seldom have to do housework. The result: Closets and cabinet shelves so high and so deep that no ordinary female can use them without a ladder."

Those gripes were voiced at the Fannie Mae forum on Housing for the Retired. "No subject aroused such universal criticism as the placing of kitchen cabinets," Fannie Mae said. Participants added these design suggestions:

> It is proposed that the bottoms of upper cabinets be placed 14 inches above the work counters and that adjustable shelves be provided in 30-inch high wall cabinets. It was also proposed that base cabinets be equipped with drawers or shelves on gliders, making it easier to reach stored items.
>
> With regard to kitchen cabinets, there were complaints about small round knobs and rectangular wood handles on doors and drawers. Stiff and arthritic hands can't grasp them. Open handles or flat knobs with finger space behind were recommended by the participants.

As for the layout of the kitchen itself, we surveyed older people about what kind of kitchen design they would prefer. One question asked about the kitchen layout and eating area. A second question asked about other family-room combinations. (See Figures 7·1 and 7·2.)

Figure 7·1

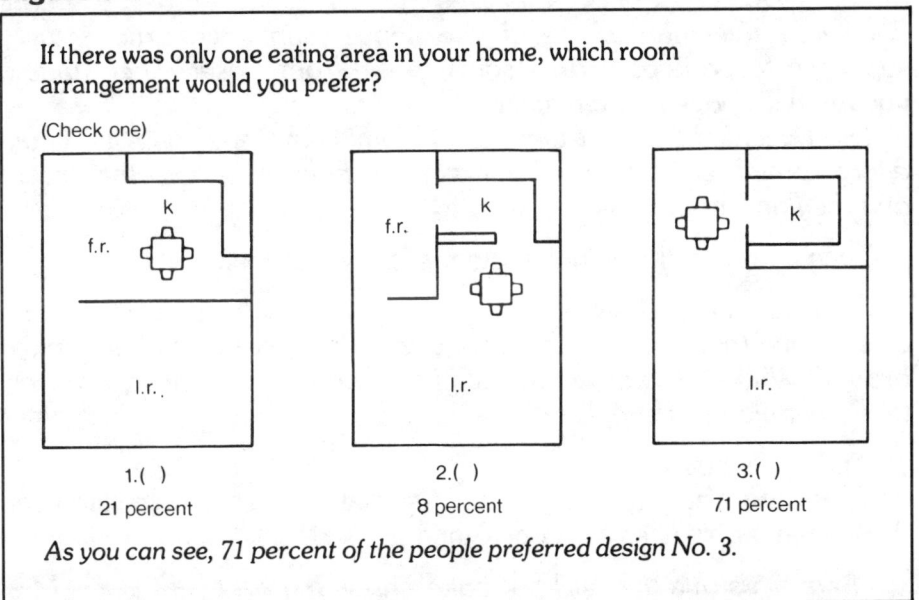

If there was only one eating area in your home, which room arrangement would you prefer?

(Check one)

1.( ) 21 percent

2.( ) 8 percent

3.( ) 71 percent

As you can see, 71 percent of the people preferred design No. 3.

Figure 7·2

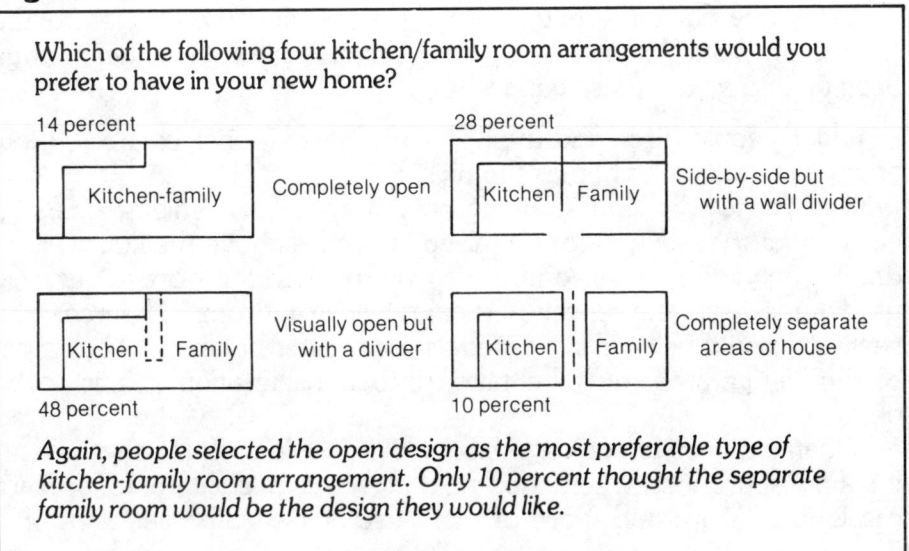

Which of the following four kitchen/family room arrangements would you prefer to have in your new home?

14 percent — Kitchen-family, Completely open

28 percent — Kitchen | Family, Side-by-side but with a wall divider

48 percent — Kitchen | Family, Visually open but with a divider

10 percent — Kitchen | Family, Completely separate areas of house

Again, people selected the open design as the most preferable type of kitchen-family room arrangement. Only 10 percent thought the separate family room would be the design they would like.

In both cases, people opted for openness, rather than a walled-off design.

The stupid broom closet. There were more complaints about things in the kitchen—or things that should be in the kitchen.

"Find a good place for a broom closet that will hold a broom, mop, vacuum cleaner with all attachments, dust cloth, and so on," declared Dorothy Paulsboe of Des Plaines, Illinois. *"I asked a condominium salesman where all the above mentioned articles were supposed to be kept and he said—in the front closet. There was a vacant wall space in the kitchen.*

"So I decided I do not want a condominium," she said. *"If I could afford a mink coat, I would not want to hang it next to the broom and the floor mop."*

Even a broom closet in the kitchen isn't much better.

Said Jane N. Weiss of Flushing, New York: "Why does the broom closet have to live up to it's name and be big enough to hold only a broom? What is a woman to do with the vacuum cleaner, brushes, and other cleaning supplies?"

And that's not all.

Stooping and crawling. Mrs. Weiss and other people said even the kitchen appliances aren't designed properly.

"I have a stove that will not bake unless the pilot light is lit," Mrs. Weiss added. *"Since the pilot is in the back of the stove on the bottom, I have to crawl on my belly if I want to use the oven for roasting or baking.*

"And why can't the gauges on the stove and the refrigerator be toward the front?" she asked. *"My eyesight is poor, and I never have been able to adjust these gauges."*

Older people often find the lower refrigerator shelves are too low and the ranges in the homes too big.

"For those who find stooping painful and inconvenient, it is suggested that the refrigerator be raised 18 inches above the floor, with a drawer on gliders installed in the space beneath for storage of rarely used items," said the report on the Fannie Mae forum. "The freezer, if separate, could be similarly raised with a drawer beneath." The height of the refrigerator must be taken into consideration if it is to be elevated.

When it comes to cooking, many older people prefer "convenience" cooking appliances when they no longer have children to prepare meals for. "More and more of them use a toaster-broiler-oven or a microwave oven," the Fannie Mae report said, "One participant said, 'I love baked potatoes, but who wants to heat a big oven to bake a potato?' Another participant remarked that she 'can bake a pie in the larger toaster-oven.'"

Living Together Areas

"Great Rooms." To many older people, the big separate dining room and family room, in addition to the living room, add up to a lot of wasted space—space that can be costly to heat, cool, and maintain. Many suggest combining these rooms into one "Great Room."

"After children have left, the need for the family room is gone," said Mrs. S. H. Crowell of Sierra Vista, Arizona. *"Older couples very seldom use their living rooms and occasionally use the dining room. Why pay taxes and have the expense of heating and cooling areas that can be eliminated?"*

With the convertible furniture available today, Mrs. Crowell suggested, *"a lovely, practical, comfortable 'Big Room' with areas designated for relaxing, dining, game area, and so on, would be ideal for us older Americans. They are hard to find."*

"The Big Room," she said, *"takes care of your living area, doing away with the formal dining room and the family room altogether. Ideally, the kitchen opens onto this big room, being separated by hanging cupboards and serving counter."*

Evelyn Kozlowski of Atlanta agreed:

"I would like to suggest having a 'Great Room,' combining the living/dining/kitchen areas."

The pattern desired by many older people seems to be fewer walled-in areas and more open space. The same finding emerged from the MIT study of apartments for older people. What such people are saying is "Don't Fence Me In."

Mrs. Marion G. Rudnick of Cape Neddick, Maine, called this design a "Living Together" area.

"My late husband and I successfully planned and built a one-level, 28 foot by 40 foot retirement home on a half-acre lot in a wooded area on the coast of Maine," she said. *"Our priority was a plan that would use as much of the space as possible for a 'living together' area. We wanted space to accommodate a 6 foot 2 inch grand piano for my pianist-husband, a fireplace, uncrowded sitting areas, a dining section, and an open kitchen."*

Neglected requirements. Mr. Aldro Lingard of Valparaiso, Florida, offered a variation that would adapt the traditional family room to older residents.

"There are two requirements which I feel are especially important and which are universally neglected," he said. "First is the room in which my wife and I would spend most of our waking hours—I would call it the 'Family Room.' But I have seen no so-called Family Rooms that meet the requirement, and the 'Great Rooms' I have seen do not meet it either.

"This family room would accommodate:"

> TV watching—two comfortable reclining chairs directly facing the TV set, which in turn directly faces the chairs—no neck-craning or looking at the side of the set.
>
> Reading—the same two chairs will do, but there must be *good* reading lights plus enough shelf or table space so that we can momentarily put down what we are reading, and maybe leave it, without creating a mess.
>
> Desk work for both of us at the same time—a small desk tucked into a corner of the kitchen, or a knee-hole desk in the living room, designed for ornamentation rather than function, is not what I'm referring to. Any family today needs a full-fledged office for writing letters to the children, answering them, and maintaining files of all the myriad things we want to keep. (A friend of mine has copies of the *National Geographic* going back 30 years.)

"We now have a TV-watching room and a den. Both are too small, and they are, by necessity on different floors and are as far apart as they can be and still be in the same house. In the den, I have a full-size office desk, files, and bookshelves," Mr. Lingard said. "We need all this plus a second desk for my wife, and we need it all in the same room that we use for watching TV—or perhaps separated from it by nothing more than an accordion-folding wall. Further, this combined area should be adjacent to the kitchen and the dining area."

What is Mr. Lingard's second requirement? It's a workshop.

"Every family has at least one member who spends (or would like to spend) a considerable amount of time doing the things that can't very well be done in the living room, the dining room, the family room, the kitchen or the spare bedroom," he said. "It is important that the workshop be viewed as a family space, not the exclusive retreat of a lone hobbyist."

How Many Bedrooms?

When it comes to bedrooms, even for most retired couples or older single people, one is not enough. Most want at least two bedrooms and some want three.

At least two bedrooms—"each with a closet"—are needed, said Mrs. Koslowski of Atlanta, Georgia, because "then if one or the other person is ill (or snores), it would be much more comfortable for the older people."

"We need two bedrooms for health reasons. We don't sleep well, and if one of us is unable to sleep, he or she disturbs the other," said a Herndon, Virginia, retiree. "Most of us need that extra bedroom for a lot of other reasons also," such as for a hobby room or office.

The extra space is needed for visitors, too.

"We find that our children still love to come home for special occasions, and now that we have grandchildren, we like to have them visit," said Mary Louise Cox of Chappaqua, New York. "This increases the need for well-designed living space."

Even more space is desired by some older people who count on a lot of visitors.

"Our three children are grown; two of them live in California and one in France. All three of them visit us about once a year, all at the same time, if possible," said Mr. Lingard of Valparaiso, Florida.

"Our ideal home, therefore, should be able to accommodate our three children, their spouses, and their children in reasonable comfort for about one to three times a year," he said. "During the rest of the year, unneeded space should be closed off and neither heated nor air-conditioned."

Others want spare bedrooms for an office or work-or-hobby area or for psychological reasons.

Said Lydia King Penny of Florida: "I like the two bedrooms even though my husband is dead. I lived for a while in a garage apartment and only had one bedroom. I felt like I was caged."

Rub Out the Tub?

Bathtubs. Older people have very strong feelings about bathrooms. Houston's Geraldine Beeman asserted:

"Who needs the tub? The only sanitary way to bathe is a good shower. A sensibly-sized shower with a good seat and spigot located within arm's reach would give a refreshing bath to one of almost any age or physical condition."

As for the rest of the bathroom?

"Builders allow stupid plumbers to ruin the most desirable wall space by placing one towel rack in the center," Miss Beeman declared. "Any bathroom needs not less than two good-sized racks and preferably three."

Now many older people prefer to soak in a tub, but surveys of homeowners do show a preference for showers. When asked to choose from several designs, 33 percent of people over age 55 chose a separate shower stall, while only 5 percent of younger people did so.

The surveys showed the older people also opted for privacy, 53 percent wanting the commode separated from the tub.

Faucet faults. Older people aren't impressed by fancy modern faucets that may look nice but aren't practical to use.

"Faucets in the bathroom are an incredible hazard to old knuckles with their unreachable nooks and crannies," said Mrs. Strang of Reston, Virginia.

Our surveys of homeowners show a preference for single-handle faucets. But older people—55 percent—are less enthusiastic than young people for double-handle faucets.

Medicine cabinets. Again, storage space often is inadequate.

"The dinkiest of medicine chests makes it impossible to move in an array of solutions, pills, balms, lotions, and utensils still thought to be necessary," stated Mrs. Strang.

And Elsie Grapentin of Cleveland, Ohio added a suggestion:

"The mirror on the medicine cabinet in the bathroom should be at the lavatory level so a man can shave sitting down and a woman apply make-up and dress her hair sitting down." Another retiree also suggested, "A bathroom mirror low enough for those of us getting shorter."

Wash basins. One bowl or two? Older people prefer the wash basin to be in a bathroom off the master bedroom, and 78 percent of those we surveyed like a basin with one bowl only. This is just the opposite of younger homeowners surveyed; 65 percent of them want vanities with two bowls.

The same generation gap is true when it comes to the preferred color of the sink. Younger people prefer colors, and older people want white.

One bathroom or two? Indeed, when it comes to the desired number of bathrooms in a house, older people are more likely to want fewer than two. Asked how many bathrooms they would like in their next home, 69 percent of homeowners age 65 to 69 said they wanted

1 or 1½ bathrooms. But 48 percent of those in the typical pre-retirement age of 56 to 64 would like two bathrooms.

Laundry Laments

When it comes to easy use of laundry appliances—clothes washer and dryer—most older people agreed with Rose Pastula of South Windsor, Connecticut:

"My suggestion is have the laundry on the first floor and not in the basement, which means climbing stairs."

When people over age 55 were asked where they wanted laundry appliances to be located, 54 percent preferred them on the first floor, and 22 percent wanted them in the kitchen. Only 7 percent preferred the garage.

Recreation

Many older people sing the virtues of a small garden or small yard where they can putter around—but nobody wants a big yard. Exercise is important, they said, whether it is tennis, golf, or just walking.

Hiram Bingham of Sportatron Company of America, Inc., in Salem, Connecticut, thinks older people need a place to exercise in their homes.

"Back in the days when Eisenhower was President, I built the first multipurpose play court for our children," Mr. Bingham said. *"I am now 76 and practice tennis on it nearly every day. So I know that older people can benefit from a few minutes of fun and exercise close to home or with their children and grandchildren."*

Parking

As long as they continue to drive, convenient and, if possible, sheltered parking is desired by older people.

"Parking is very important for older people because the buses don't run on all the streets," said Mrs. Oczytko of Arlington, Virginia.

A carport or garage is best for a house. At condominium and apartment developments, parking near the living unit is essential.

"One of my greatest problems is to get my groceries from my car to my apartment," said Mrs. H. Hendricson of Silver Spring, Maryland.

Thinking Ahead, About Disabilities

We all hope we will always be spry and healthful. But age sometimes doesn't cooperate. Houses should be designed to accommodate the special needs of those with physical disabilities, older people suggest.

Geraldine Beeman of Houston advised:

"All outside doors should be sufficiently wide to accept wheelchairs with ease. All inside doors should be easily accessible to wheelchairs, most particularly bathrooms."

Narrow hallways can be a major barrier for people in wheelchairs.

"My mother is confined to a wheelchair and needs wide doorways, open spaces and large bathrooms," said one Flournay, Maryland, woman.

In most houses, "the bathroom doors are narrower than other doors," said Barry Robinson of the American Association of Retired Persons. "If you are in a wheelchair, you might find yourself trapped outside your own bathroom."

"It should be mandatory to include in all buildings, help, not just for the elderly, but for the handicapped of all ages," declared a San Rafael, California, man. "Curbs should be done away with; ramps constructed for those in wheelchairs who cannot go up stairs; doorways made wide enough for wheelchairs to go through."

Some experts think that new housing should be constructed with "adaptability guidelines" that would allow the house to be adapted to use by the handicapped, young or old. Such houses would be designed with wider doorways, counters that could be relocated to lower levels, if necessary, entrances that could be adjusted easily to allow for access for wheelchairs and walkers, and backing for grab bars in the bathrooms near tubs, showers, and commodes.

Saving Energy

With today's rapidly rising fuel bills, there is one overriding thing that older people want in homes—energy-efficient design. Smaller houses, they feel, will help keep down utility bills, especially if the houses are well insulated.

And older people are more than ready to try new energy-saving ideas—like capturing the heat of the sun.

"I find that 100 square feet of south-facing glass, plus a couple of skylights in the bathroom, really cut gas and electric bills," reported Oliver K. Ash, a retiree in Albuquerque, New Mexico.

Indeed, the "new" idea of solar energy is old hat to retirees like Evelyn S. Pease of Oxon Hill, Maryland, near Washington, D.C.

"In 1947 we built what is now called a passive solar home to take advantage of a 7¼ mile view of the south down the Potomac River. We put nine Libbey-Owens Ford picture windows on the southern wall. Overhead depth of an overhang was matched to the height of the window to cut out the summer sun, too, for our latitude.

"The windows warm the rooms from about 9:30 A.M. till sundown and the house holds the heat, if I close the drapes and it's not windy, till 10 P.M. I also put foam panels over the foundation on the northwest and east sides of the house and loosely plastic-bagged oak leaves against the panels and behind the shrubbery to keep the foundation and the area just above the ground warm.

"I pin blackout linings to the backs of the drapes—I also put in blackout window blinds. I have storm doors and windows and tightly insulate and weatherproof parts of the house, and have thermopane windows.

"It is the south and east thermopane windows and overhang that has earned money, based on heating and cooling, many, many, many times beyond their initial costs.

"When oil was nine cents a gallon, this was a savings," Mrs. Pease said. "Now it's a boon."

The goal is to rely on "free" solar energy rather than building costly collectors, advised Roger A. Parsons of Deming, New Mexico.

In an area where the neighbors are paying as much as $100 a month for space heating, the average for our 1,850-square-foot house is $109 a year," Mr. Parsons said. "The sun supplies more than half our needs, without any solar-heating gadgets, and electric baseboards supply the rest.

"The features are: Large unobstructed southern exposure, with lots of glass; all glass double and tight-fitting; complete thick ceiling and wall insulation; concrete floor with slab on the ground, with exposed edges insulated; two-foot eave overhang for summer protection; and a thermostat in each room to control the electric baseboard units.

"The free solar heating option should appeal particularly to retirees on fixed incomes, such as ourselves, who might not ever recover the expenses involved with other systems," Mr. Parsons said.

The EVAC House

John F. Strickler, Jr., a retiree in Camano Island, Washington, has designed his own energy-efficient house. Buried on three sides by dirt, the house has south-facing patio windows to catch the sun and heat his home. He calls it an EVAC—Energy at a Very Acceptable Cost—house.

Mr. Strickler, now in his 60s, is a former aerospace manager and holds an engineering degree from MIT.

"The idea for EVAC was born in 1973 with the Arab oil embargo and the long lines at the gasoline pumps," he said. He had his 1,536-square-foot, three-bedroom home built in 1976.

"The EVAC concept is simple," he said. "Design and build a home which requires little energy to keep the occupants warm. Obtain as much of that energy from the sun as you can without spending anything for collectors or a storage system.

"The fact that the sun is lower in the sky in winter than it is in summer makes this possible," Mr. Strickler said. "The concrete floor and wall structures, well-insulated on the outer surface, collect the heat from the sun, which enters through the patio glass doors, stores the heat, then radiates it to the occupants, all without needing pumps, blowers, or other 'active' components."

Despite soaring fuel costs, Jack and Billie Strickler's winter electric-heating bills have been under $180 for an entire year. They plan to build windmills to generate even more low-cost energy. Mr. Strickler said the house can be built for under $30 a square foot. Not bad, compared to the average cost of over $50 a square foot for a typical new single-family house.

Figure 7-3 is a design of the Strickler EVAC house. Further details are available from Mr. Strickler at 338 N. Wind Sun Way, Camano Island, WA 98292.

Housing Should Be . . .

What kind of housing do older people want? Clearly, they want homes smaller in size to fit their needs, and smaller in price to fit their pocketbooks.

"Most magazines show how to expand homes, but after your family has grown, how do you shrink the rooms that were so important at the time?" asked K. S. Field of Attleboro, Massachusetts.

Figure 7·3

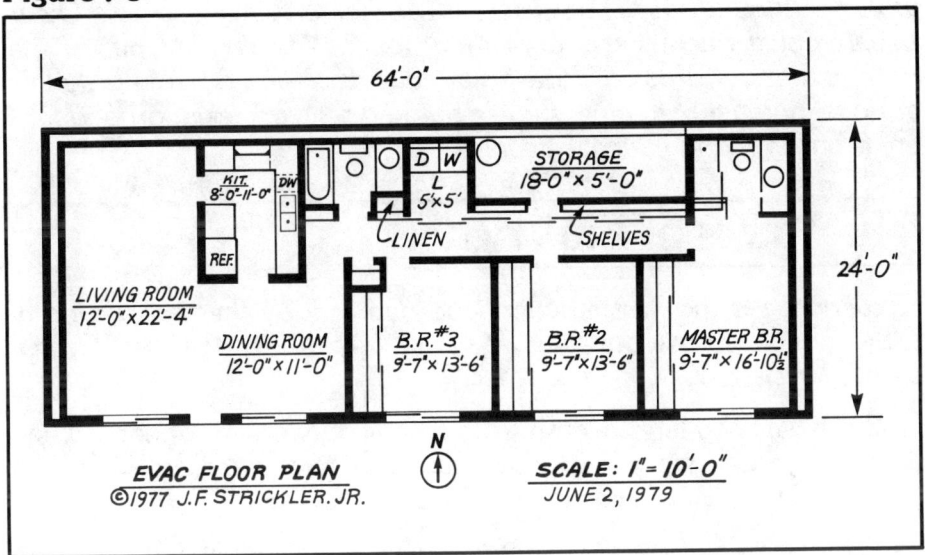

EVAC FLOOR PLAN
©1977 J.F. STRICKLER. JR.
SCALE: 1"= 10'-0"
JUNE 2, 1979

And older people are upset and even angry, because of a belief that the housing industry isn't providing them with the homes they need.

"Today I feel there should be small homes, built for older citizens—say five rooms, no basement, car garage, bath, utility space, and be reasonable," said Mrs. Florence Wallace of West Caldwell, New Jersey. "Homes should be built in clusters with small gardens, walks, recreation shops, but not like retirement villages."

One problem that both builders and older people face is that, in many communities, zoning ordinances require minimum lot sizes that often are bigger than necessary. Land is becoming so expensive that it is hard to build new homes priced within the budgets of many older people.

"The *big problem* coming up for all communities both large and small, is anti-zoning of small but very adequate lots for our elderly people," said Russell Hughes, a Realtor in Winthrop, Massachusetts. "Large high-rise developments may be cheaper to build, but I contend that small one-story homes are preferable to maintain dignity and respect for our elderly. Smaller home lots, houses well-oriented on cul-de-sacs with some common recreational space is what they need and deserve."

Small apartment buildings that aren't segregated and out of the mainstream of everyday living would suit some older people.

"An apartment building of four to six units in a regular environment would be great," said Mrs. Marvin Meeker of Union, Ohio. "Older people could occupy this apartment without feeling left out of the normal world. If I could choose my housing, I would live in a double cottage, not just with older people but in a regular neighborhood for I enjoy children and younger people."

The Voices of Experience

"Experience is the best teacher—too bad that by the time we learn, we're too old to use our learning," said Mrs. T. B. Wigley of Greenwood, Mississippi.

But it isn't too late to learn from the wisdom of older people when it comes to designing future houses. They have very specific ideas. Listen to Mrs. Elsie Grapentin of Cleveland, Ohio:

"This is a plea for builders and developers to supply and include in their housing developments, sections of new, 5-room, basementless, 1-floor, 1½ bath homes costing less than $60,000, situated on the center of a 60-by-75-foot lot within walking distance to shopping centers, churches, and public transportation.

"Some important features should be:

Street or sidewalk level entrance.
Ramps instead of stairs.
Wide doors to accommodate walking aids.
Optional air conditioner.
Heated preferably with gas.
Inward tilted windows.
Self-storing storms and screens or thermopane window glass.

"There is a very good market for this type of home among older citizens (age 55 and up) of this country who are able to afford a lifestyle less expensive but quality-wise equal to that experienced in their working career," said Mrs. Grapentin.

A Growing Market for Older-people Housing

Indeed, statistics show, in terms of sheer numbers, that there is a burgeoning market for housing for older people. For example, the Census Bureau reported 83.5 million total U.S. households in 1982.

Of this, 17.3 million were people age 65 or over; by 1985 they will number 18.1 million, and 20.2 million by 1990.

The challenge is to produce the kind of housing that older people want and can afford.

"I am 68 years old and my wife is 70. We use about 837 square feet of the 2,080 square feet available" in our current house, said Charles A. Grimes of Roswell, New Mexico. *"We would choose a smaller house on a smaller lot. Our ideal house is a unit 28 feet by 28 feet."*

A house exactly that size was, in fact, designed by Joseph H. Orendorff, a specialist in residential design, for the Fannie Mae forum on Housing for Retired People. It was one of several sizes of "Options" houses designed by Mr. Orendorff, of the American Institute of Architects, based on the comments of older people at the forum.

"The 'Options' house demonstrates that once a good compact plan has been achieved, the house can be expanded easily," Fannie Mae noted. And "the house is suitable for and can be built as single-family dwellings, as duplexes, even triplexes and in cluster arrangements."

The "Options" house is attractive on the outside and practical on the inside. For further information on these designs, write the Federal National Mortgage Association, Office of Urban Activities, 3900 Wisconsin Avenue, N.W., Washington, DC. Copies of Fannie Mae's "Forum III—Housing for the Retired," which includes pictures of the "Option" houses, are also available for $3.50 per copy from the same address. (See Figure 7·4 on pages 154–156.)

Innovative Home Design

The authors agree that more should be done to encourage innovative design for homes for older people. And to help get the innovation ball rolling, we asked Herman York, a respected architect in Garden City, New York, to design specifically for this book a moderate-priced home for older people based on the comments of the people who wrote to us. Mr. York, who writes (and draws) a newspaper column on design and who is in his 60s, created with Raymond Schenke an attractive and practical design for a retirement house.

This home can not only offer a solution for older people who are looking for smaller and well-designed houses, but—since it is easily expandable—it can also be a starter home for young first-time buyers. The bonus would be mixed communities of such homes, where both older and younger people could help—and learn from—each other.

154 Planning Your Retirement Housing

Figure 7·4: The "Options" House

Housing for the retired

There is no one solution to the problems of housing for retirees. The basic plans of the "Options" House should be considered as guidelines to the development of a wide range of retirement dwellings that are suitable for various income levels, family compositions, and styles of living. The basic plans are flexible enough for single-family dwellings and for combining into duplexes, triplexes, row or townhouses, grouping in cluster arrangements, and for converting to garden and high-rise rental apartments or condominiums.

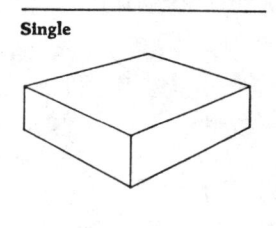

Single

(continued)

Designed for Mature Living 155

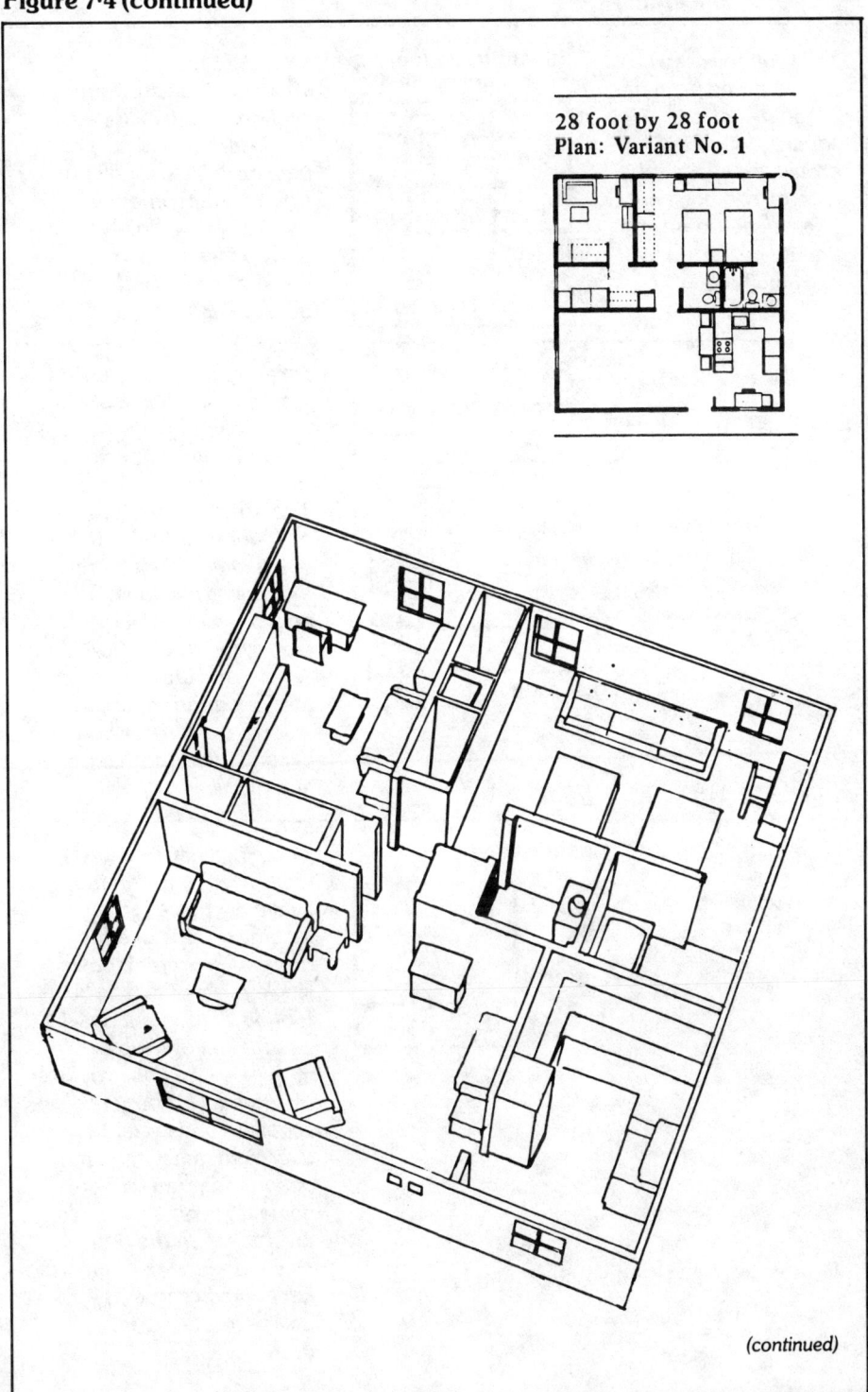

Figure 7·4 (continued)

28 foot by 28 foot
Plan: Variant No. 1

(continued)

Figure 7·4 (concluded)

28 foot by 28 foot Plan: Variant No. 2

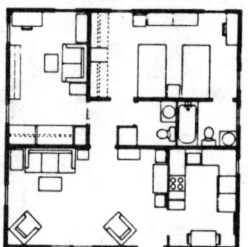

The Options area has been omitted from this 28 foot by 28 foot square plan, but it provides a separate laundry room, a den or small bedroom, a private bath, and an extra half-bath.

Here a 16-foot span is shown in the bedroom section, which includes two bedrooms, a full private bath, also a half-bath. Laundry equipment is stacked in the half-bath, and spaces are provided in the kitchen for optional appliances.

Front Extensions

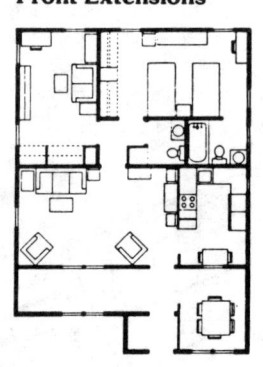

An entry foyer, requested for cold climates, is shown in combination with a bay-window-type extension to the kitchen-dining area. These may be used singly or in combination with any of the plans. Together with the rear extension of the basic 24 foot by 24 foot plan, shown in Option No. 4, they provide opportunities for variations in the exteriors of cluster housing and offer another option for all.

Efficiency

This efficiency unit was developed to widen the range of choice for lower income groups and for those who prefer a basic single room unit. The 20 foot by 20 foot unit has 400 square feet of usable interior space and provides an unusual amount of livability for its size. An overnight guest can be accommodated without going through the sleeping area to reach the bathroom, and the closet in the kitchen can serve as a utility closet or pantry, or both.

One-floor Living

Architects Herman York and Raymond Schenke designed this house (Plan 5491) after taking into consideration the needs of older persons. The floor layout has been carefully planned to comply with surveys that gather opinions expressed by retirees. See Figures 7·5, 7·6, and 7·7.

This is a one-story house, without basement, with no stairs to climb, barrier-free, designed to accommodate wheelchairs if needed, yet retaining the basic appearance of a normal primary home. Most senior citizens do not want their houses to take on the appearance of a nursing home, but they accept inconspicuous aids to assist them in moving about in comfort.

The architects have included many such subtle features, all planned around a center hall house, with a minimum of hall space and a maximum of light and air.

The "Retirement Room" is in an open-plan arrangement with the dining area, additional less-formal dining being available in the kitchen. A laundry and toilet/lavatory is nearby.

The house is energy efficient, with, among other things, maximum insulation, insulated glazing throughout, weatherstripped windows, fireplace designed for energy efficiency, and so on. All ceilings are flat to reduce the overall cubic content, thereby conserving heat.

Generous closet space is provided throughout this house, with a huge broom closet—large enough to store vacuum cleaner, mops, and the like, all near the kitchen area. Additional storage space is shown in the garage for the many items of garden equipment.

The overall size of the house is less than 1,300 square feet of habitable area—modest, yet spacious enough to include some of the luxury areas, which the owners may have previously enjoyed.

The exterior is designed with a generous amount of brick on the facade, thus minimizing maintenance cost. Vertical wood boards are used to insure an attractive exterior appearance; these can be stained, which will also reduce upkeep expenses.

The architects recommend a light-colored roof to reflect the heat of the summer sun. Moreover, to obtain the greatest benefit from sun in winter months, this house would best be faced with its rear elevation toward the south. The rear, private area has been designed for outdoor lounging and dining.

Table 7·1 gives the statistics of the house (Plan 5491).

158 Planning Your Retirement Housing

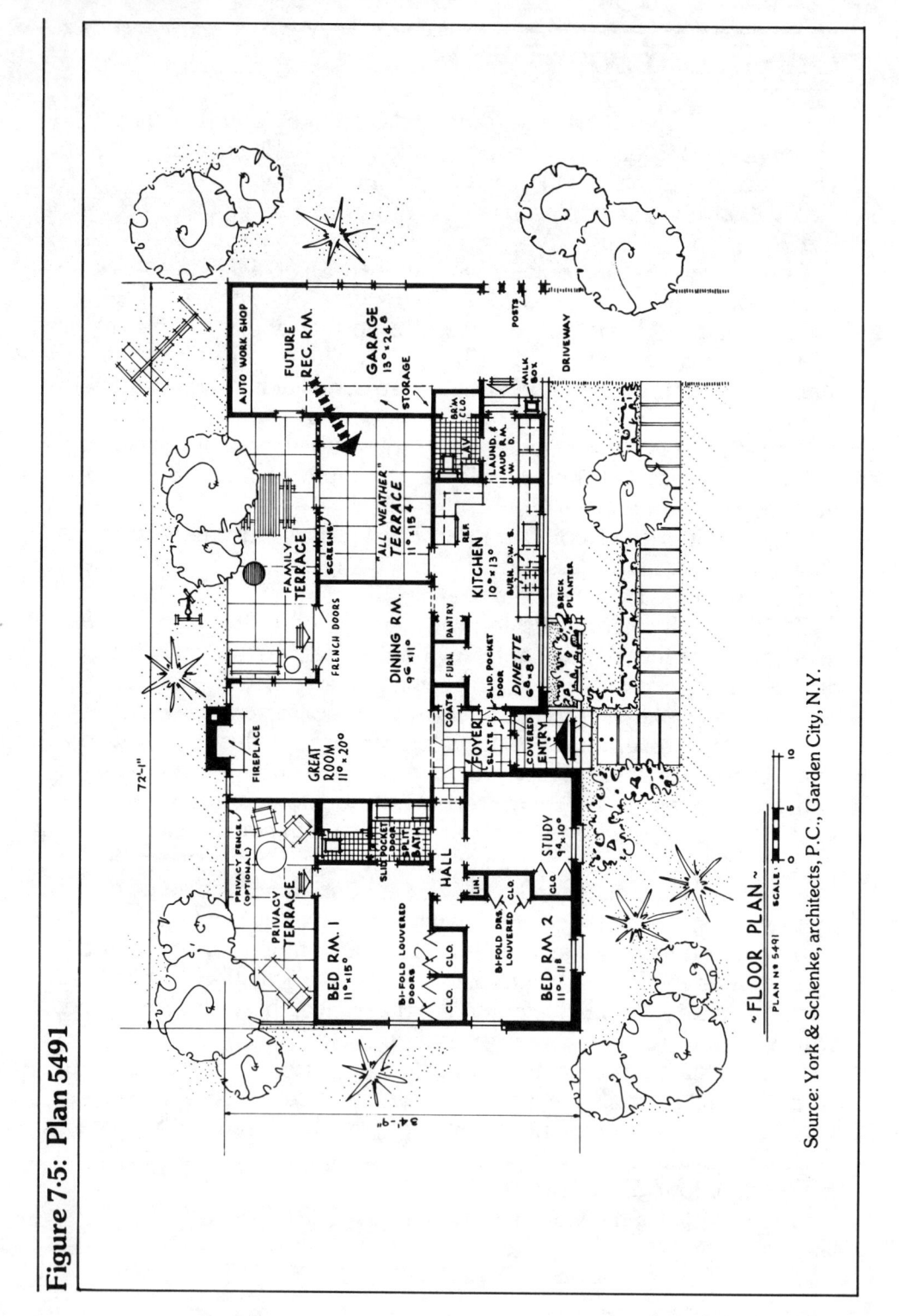

Figure 7-5: Plan 5491

Designed for Mature Living 159

Figure 7·6

Figure 7·7

Table 7·1 Statistics of Plan 5491

Overall length	72 feet, 1 inch
Overall depth	34 feet, 9 inches
Habitable area	1,262 square feet
All-weather terrace	173 square feet
Garage	347 square feet

Another Design—Especially for Us

We asked another architect, Walter J. Litwin of Washington, D.C., to design a group of houses for us. We gave him a copy of Chapter 7, "Designed for Mature Living," to read as well as some of the letters written to us about design.

What follows is Mr. Litwin's description of three types of homes designed for mature living.

The Litwin Plan

The goals of the first-time, young home buyer are quite similar to those of the mature market in many respects. That is,

The young require affordable housing with expansion potential to house the growing family economically and comfortably.

The mature market should be provided custom-designed housing with growth potential to insure or appreciate their estate.

Three examples of innovative housing are presented here: The Surety I, The Surety II (Figures 7·8, 7·9, 7·10), and The Concept House (Figures 7·11, 7·12, 7·13). These housing examples are designed primarily for mature home buyers and for potential first-home purchasers. Key elements include originality of design, built-in equity, potential income production, and insurance of appreciation with low-cost maintenance. Also presented are some planning considerations involved in the development of the examples. (Some architectural terminology is used in the presentation of the Litwin Plan.)

Basic Planning and Design Development

The examples illustrated are primarily planned as single-family detached houses on either minimal ground or property of choice; however, with modifications, these plans can be adapted to planned unit developments, zero lot lines, duplexes, and quadraplexes.

Designed for Mature Living 161

Figure 7·8: The Surety I

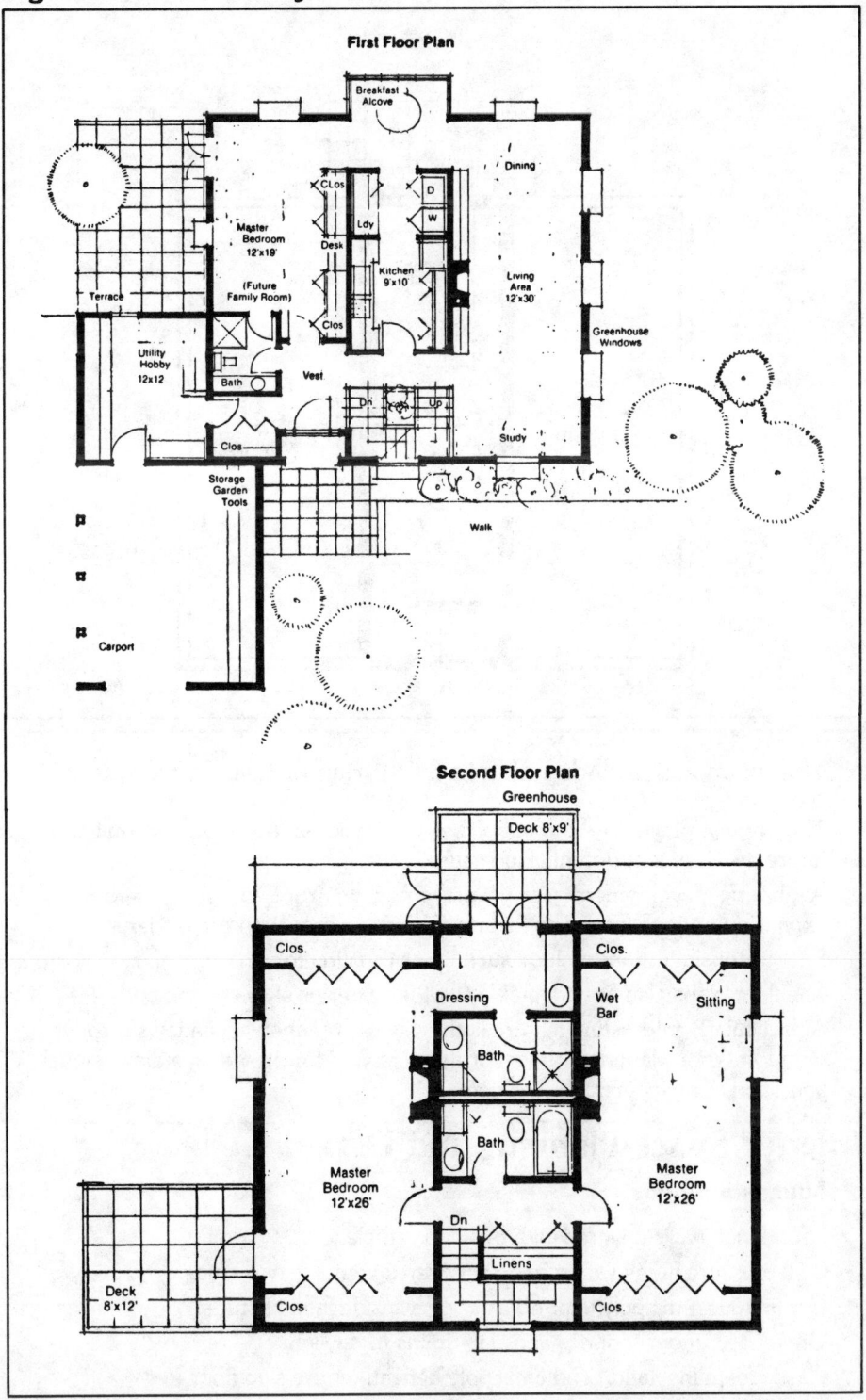

Figure 7-9: The Surety I & II Expansion Plan

[Floor plan showing BASEMENT (optional), Terrace, Basement 9'x30', Utility Room, H/W, Furn, Dry Storage, and UNEXCAVATED areas on both sides]

(continued)

The examples are adaptable to flat terrain or hilly environment.

The original phase in the examples is the basic 32 foot × 32 foot unit with future development potential indicated.

A phasing development plan is presented up front for purchasers' total expansion options for equity insurance and leverage with the lender.

Energy considerations include such items as siting for solar benefits.

The floor plans also are adaptable to other exterior styles of choice.

A particularly interesting feature is the use of greenhouse windows throughout for interior plantings, space for artifacts, and for providing a dimensional and open atmosphere.

Interior Space Planning and Design

Foundation/floor

Foundation walls covered with 6-mil polyethylene below grade.
R-30 pressure fit insulation batts between 2 inch × 8 inch studs.
Continuous 4-mil poly vapor barrier over inside face of studs.
Gravel bed under footings and slab drains to daylight.
Plastic foam insulation and 6-mil poly beneath entire slab floor.

Figure 7·9 (continued)

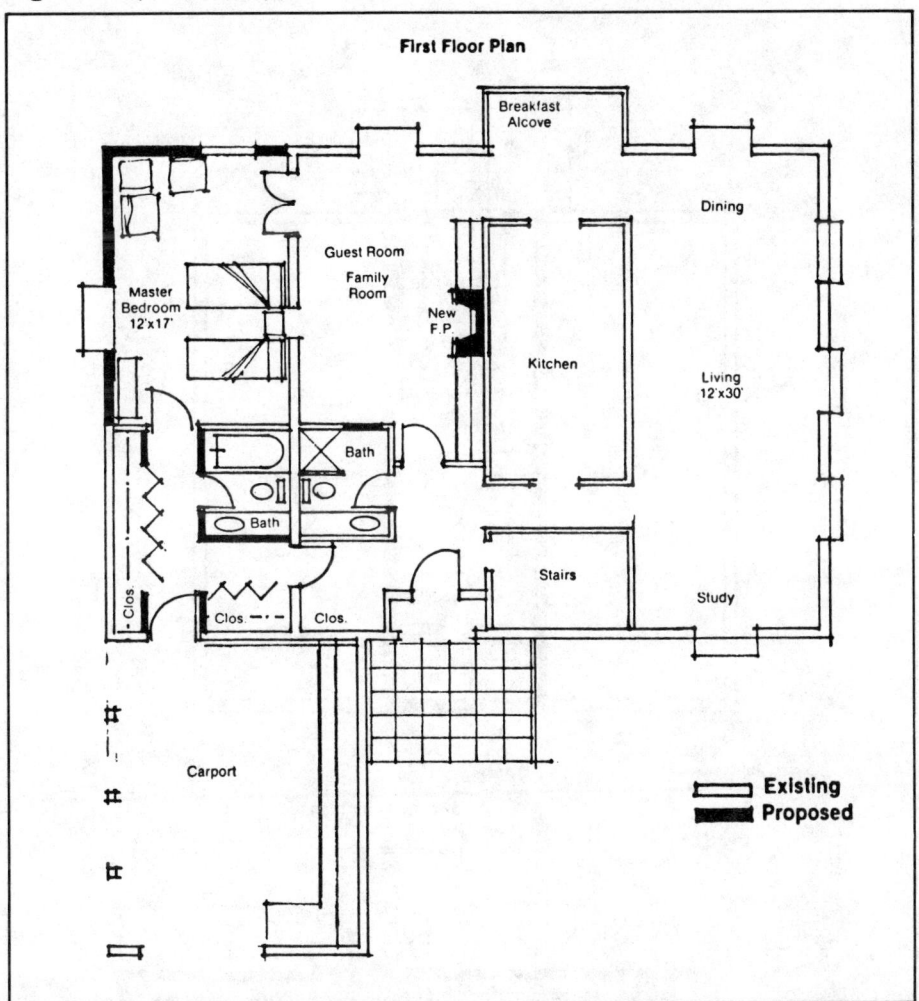

First Floor Plan

Plastic foam insulation around exposed slab edge.

Plastic foam insulation over band joists.

Continuous 28 foot long, 2 inch × 10 inch on 24 inch centers floor joists of COMPLY lumber.

Single-layer floor of ¾ inch T&G COMPLY panels on sleepers over concrete slab with insulation between sleepers.

Single-layer floor of ¾ inch T&G COMPLY panels glue-nailed to joists on second floor.

Eight-inch-thick concrete slab in lower level.

Exterior walls

In frame construction—2 inch × 6 inch on 24 inch centers studs and single 2 inch × 6 inch top plate of COMPLY lumber.

164 Planning Your Retirement Housing

Figure 7·10: The Surety II

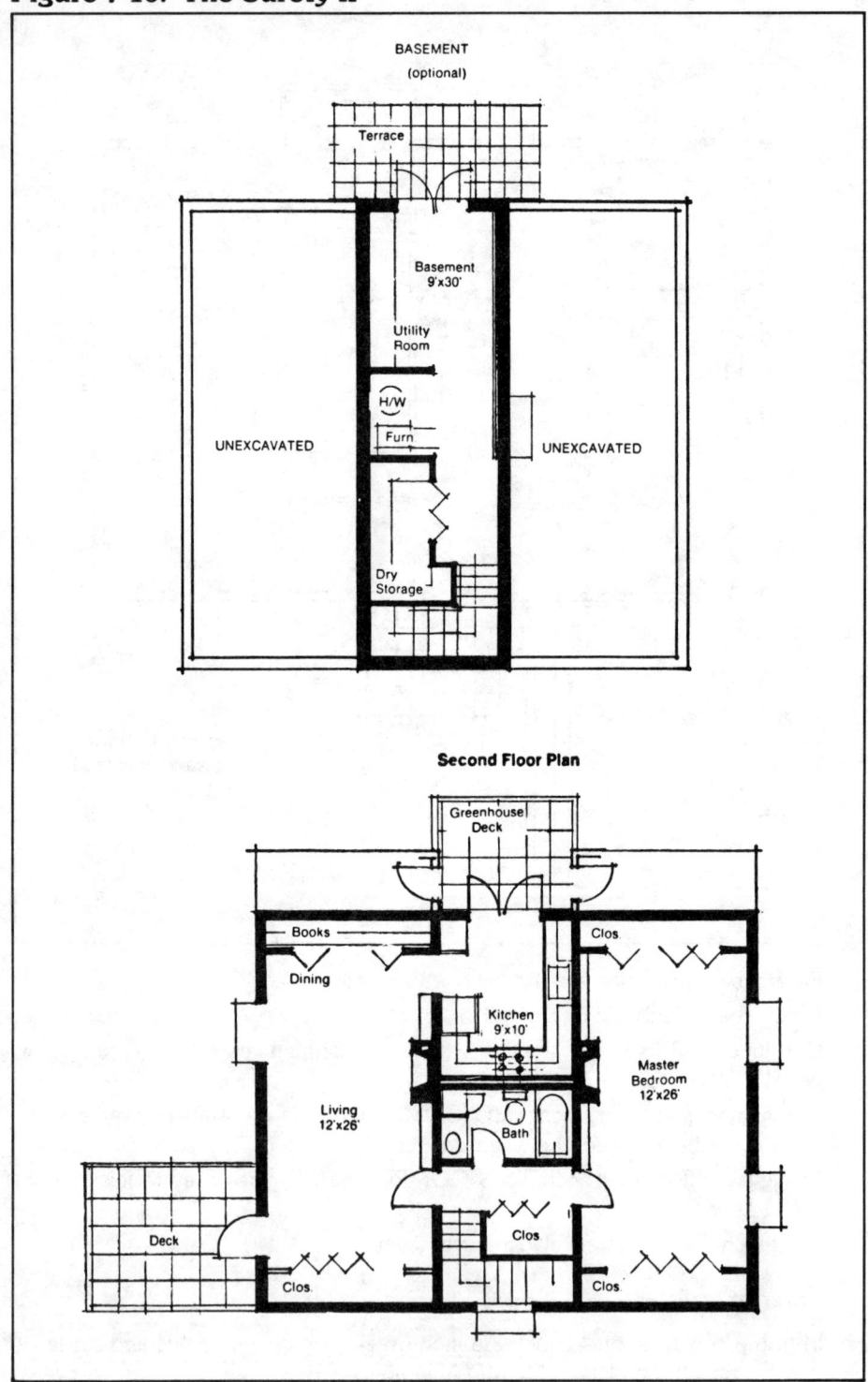

Plastic foam insulating sheathing, cedar bevel siding.

Pressure-fit insulation batts between 2 inch × 6 inch studs.

Continuous 4-mil vapor barrier over inside face of studs.

Plywood box headers over window and door openings fully insulated with R-19 batts.

Special corner post construction and deletion of partition posts to avoid disrupting insulation.

Central core unit

The first and second floor core houses the kitchen, all mechanical equipment, and baths, and provides for centrally located plumbing and heating equipment, affording short runs which result in efficiency of operation, installation, and maintenance.

Open plan

It provides flexibility, diversity in furniture arrangements, space utilization, and casual entertaining features.

Adequate living space is provided within the initial first-floor development for the mature couple.

The second floor can be unfinished initially with all plumbing and heating roughed in for future development, or finished initially for rental purposes and income production.

Doors/windows

Insulated steel entrance door with magnetic weatherstripping.

Low infiltration glass doors with double insulating glass.

Low infiltration greenhouse windows with double insulating glass and operable tops for circulation.

Adjustable blinds protect east/west windows from excessive solar gain.

Thermal shutters close over windows from inside.

Cracks around all door and window frames filled with insulation.

Roof/ceiling

Trusses fabricated from 2 inch × 4 inch COMPLY lumber for end sections of roof.

Large gable end vents provide ventilation for end sections.

Batt insulation installed in all ceilings; no vapor barrier.

Attic access door insulated and weatherstripped.

Roof overhangs shade south windows in summer.

Kitchen

Design features—compact, ease of circulation, access to storage facilities.

Pantry—features folding shutter doors for easy and complete accessibility to total storage.

Storage—abundant space provided with adjustable hardware for shelving and hanging goods; pegboard walls for versatile storage planning.

Appliances—high-efficiency range, refrigerator, dishwasher, and microwave oven.

Laundry

Washer/dryer—convenient and concealed by folding shutter doors; the interior finish pegboard with adjustable hardware for flexible shelving arrangements.

Laundry tub provided with adjoining serviceable work space.

Laundry chute from second-floor bath area.

Heat recycling from laundry in winter season to adjacent rooms; venting in summer months to exterior.

Closets

All closets have folding shutter or panel doors, prefinished pegboard walls, and adjustable hardware for total flexibility and use of space.

Greenhouse

The greenhouse provides dining space on the lower level and lounge or dining area on the upper level. It not only provides daylight but also acts as a solar collector.

Baths

Ample space.

Maintenance-free tile floors and walls.

One-piece shower and tub.

Water-saving fixtures.

Linen storage in each bath.

Dressing alcove and vanity on second floor.

Laundry chute to laundry on first floor.

Ample convenience outlets and ventilation fixtures.

Bedrooms

Master-size bedrooms.

Greenhouse windows for custom decor.

More than 20 feet of closet space in each bedroom.

Sliding shutters over windows for additional energy conservation.

Living area

For living, dining, study.

Folding-shutter divider walls if required or etagers.

Wall spaces for books, artifacts, display, etc.

Greenhouse windows with operable top for ventilation; sliding shutters for energy and light control.

Fireplace with ducts to adjacent rooms for heat distribution and ducts from exterior to hearth for outside supply of air for combustion saving, inside heated air.

Architectural paneled walls as design requirements using six-panel door skins, providing traditional luxury treatment with economical considerations. Wainscoting, using door skins, where desired.

Utility-hobby room

Work bench with ample adjustable shelves and pegboard walls.
Radiant heating.
Serves as mud room.
Provision of space for future bath.
Adjacent to carport.

Carport

Ample garden and miscellaneous tool storage and working space.
All walls prefinished pegboard with adjustable hardware.
Radiant heating panels over work space.

Energy conservation

Design and planning features: With proper planning and siting, passive solar can provide active savings in energy costs.

General

Compact bi-level design utilizes space efficiently and minimizes exterior surface area.

Partial earth sheltering on north side helps protect lower level from temperature extremes.

Attached garage shields north wall of first level and house entrance from winter winds.

Vestibule air-lock entrance prevents direct air exchange between indoors and outdoors.

South orientation of two-story rear wall for maximum solar exposure.

All rooms except kitchen (which has internal heat gains) can be situated on south wall for solar heating.

Large greenhouse windows located to maximize direct solar gain in winter.

Thermal shutters at windows block heat loss on winter nights and sunless days.

Greenhouses on upper and lower levels act as passive solar collectors.

Open planning and stairwell promote natural circulation throughout both of the levels.

Roof, balcony, and structural overhangs shade south facing windows in summer.

Operable windows and doors provide effective summer ventilation.

Heating/cooling systems

Heat pump centrally located for efficiency through shorter duct runs.

Energy-Kote radiant heating panels (to heat people instead of houses) located in each room with individual thermostats, affording control of individual rooms, eliminating heating the entire house to keep one room warm.

Separate central control panel in kitchen for remote control of all individual rooms in the house.

Water heating/appliances

Heavily insulated electric water heater with temperature set back to 120°F., centrally located, saving piping runs and time for delivery of hot water.

Passive solar water preheater operates only during warm season; winter drain-down avoids cold-weather problems and inefficiencies.

Flow restrictors on faucets and shower heads reduce hot water use.

High-efficiency refrigerator, range, dishwasher, and microwave oven.

All baths stacked, affording economies of installation and maintenance.

Fireplaces

Prefab with registers to spread heat into adjacent rooms.

Ducting to outside for fresh air intake to hearth, saving inside heated air.

The Concept House

The ultimate development of the concept house can be achieved in three optional phases with income provision in the interim for financial support of future expansion.

The concept house approach is ideal for the first-time home buyer, the mature family, and also the mature professional (physician, dentist, psychiatrist) who eventually wishes to practice at the same location as he or she resides. The lower floor can easily be adapted to accommodate a professional's practice. In addition to the convenience, it also provides a proportionate tax write-off. This particular house has been built and occupied by a doctor who is utilizing the entire lower level for his practice.

First phase

Build the basic 32 foot × 32 foot structure, preferably on a hillside or sloping ground to afford walkout or complete exposure in rear of house for maximum daylight and for energy-conserving purposes.

First floor finished for occupancy.

Designed for Mature Living 169

Figure 7·11: The Concept House—Phase I

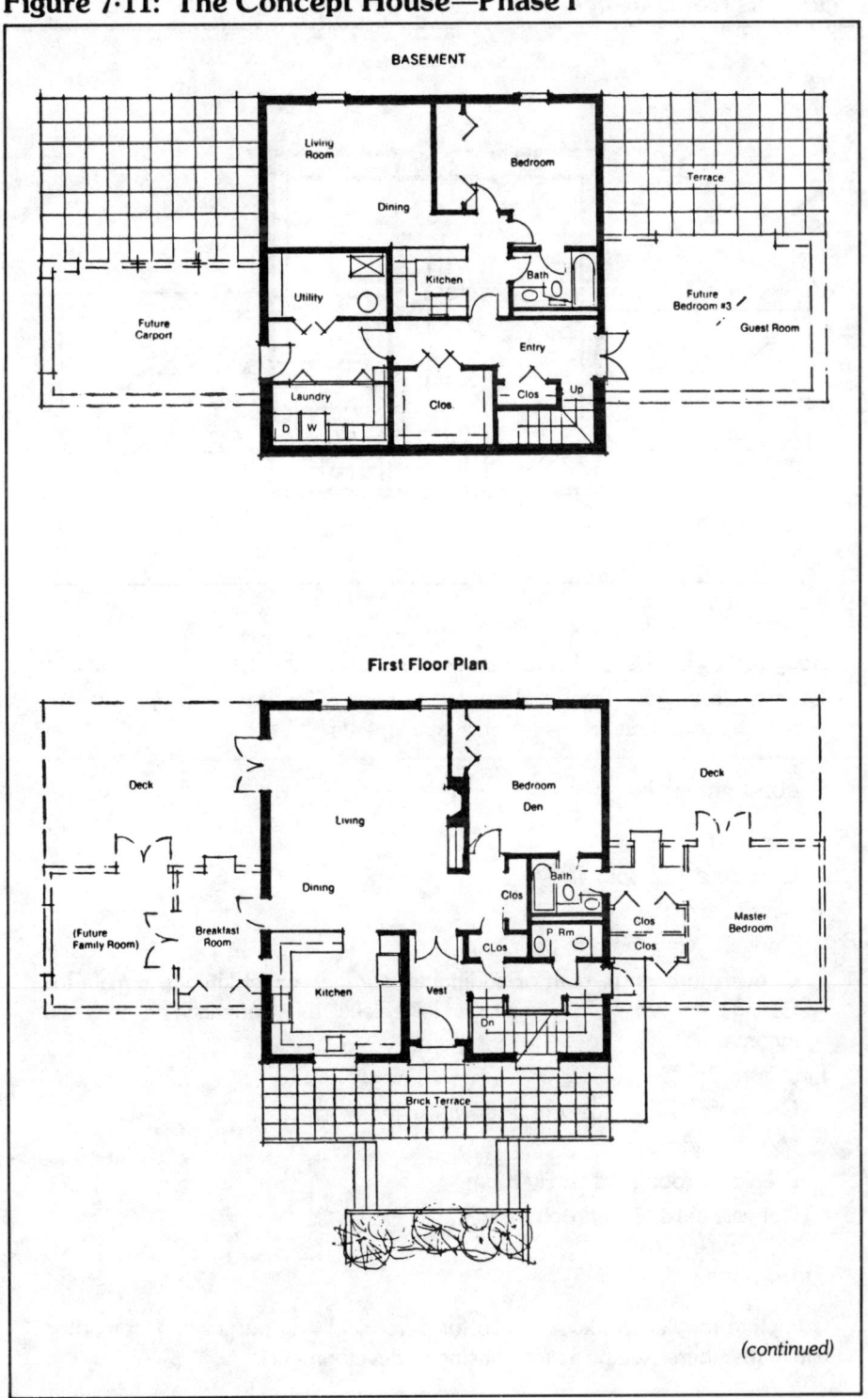

(continued)

Figure 7·11 (continued)

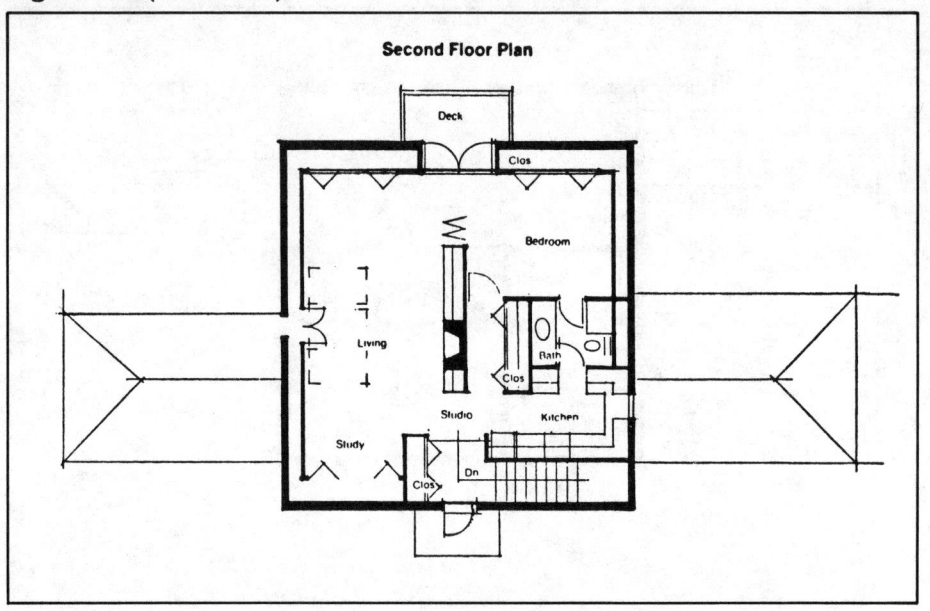

Second Floor Plan

Rough in lower level and studio on second floor.

Or complete lower level and studio as shown for leasing purposes with provision for private access for both apartments.

Second phase

Lower level
    Complete bedroom 3.
    Finish carport.
    Convert living room to bedroom.
    Convert kitchen to bath or additional storage—or let kitchen remain for leasing purposes of entire expanded lower level, thus commanding increased income.

First floor
    Complete development of both wings.
    Master bedroom.
    Breakfast room and family room.
    Convert existing bedroom to den.

Third phase

Complete the second floor studio for personal living purposes or for other family members (see plans for phasing of development).

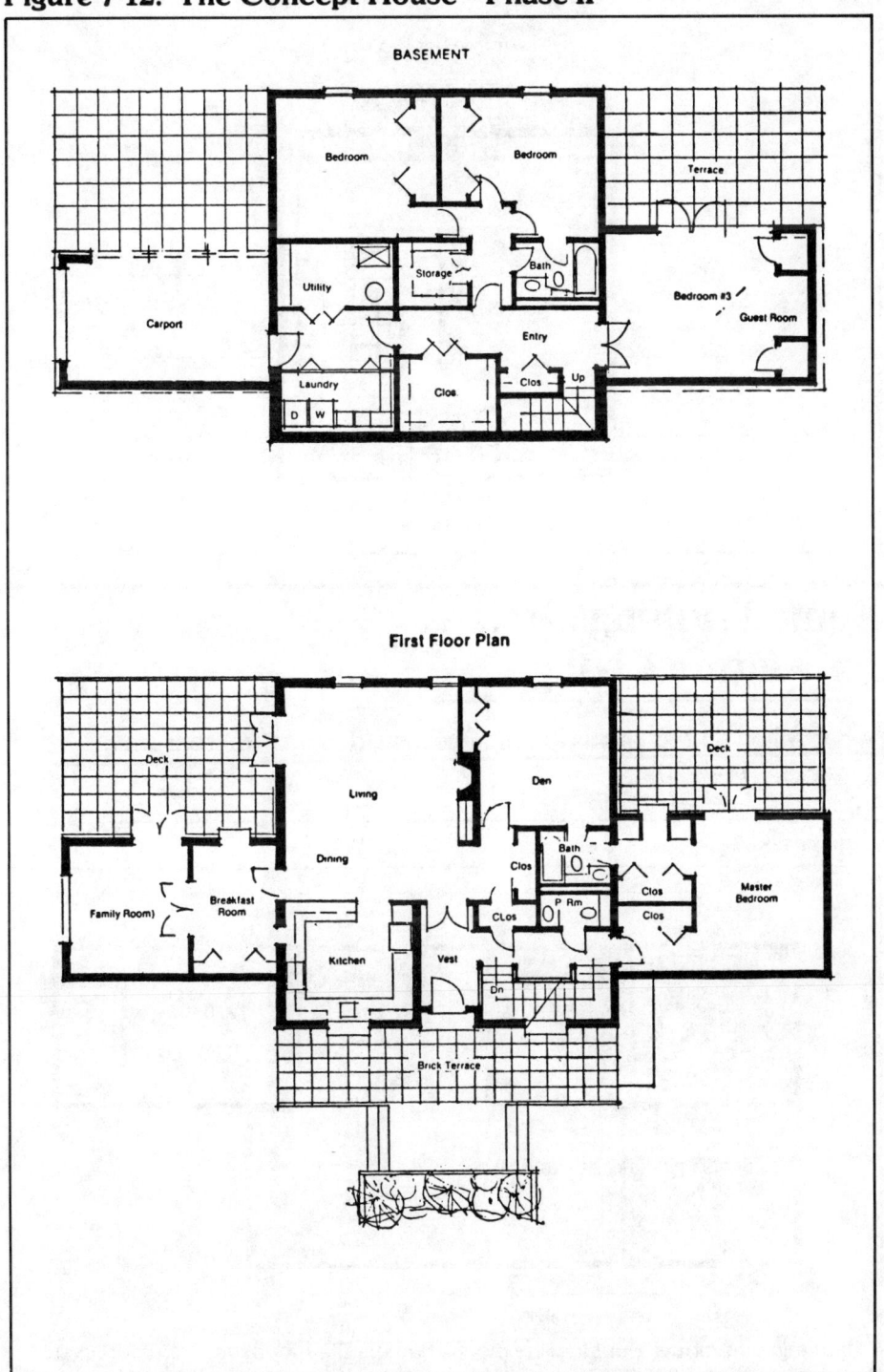

Figure 7·12: The Concept House—Phase II

172 Planning Your Retirement Housing

Figure 7·13: The Concept House—Phase III

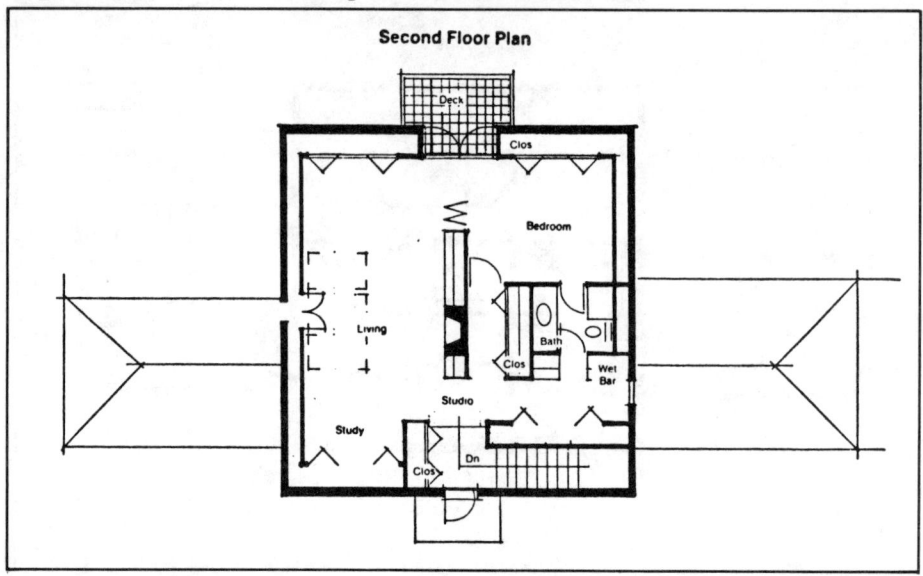

[Second Floor Plan showing Deck, Closet, Bedroom, Living, Bath, Wet Bar, Studio, Study, Closet, Dn (stairs)]

Some Winning Designs for Mature Living

What follows next are additional plans—designs for retirement living (Figures 7·14–7·20).

Figure 7·14

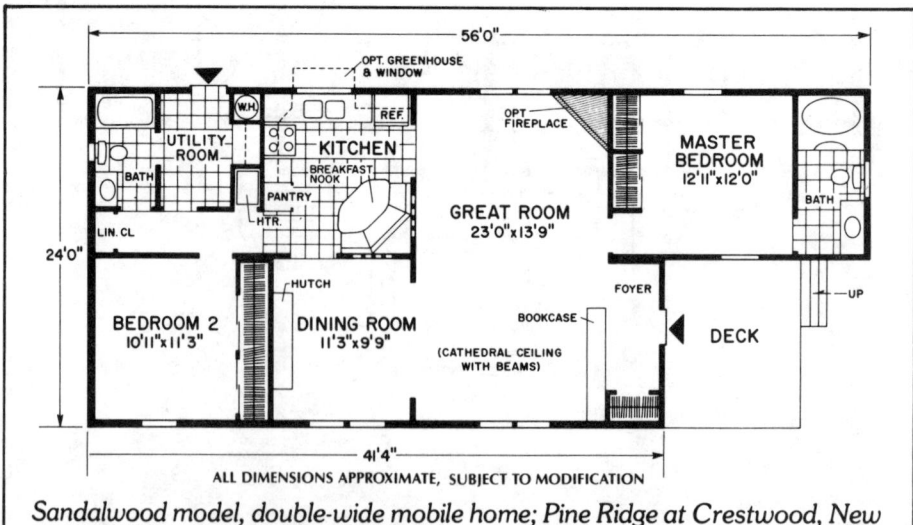

[Floor plan, 56'0" × 24'0", showing Utility Room, Bath, Kitchen with Breakfast Nook, Pantry, Opt. Greenhouse & Window, Opt. Fireplace, Master Bedroom 12'11"×12'0", Bath, Great Room 23'0"×13'9", Bedroom 2 10'11"×11'3", Dining Room 11'3"×9'9" (Cathedral Ceiling with Beams), Hutch, Bookcase, Foyer, Deck, Up. 41'4" dimension shown. ALL DIMENSIONS APPROXIMATE, SUBJECT TO MODIFICATION]

Sandalwood model, double-wide mobile home; Pine Ridge at Crestwood, New Jersey; selling at $35,790 on leased land.
Source: Crestwood Village, New Jersey.

Figure 7·15

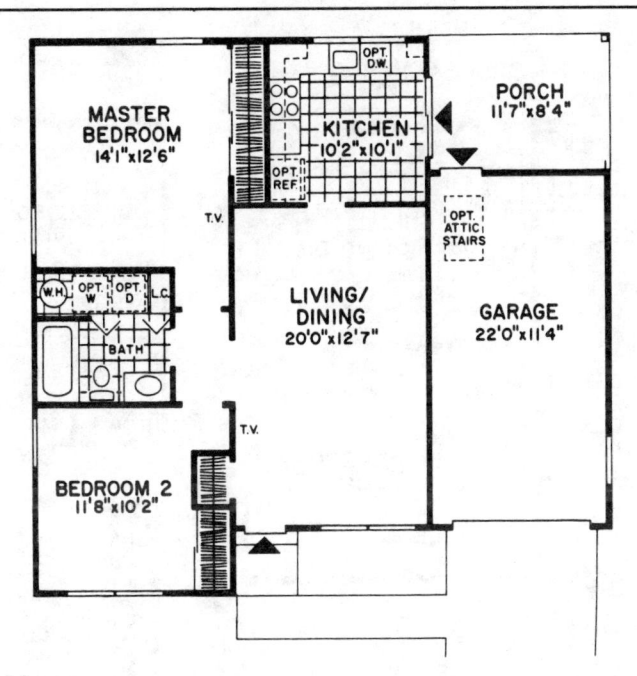

A two-bedroom, one-bath, single-family detached home built in the retirement community of Crestwood, New Jersey. Sales price as of May, 1983: $47,990. Monthly community service charges:* $44.02; homeownership cost:** $78.66.

*Exterior repairs, roof repairs, bus service, snow clearing, lawn cutting and fertilizing, street maintenance and lighting, 24-hour emergency repairs, club membership, outside maintenance.
**Real estate taxes, water and sewer, garbage removal, insurance, and cable TV.

Source: Crestwood Village, New Jersey.

Figure 7·16

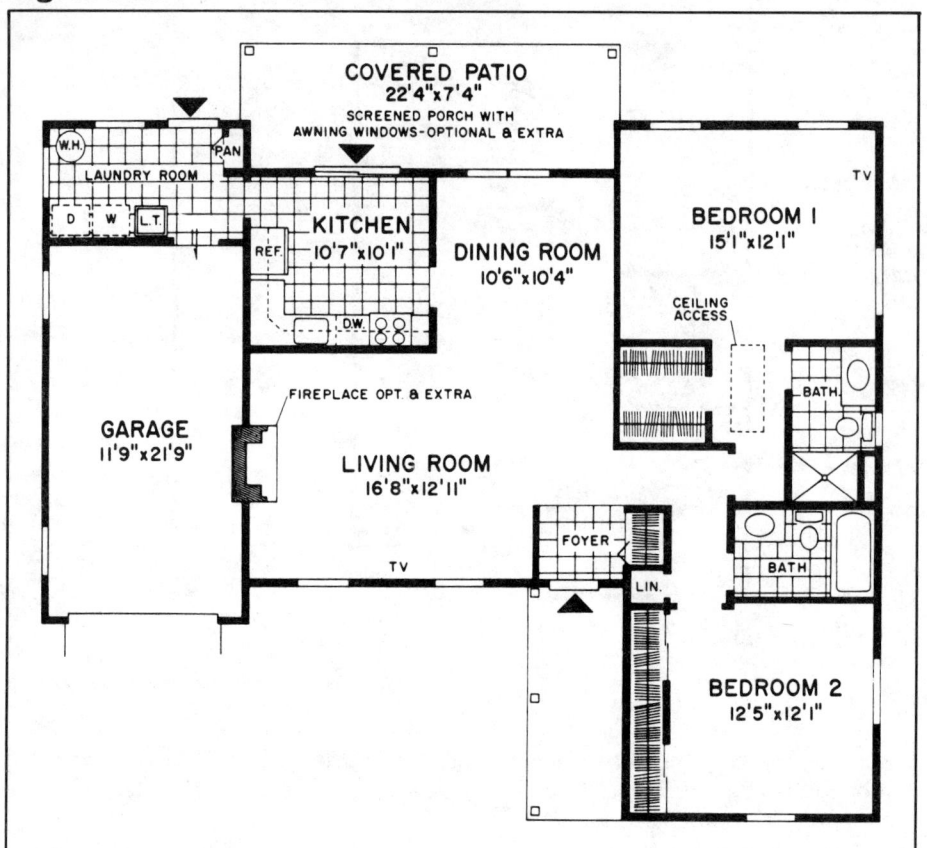

Crestwood Village, a retirement community in Frederick, Maryland. Single-family detached home called The Yardley, selling in Spring of 1983 for $73,490. Monthly community service charges: $42.07; estimated homeownership cost: $108.84.

Source: Crestwood Village, Frederick, Maryland.

Designed for Mature Living 175

Figure 7·17

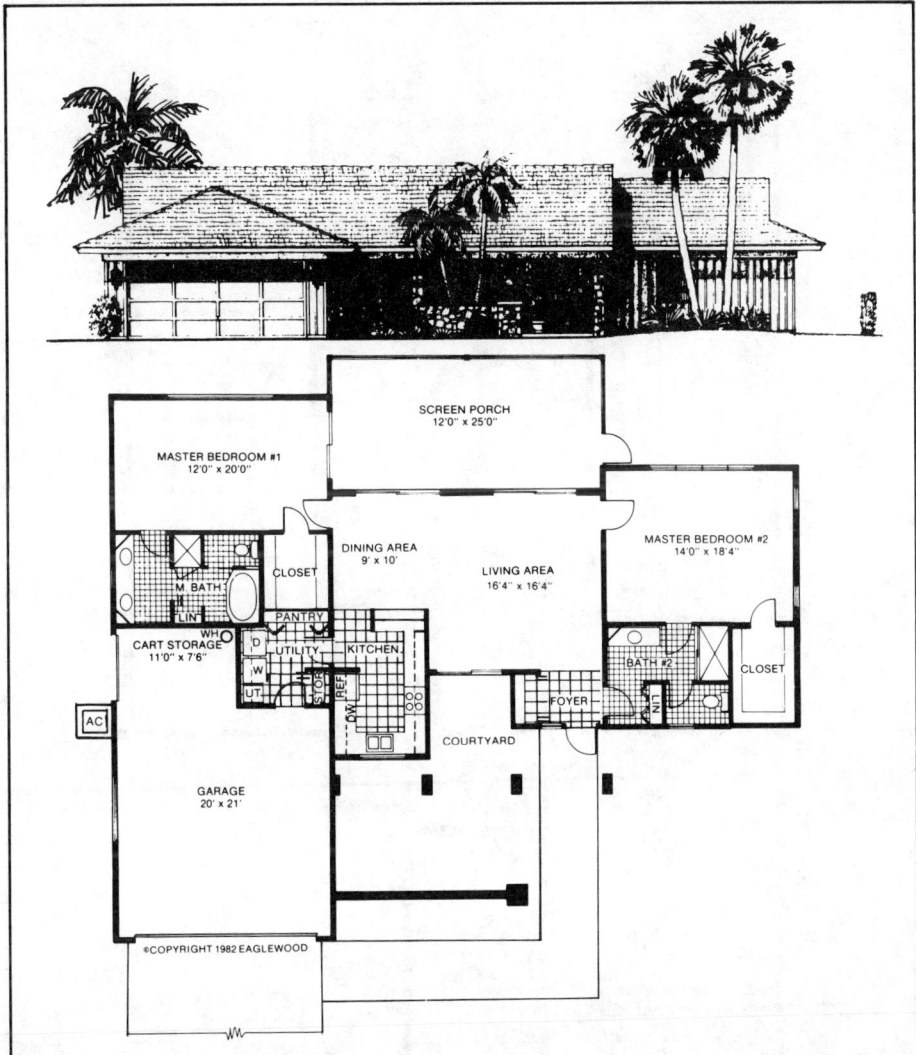

Plan 103: Two-bedroom, two-bathroom, single-family detached unit built in the "Eaglewood" subdivision, Hobe Sound, Florida and selling for $113,000.

Source: Robert W. Jahn, President, Eaglewood of Hopetown Sound, Inc., Florida.

Figure 7·18

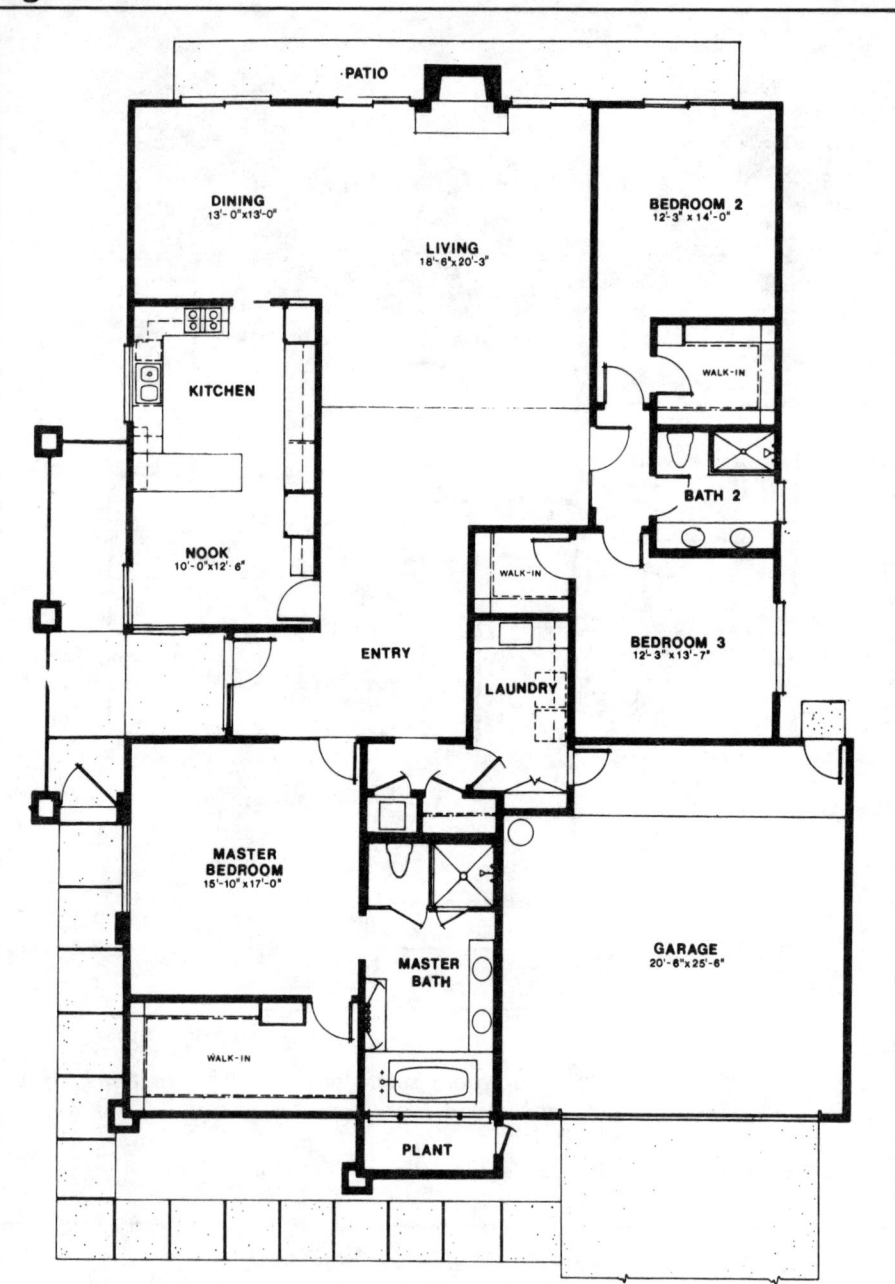

Luxury single-family home, developed by Rossmoor Corporation in Laguna Hills, California. Sales price in 1980—$299,900; in Summer, 1983—$350,900.

Source: Rossmoor Corporation; the Grand Finale Villages of Leisure World—Casa Monaco.

Designed for Mature Living 177

Figure 7·19

The exterior view and the interior atrium of a rehabilitated automobile dealership building in Taunton, Massachusetts. This development, located within a two-minute walk of the main thoroughfare at the center of the city, provides 75 units of housing for older people (one- and two-bedroom units).

Architects: Vitols Associates Architects/Planners

178 Planning Your Retirement Housing

Figure 7·20

WARM HEARTH VILLAGE
NEIGHBORHOOD I

1" = 50'

A new concept in the layout of retirement housing: High density with a lot of common ground. Warm Hearth Village: Neighborhood I, between Blacksburg and Christianburg, Virginia, is representative of retirement developments set in wooded areas with each housing group designed around a landscaped center courtyard and connected with the rest of the development by walkways. Such developments are within easy access of doctors' offices, shopping, banks, schools, restaurants, and recreation.

Design by Collins & Kronstadt, of Silver Spring, Maryland.

Keeping Up The Old Homestead

8

My home is my friend—letting my home run down is my greatest anxiety.
A retired homeowner at a Fannie Mae housing forum

Whether you stay where you are or buy another home, you must know the condition of the home where you plan to live in retirement. If you purchase another home, you want to make certain the new abode is in good shape so you won't get socked with costly repairs—and excessive utility bills—later. If you plan to stay in your pre-retirement house, especially if you live in an older house, you might want to consider renting part of a big old house to help generate some income to help with the upkeep.

A Solid Foundation

By getting your home into tip-top shape in the early years of retirement, you can beat some of the rising costs of home remodeling, repairs, replacement, and even energy.

The most important part of the house to check is the basic structure. Consider hiring a reputable home-inspection or engineering firm to give you a full report on the condition of the house where you plan to live in retirement. They can tell you what specific repairs are needed—and whether the repairs are worth making.

Writing in the U.S. government's *1978 Agriculture Yearbook*, Gerald E. Sherwood, an engineer in the Forest Products Laboratory of the U.S. Forest Service, Madison, Wisconsin, suggested inspecting these items:

1. Foundation. "The foundation is vital because it supports the entire structure," Mr. Sherwood noted. The foundation should be sound. "If pillars are used under the house or under porches, check to see that they are sound, also. Sometimes replacement is more difficult than it appears."

2. Standard wood frame. "Any foundation failures may destroy the house frame, resulting in problems with doors and windows, loosening of siding and interior finish, and cracks that allow air to blow through the house," Mr. Sherwood said.

Also, check for decay from moisture or insects. Check the wood for decay at points where the wood connects with concrete.

3. Interior. Check all surfaces for wear, distortion, and the presence of moisture. Inspect wood floors for buckling, or cupping of boards. Large cracks in the ceilings or walls could indicate structural damage. But often there are minor cracks that don't pose any problem.

4. Decay and insect damage. Look for decay in any part of the house where wood has remained wet for a long time. If you suspect damage, call a professional exterminator for an inspection.

5. Plumbing and electricity. Make sure the water service is sufficient. Also that the wiring isn't out of date for modern living or that the wiring isn't worn and dangerous. "Some wiring is usually exposed in the attic and basement where it can be checked," Mr. Sherwood said. "If the cable insulation is deteriorated, damaged, brittle, or crumbling, or if armored cable or conduit is badly rusted, wiring should be replaced."

6. Utilities and heating. Check to see if the heating system is in reasonable working order or if you will have to shell out some money before too long to replace it.

Wear-out Worries

Is your roof getting along in years? You might want to retire it and put on a new one that will last 20 or 25 years. If your furnace is pushing the quarter-century mark, it might need replacing before long. If you bought your refrigerator when Betty Furness was selling them on television, you probably can't expect it to last much longer.

To help you determine how much life is left in parts of your house, Table 8·1 provides a list of "Life Expectancies of Various Parts of the House," compiled by Dean Christ of the National Association of Home Builders' economic division. Table 8·2 lists common problems found in older homes.

Table 8·1 Life expectancies of various parts of the house

Item	Useful life	Remarks
Footings and foundations		First four items are likely to last up to 250 years. There are homes in the United States over 300 years old. Structural defects that do develop are a result of poor soil conditions.
Footings	life	
Foundation	life	
Concrete block	life	
Waterproofing:		
Bituminous coating	5 years	
Pargeting with Ionite	life	
Termite-proofing	5 years	Maybe earlier in damp climates.
Gravel outside	30–40 years	Depends on usage.
Cement block	life	Less strong than concrete block.
Rough structure		
Floor system (basement)	life	
Framing exterior walls	life	Usually plaster directly on masonry. Plaster is solid and will last forever. Provides tighter seal than drywall and better insulation.
Framing interior walls	life	In older homes, usually plaster on wood lath. Lath strips lose resilience, causing waves in ceilings and walls.
Concrete work:		
Slab	life	(200 years)
Precast decks	10–15 years	
Precast porches	10–15 years	
Site-built porches and steps	20 years	
Sheet metal		
Gutter and downspouts and flashing:		
Aluminum	20–30 years	Never requires painting, but dents and pits. May need to be replaced sooner for appearance.
Copper	life	Very durable and expensive. Requires regular cleaning and alignment.
Galvanized iron	15–25 years	Rusts easily and must be kept painted every 3 to 4 years.
Rough electrical		
Wiring:		
Copper	life	
Aluminum	life	
Romex	life	

(continued)

Table 8·1 (continued)

Item	Useful life	Remarks
Circuit-breaker		
Breaker panel	30–40 years	
Individual breaker	25–30 years	
Rough plumbing		
Pressure pipes:		
Copper	life	Strongest and most common. Needs no maintenance.
Galvanized iron	30–50 years	Rusts easily and is major expense in older homes. Most common until 1940.
Plastic	30–40 years	
Waste pipe:		
Concrete	20 years	
Vitreous china	25–30 years	
Plastic	50–70 years	Usage depends upon soil conditions. Acid soils can eat through plastic.
Cast iron	life	
Lead	life	A leak cannot be patched. If bathroom is remodeled, lead must be replaced.
Heating and venting		
Duct work		
Galvanized	50–70 years	
Plastic	40–60 years	Type used depends upon climate.
Fiberglass	40–60 years	
AC rough-in		Same as Duct Work
Roof		
Asphalt shingles	15–25 years	Most common. Deterioration subject to climate. Granules come off shingles. Check downspouts.
Wood shingles and shakes	30–40 years	Expensive. Contracts and expands due to climate.
Tile	30–50 years	Tendency to crack on sides.
Slate	life	High quality. Maintenance every 2 to 3 years as nails rust.
Metal	life	Shorter life if allowed to rust.
Built-up asphalt	20–30 years	Maintenance required— especially after winter.
Felt	30–40 years	
Tar and gravel	10–15 years	
Asbestos shingle	30–40 years	Shingles get brittle when walked on. Maintenance every 1 to 3 years.
Composition shingles	12–16 years	

(continued)

Table 8·1 (continued)

Item	Useful life	Remarks
Roof *(cont.)*		
Tin	life	Will rust easily if not kept painted regularly. Found a lot in inner-city row houses.
4 or 5 built-up ply	15–25 years	Layers of tar paper on tar.
Masonry		
Chimney	life	
Fireplace	20–30 years	
Fire brick	life	
Ash dump	life	
Metal fireplace	life	
Flue tile	life	
Brick veneer	life	Joints must be pointed every 5 to 6 years.
Brick	life	
Stone	life	Unless a porous grade stone like limestone.
Block wall	life	
Masonry floors	life	Must be kept waxed every 1 to 2 years.

Stucco	life	Requires painting every 8 to 10 years. More susceptible to cracking than brick. Replacement is expensive. Maintenance cycles for all types of masonry structures, including those found in urban areas, subjected to dirt, soot, and chemicals:
		  Caulking—every 20 years
		  Pointing—every 35 years
		  Sandblasting—every 35 years

Windows and doors		
Window glazing	5–6 years	
Storm windows and gaskets	life	Aluminum and wood.
Screen doors	5–8 years	
Storm doors	10–15 years	
Interior doors (Luan)	10 years	
Sliding doors	30–50 years	
Folding doors	30–40 years	
Sliding screens	30 years	
Garage doors	20–25 years	Depends upon initial placement of springs, tracts, and rollers.
Steel casement windows	40–50 years	Have leakage and condensation problems. Installed mostly in 1940s and 1950s.

(continued)

Table 8·1 (continued)

Item	Useful life	Remarks
Windows and doors *(cont.)*		
Wood casement windows	40–50 years	Older types very drafty.
Jalousie	30–40 years	Fair quality available in wood and aluminum. Used mostly for porches.
Wooden double-hung windows	40–50 years	
Insulation		
Foundation	life	
Roof, ceiling	life	
Roof—electric vent—automatic	10–15 years	
Walls	life	
Floor	life	
Weatherstripping:		
Metal	8–9 years	
Plastic gasket	5–8 years	
Exterior trim		
Wood siding	life	Must be kept painted regularly—every 5–7 years.
Metal siding	life	May rust due to climate.
Aluminum siding	life	Maintenance free if baked-on finish.
Shutters:		
Wood	20 years	
Metal	20–30 years	
Plastic	life	
Aluminum	life	
Posts and columns	life	
Gable vents:		
Wood	10–14 years	
Aluminum	life	
Gable vent screens	Same as gable vents	
Cornice and rake trim	life	
Trellis	20 years	Will rot in back even if painted because of moisture.
Exterior paint		
Wood	3–4 years	Climate a strong factor.
Brick	3–4 years	
Aluminum	10–12 years	
Gutters and downspouts and flashing:		
Aluminum	10–12 years	
Copper	life	No painting required.
Stairs		Usage is a critical factor.
Stringer	50 years	
Risers	50 years	

(continued)

Table 8·1 (continued)

Item	Useful life	Remarks
Stairs *(cont.)*		
Treads	50 years	
Baluster	50 years	
Rails	30–40 years	
Starting levels	50 years	
Disappearing stairs	30–40 years	
Drywall and plaster		
Drywall	40–50 years	Lifetime is adequately protected by exterior walls and roof. Cracks must be regularly spackled.
Plaster	life	Thicker and more durable than drywall. Exterior must be properly maintained.
Ceiling suspension	life	
Acoustical ceiling	life	
Luminous ceiling	10–20 years	Discolors easily.
Ceramic tile		
Tub alcove and shower stall	life	Proper installment and maintenance required for long life. Cracks appear due to moisture and joints; must be grouted every 3–4 years.
Bath wainscote	life	
Ceramic floor	life	
Ceramic tile	life	
Finish carpentry		
Baseboard and shoe	40–50 years	
Door and window trim	40–50 years	
Wood paneling	40–50 years	
Closet shelves	40–50 years	
Fireplace mantel	30–40 years	
Flooring		
Oak floor	life	In most older homes, 1st-story floor is oak and 2d- and 3d-story floors are hard pine.
Pine floor	life	
Slate flagstone floor	40–50 years	
Resilient (vinyl)	10–15 years	Because of scuffing may have to be replaced earlier.
Terrazzo	life	
Carpeting	5–8 years	Standard carpeting.
Cabinets and vanities		
Kitchen cabinets	18–30 years	
Bath vanities	18–30 years	
Countertop	18–30 years	
Medicine cabinets	15–20 years	
Mirrors	10–15 years	
Tub enclosures	18–25 years	
Shower doors	18–25 years	
Bookshelves	life	Depends on wood used.

(continued)

Table 8·1 (continued)

Item	Useful life	Remarks
Interior painting		
Wall paint	3–5 years	
Trim and door	3–5 years	
Wallpaper	3–7 years	
Electrical finish		
Electric range and oven	12–20 years	
Vent hood	15–20 years	
Disposal	5–12 years	
Exhaust fan	8–10 years	
Water heater	10–12 years	
Electric fixtures	20–30 years	
Doorbell and chimes	8–10 years	
Fluorescent bulbs	3–5 years	
Plumbing finish		
Dishwasher	5–15 years	
Gas water heater	8–12 years	
Gas refrigerator	15–25 years	
Toilet seats	8–10 years	
Commode	15–25 years	
Steel sinks	15–20 years	
China sinks	15–20 years	
Faucets	life	Washers must be replaced frequently.
Flush valves	18–25 years	
Well and septic system	15–30 years	Depends on soil and rock formations.
Hot water boilers	30–50 years	Becomes increasingly inefficient with age and may have to be replaced before it actually breaks down.
Heating finish		
Wall heaters	12–17 years	
Warm air furnaces	25–30 years	Most common today.
Radiant heating:		
Ceiling	20–30 years	
Baseboard	20–40 years	
AC unit	8–18 years	
AC compressors	10–18 years	Regular maintenance required.
Humidifier	7–8 years	
Electric air cleaners	8–10 years	
Appliances		
Refrigerator	15–25 years	
Washer	8–12 years	
Dryer	8–12 years	
Combo washer and dryer	7–10 years	
Garage door opener	8–10 years	
Disposal units	8–12 years	
Dishwasher	8–12 years	
Lawn mower	7–10 years	Must be serviced regularly.

(continued)

Table 8·1 (concluded)

Item	Useful life	Remarks
Appliances *(cont.)*		
Vacuum cleaner	6–10 years	
Music system (intercom)	30–40 years	
Appointments		
Closet rods	life	
Blinds	10–15 years	
Drapes	5–10 years	
Towel bars	10–15 years	
Soap grab	10–12 years	
Others		
Fences and screens	20–30 years	
Splash blocks	6–7 years	
Patios (concrete)	15–50 years	
Gravel walks	3–5 years	
Concrete walks	10–25 years	
Sprinkler system	15–25 years	
Asphalt driveway	5–6 years	With patchwork may last 15 to 20 years.
Tennis court	20–40 years	

Table 8·2 Some common problems found in older homes

1. *Water.* A very common problem in older homes. Often it is a result of poor gutter alignment, poor downspout direction, and/or poor surface grading. Water can be detected by discoloration of floor tile, stained paneling at floor level, dark spots on cinder block, and other signs in basement.
2. *Plumbing.* In older homes pressure tends to drop substantially because of rusty galvanized pipes. Considered major expense in older homes. Test for leaks and water pressure. A leak in lead waste piping can not be patched. If bathroom is remodeled, lead pipes must be replaced.
3. *Termite activity.* Combinations of wood, dirt, darkness, and dampness will bring termites. Particularly acute if there is crawl space with dirt very close to wood floor joists.
4. *Roofs.* Older homes may have roofs that have water leaks. Check metal roofs for rust; tile roofs for cracking on sides; slate roofs for rusty nails and tar coming off ridge; tin roofs for rusting; and built-up roof with gravel for spongy spaces and bubbles.
5. *Retaining walls.* Large cracks sometimes form, which usually indicates that surface water is collecting behind the wall, freezing and causing pressure. Can be demonstrative of poor structural work.
6. *Interior walls and ceilings.* Most older homes have plaster on wood lath. Over the years wood lath strips lose resilience and pull away from joists and studs, causing waves in walls and ceilings. Wood lath is very sensitive to moisture.

(continued)

Table 8·2 (continued)

7. *Electrical wiring.* Most older homes have inadequate wiring. Usually only one or two outlets per room and this does not meet many codes. Most newer homes have outlets installed every 12 feet of any doorway. This is so you never need an extension cord.
8. *Insulation.* Older homes are not as well insulated as newer ones. Lack of insulation between masonry walls and interior walls.
9. *Appliances.* Older homes do not have the variety as well as the quality of appliances that newer ones do. Technological changes are such that newer and better appliances are available to consumers.
10. *Windows.* Older homes usually have windows that readily conduct cold air into the house. Replacement is expensive.

Preventive Remodeling

Once you know what is likely to need replacing, the next step is to make improvements that will put your home in top shape. In considering which improvements to make, think of safety first.

Check the wiring. For example, make sure your home's wiring meets current safety standards. If you have an older house, you may need to increase the electrical service and put in a new fuse box or circuit breakers. Also, check to see if you have aluminum wiring instead of copper wiring. The U.S. Consumer Product Safety Commission warned that aluminum wiring may be an "imminent fire hazard" in more than 1.5 million homes built during the 1965–1973 period.

Replacing wiring can be costly, but it also could save your life. The Product Safety Commission estimated that 75,000 fires per year and 11,000 injuries are associated with home electrical systems of all kinds. These fires result in 700 to 800 deaths annually.

The commission warned "especially if you've noticed any electrical problems, such as the frequent blowing of fuses, tripping of circuit breakers, heating of switch plates or outlet covers, and flickering lights, you better have your electrical system checked."

Install smoke detectors. The cheapest fire protection you can get are smoke detectors that will sound an early-warning alarm that will give you time to escape a fire in your home. This can be especially important for older people who may take longer to flee. There are two basic kinds of smoke detectors on the market: the "ionization" detector, which is best at sensing openly burning fires; and the "photoelectric" detector, which is best at sensing smoldering fires.

A subcommittee of the International Association of Fire Chiefs endorsed the photoelectric device over the ionization type. Its report concluded: "It is the subcommittee's belief that only the photoelectric detector will meet the requirements reliably when subjected to both open flame and smoldering fires."

The fire chiefs preferred the photoelectric detector because smoldering fires are becoming the most common kind in American homes. Others disagree. Our advice: Buy one of each type and put them up in different parts of your home for the best overall protection.

Burglar-proof your house. Older people are often targets of burglars. Make sure your windows and doors are as burglar-proof as possible.

"One of the things I would have if I was building new is a very sturdy front door and any other doors that lead to the outside, and the doors would have the very best locks that money can buy," said Lydia King Penny, a retiree in Jacksonville, Florida. *"And I would investigate to see which windows give crooks the most trouble to get in."*

Your local law-enforcement agency can advise you on what are the best safeguards to make.

A "Carefree" House

Other improvements should be made with an eye to holding down maintenance costs.

"We bought our present home four years ago after living 19 years in a custom-made house that became too large for us," wrote Jean Whitford of Tacoma, Washington. *"We have had the following improvements made:*

1. Vinyl siding on the outside to eliminate painting and to provide extra insulation.
2. Modernized kitchen to provide more cupboard space, floors that don't need waxing, self-cleaning oven (the BEST improvement in our house) and a glass-top stove that is simple to keep clean.
3. Added a family room that doubles as a dining room, library, and guest room.

"We are near retirement, so we are interested in having a carefree house as much as possible," Mrs. Whitford explained.

Some federal booklets are available that can help you develop a "carefree" house. They are "Protecting Your Housing Investment" (27 pages, free), "How to Crimeproof Your Home" (18 pages, $2.50), and "Smoke Detectors" (30 pages, $2.50). All are available from the U.S.

Consumer Information Center in Pueblo, Colorado. (See page 250 for instructions on ordering.)

Home-improvement Costs

Consider your retirement needs. Will you need a modernized kitchen? A new bathroom? What about a first-floor bedroom if you have a two-story house? But don't get carried away. Remember, you may not need more room, and too big an addition could boost your property taxes and maintenance costs.

Maurice Gantz, who runs a home-maintenance program for older homeowners in Brevard County, Florida, advised: "Bring the appearance of your home up to its best possible state. This will include exterior and interior painting and decoration, and replacement or discarding of accumulated junk and eyesores.

"In general, stop thinking and living as who you were, and think of and respond to the needs, wishes of who you will be, both as man and wife, healthy and ill—and as a possible survivor, widow or widower. Make the home pleasing to the eye and easy to care for."

Probably the best way to finance a remodeling job is with a Federal Housing Administration (FHA) Title 1 loan. You can borrow up to $15,000 for up to 15 years with an FHA-insured loan, which you obtain from your banker, savings and loan association, or credit union. You also can get a regular home-improvement loan from lenders, or you could take out a second mortgage.

To give you an idea of how much typical home improvements are likely to set you back, see Table 8-3, "Costs of Remodeling or Repair," prepared by the Home-Tech Systems of Bethesda, Maryland. The figures are based on what a contractor would charge a homeowner in the Washington, D.C.-Baltimore area in 1983. Prices may be lower or higher in your area.

Home-Tech said the costs generally include one third for materials, one third for labor, and one third for profit. So you have room to bargain a cheaper price. And if you are a do-it-yourselfer, you may be able to save money on some jobs.

A Tax Tip

When you shell out a lot of money for home improvements, make sure you don't lose some tax advantages. Here's a blueprint for deducting sales taxes on building materials.[1]

Table 8.3 Costs of remodeling or repair (Washington–Baltimore area, 1983)

Remodel kitchen	$ 4,000–	$ 6,000
Remodel bath	2,500–	4,500
Add powder room	1,500–	2,500
Add full bath	2,500–	4,500
Increase electrical service to 200 amps	400–	500
Run separate electrical line for dryer	75–	100
Run separate electrical line for a/c	75–	125
Install new warm air furnace	800–	1,200
Install central air-conditioning, electric	1,000–	1,500
Install central air-conditioning, gas	1,500–	2,000
Install humidifier	180–	200
Install electrostatic air cleaner	400–	550
Install new 40-gallon hot water heater	200–	275
Install new 30-gallon hot water heater	175–	225
Install attic ventilating fan	150–	250
Install storm windows, each	30–	40
Install replacement windows, each	175–	250
Install new gutters and downspouts, $2.50 linear ft.	300–	400
Install new asphalt shingle roof	1,000–	1,800
Dig and install new well	1,500–	2,500
Install new septic system	1,500–	2,500
Build rear addition, approx. 300 sq. ft. $35 to $45/sq. ft.	10,000–	14,000
Sand and finish floors, 50¢ to 70¢/sq. ft.	600–	1,200
Install new drywall ceiling over plaster, per room	150–	250
Regrade around exterior	250–	500
Install new sump pump	250–	390
Install French drain and sump pump	1,500–	2,500
Enclose porch	2,500–	4,000
Install new hot-water boiler	1,000–	1,800
Install new copper horizontal water pipes in basement	500–	900
Insulate attic, 50¢/square foot	350–	800
Remove interior non-loadbearing wall	300–	500
Remove exterior wall and install sliding doors	800–	1,200
New single garage	4,000–	5,000
New double garage	5,000–	8,000
Masonry fireplace	1,500–	2,500
Pre-fab fireplace	1,100–	1,500
New kitchen floor, $2/sq. ft.	200–	500
Basement apartment to meet code	15,000–	20,000
Gut and renovate two-story townhouse, $20 to $25/sq. ft.	20,000–	35,000
Replace disposal	100–	150
Install new disposal-drop waste	200–	300
Replace dishwasher	300–	500
Replace refrigerator	350–	700

(continued)

Table 8·3 (continued)

Replace cooking equipment	$300–	$900
Install countertop with stainless steel sink	250–	350
Install bath vanity	200–	300
Drop concrete floor—townhouse	2,500–	3,500
Replace laundry tub—single fiberglass	100–	150
Install plumbing for laundry—within 5 feet of plumbing	250–	450
Vent dryer—easy access	25–	50
Pour concrete patio—$2 to $3/sq. ft.	300–	800
Install overhead garage door—single	175–	250
Install overhead garage door—double	350–	500
Install garage door opener	250–	300
Replace flat roof—townhouse, selvage 4-ply built-up ($2/sq. ft.) galvanized	1,200–	1,800
Install storm door	75–	125
Reline fireplace with terra cotta	1,000–	1,400
Repoint brick exterior, $1 to $2/sq. ft.	300–	500
Install skylight	500–	800
Install bars on windows, $4 to $6/sq. ft. (ea.)	60–	75
Install wrought-iron door (ea.)	150–	200
Install ceramic tile in tub area—mastic	250–	350
mud	350–	500
Change sash cords in windows (per side)	12	
Install aluminum siding, $1.50 to $2/sq. ft.	2,000–	4,000
Paint interior of house—small	1,000–	1,800
medium	1,500–	2,500
large	2,000–	4,000
Replace slate roof, $3/sq. ft.	3,000–	7,000
Replace cedar shake roof, $2/sq. ft.	2,000–	6,000
Install disappearing stairway to attic	125–	150
Build redwood or pressure-treated deck (sq. ft.)	10–	12
Basement conversion—component items	($ 1,500–	4,000)
Kitchen $3,000–$5,000		
Bath 2,000– 3,500		
Electrical 1,200– 1,800		
Heating and A/C–separate 1,500– 2,500		
Heat–copper baseboard 800– 1,500		
Paint 400– 700		
Drywall 1,500– 2,500		
Carpentry 1,500– 2,500		
Drop floor 2,500– 3,700		
Build 30-foot shell dormer–finished exterior	$ 4,000–	5,000
Run new water line to street	800–	1,500
Install burglar alarm system if tied into central–monthly	800–	1,500
charge (per mo.)	18–	25
Replace front door	200–	500
Build closet	300–	500

If you're building or improving a home, those sales taxes are deductible on your U.S. return only if itemized and if you, as the ultimate consumer under state law, pay them. In one case, a New Yorker reimbursed a contractor for itemized sales taxes, but couldn't deduct the payments: the tax court held that the New York law made the contractor the consumer in that situation.

The *CPA Journal* of New York State Society of CPAs advises taxpayers to be sure to put themselves in the position of ultimate consumer when engaging a builder. The most direct way is to buy the materials from the supplier yourself and turn them over to the contractor.

Or, if the builder requires a down payment, arrange for an escrow fund, specifying that any payments for materials are for your account.

Energy Savings

One of the wisest home improvements you can make is to make your home stop wasting energy. You can save money now by holding down your utility bills and even more later as heating and cooling costs are expected to continue to skyrocket. A 1980 study by the Mellon Institute's Energy Productivity Center estimated that $1,900 worth of energy-saving home improvements would be recovered in savings within six years.

Energy-saving improvements should be part of any remodeling plan, advised Richard Bergere, the "holdout" in his Victorian home in Flushing, New York.

"I have an ultra-modern kitchen done in Ethan Allen style and three baths that are new. I put in triple storm windows; caulked every crack, use coal in the fireplace and have gone 20 days without using the oil burner. That's how tight the house is," Mr. Bergere said.

First you need to find out where you are wasting energy. The best way is to get an energy audit. Local utilities must provide such audits for a small fee of $15 or so. Or you can hire a professional inspection firm for a higher fee. The audit inspectors will check your home and give you a report on needed improvements. Some will estimate what the improvements should cost you and how long it would take you to recover your costs. Some utilities can even arrange low-interest financing for energy-saving improvements.

The energy-saving remedies range from something as simple as turning down your thermostat at night to adding several thousand dollars of insulation. Such improvements can be especially necessary for older homes that are likely to be less energy efficient than newer ones. Improvements are also necessary for all-electric homes, which have higher utility costs than those with gas or even heating-oil furnaces.

How much can you save in energy and utility bills? A study by the research foundation of the National Association of Home Builders (NAHB), under a federal contract, showed that energy use in a typical new home can be trimmed 50 percent by taking actions for which the owners would recoup their costs in six years, which is the same time cited by the Mellon study. In the NAHB study, the foundation had two identical, all-electric homes built in Mount Airy, Maryland. One home included numerous energy-efficient improvements, the second home didn't.

Though both homes were newly built, the study's results can be adapted to most existing homes. For example, the biggest energy saving, 28 percent, came from turning down the thermostat on the water heater in the energy-efficient house to 120 degrees, compared with a setting of 160 degrees in the conventional house.

From this study and others by the foundation, here are some energy-saving proposals that you might want to consider:

Install storm windows. Storm windows decrease heat loss by conduction up to nearly 50 percent, and substantially reduce the air inflow or infiltration. In the summer, storm windows also help a little to reduce the cooling load.

In cold climates, consider replacing windows with double- or triple-paned glass. But this is expensive, so check the savings closely.

Caulk and seal air leaks. Caulking and sealing cracks, joints, and other openings throughout the house reduces air infiltration and saves energy. Caulk at the corners, at the intersection of windows and door trim with the siding, and around pipes, vents, and other penetrations of the house shell.

These little cracks waste more energy than you might think. A Dow Chemical Company study found that air infiltration accounted for the greatest heat loss (36 percent) in a modern two-story house.

Turn down the water heater. Reducing the temperature on a hot water heater to 120 or 125 degrees saves energy and prolongs the life of the heater. Also insulate the heater.

When installing a new hot water heater, get one with as small a capacity as practical and spread your use of hot water.

"The more personal habits that spread out the use of hot water, such as bathing at different times of the day, washing dishes and clothes at different times, or other staggered uses means that the water heater can be smaller. And since hot water heating may represent 40 percent of all energy used, a savings in this area can have a substantial effect," stated AA Technical Inspections of Rockville, Maryland.

Older people, when they no longer have a family to house, especially don't need a big, energy-wasting heater. Flora C. Gick, a retiree in North East, Maryland, noted:

"I learned that I can turn the electric hot water off all day and just put it on two hours in the evening, sufficient for one person."

Stop the drips. Make sure hot water faucets don't leak. A constant water drip can lose 6 million BTUs a year. Use water-saving shower heads.

Lower the thermostat. Lowering the thermostat three degrees in winter can produce annual savings of 10 percent on the heating bill. Consider installing a clock thermostat that automatically lowers the temperature at night and raises it in the morning.

Caution: When you get older, don't turn the thermostat down too low. The internal body temperature regulators of older people sometimes fail to warn them when they are getting too cold. The result can be accidental hypothermia—where the body temperature drops below 95 degrees. And it can be fatal. The rule of thumb, experts say, is that people over age 65 should keep their houses at no less than 65 degrees and people over age 75 should keep their houses above 70 degrees.

Don't install an over-sized furnace. If you buy a new furnace or air conditioner, it is better to have one with too low a capacity than too large. In many older homes, larger-than-necessary furnaces were installed (they did not have an energy crisis back then) so the furnaces would heat up quickly. Have the furnace and air conditioner checked annually to make sure they are operating at peak efficiency.

Put in a heat pump. Consider installing a heat pump if you live in an all-electric home in a very cold or very warm climate. Heat pumps take the heat out of the air on the outside of the house and transfer it to inside the house. The pumps also can be reversed to take the heat from the house to the outside, for cooling purposes. In the NAHB foundation's energy-efficient house, the heat pump produced the second largest energy savings, 22 percent.

Look at the lighting. In a typical home, lighting is the fourth-largest energy user. Fluorescent lights produce nearly four times as much light per watt as incandescent light bulbs and last much longer.

Fix the fireplace. If you have a fireplace, install a damper to cut heat loss when the fireplace isn't being used. Glass doors enclosing the fireplace cut loss even more. Otherwise, more money goes up the chimney than you save by using the heat from a fireplace.

Other savers. Other ways to lower annual energy costs, according to the NAHB Research Foundation, is to close off rooms that aren't being used, drawing drapes or shades over windows at night during the winter and when the sun is shining on the windows during summer. The cost-effectiveness of fancy storm doors is questionable if the prime door is well insulated, tight fitting, and well weather-stripped. Also, when buying a new appliance, investigate those that are more energy-efficient.

Insulation Issues

The other major energy-saving improvement is to add insulation. This is a complex area, but you can simplify it somewhat by learning to speak the language. The thickness in inches of different material has nothing to do with its insulating abilities. What you need to know is the R-value, which is the common measure of a material's ability to resist heat transfer.

By comparing the R-value per square foot of thickness, you can directly compare different insulating materials. And dividing the price per square foot by the R-value permits you to compare the cost efficiency of different insulating materials. The R-value of insulation you will need depends on where you live. The colder or hotter the climate, the higher the R-value the insulation should be.

There are basically four types of insulation: batts or blankets of fiberglass or of mineral wool; loose fill of cellulose or of mineral wool; foam; and plastic foam boards.

"The home buyer should ask the salesperson what types of insulation are being installed and what the R-values are," suggested one energy expert. "It would be a good idea to get all this written into the contract."

Generally, insulation is needed in places where an uninsulated floor, ceiling, or wall is next to an unheated area or the outside of the house.

For example, the prime candidate for insulation in many houses is an unfinished-attic floor. Rolls of insulation or loose-fill insulation can be installed to cut heat loss. The number of inches of insulation needed depends on the recommended R-value for your climate. In mild climates where energy costs are relatively low, the NAHB Research Foundation said that installing enough insulation to provide a total heat resistance of about R-19 usually is cost-effective. In colder or hotter climates, with high energy costs, the needed insulation might be R-30 or R-38.

Crawl spaces also should be insulated, as should walls next to unheated rooms, such as garages. The ceilings in unfinished and unheated basements may need insulating. Insulation into other walls of the house can be costly and should be investigated carefully to make sure the move will be cost-effective. The NAHB Research

Foundation noted: "If any insulation exists in walls, it will probably not be feasible to attempt any additional."

Two guides for helping you decide what insulation you need are available from the federal government. They are "In the Bank . . . or Up the Chimney" (77 pages, $5.50) and "Home Energy Savers' Workbook" (29 pages, $2.50). To get copies, write: Superintendent of Documents, U.S. Government Printing Office, Dept. 33. Washington, DC 20402.

You also can get a poster, "Insulate by the Number," for $2.50 from the U.S. Consumer Information Center in Pueblo, Colorado. (See page 250 for instructions on ordering.)

Insulation Cautions

Make sure you don't over-insulate. After you reach a certain level, the additional savings can be small and not worth the money. For more details, look up a copy of the February 1978 issue of *Consumer Reports* magazine and the cover-article, "The overselling of insulation —CU tells you when enough is enough."

There also are safety concerns about insulation. Thermal insulation can add to fire dangers if your wiring is faulty. And fire-hazard questions have been raised about the use of cellulose insulation, which basically is chemically treated shredded paper. In addition, the U.S. Consumer Product Safety Commission banned the use of formaldehyde foam because of a possible health hazard, although a federal court overruled the commission on legal grounds. Some homeowners who installed the foam, which is highly rated as an insulation, complained of eye irritations, rashes, and chronic headaches.

Also, the buildup of formaldehyde from both insulation and furniture can be a health hazard if the flow of air is cut off too much in energy-saving improvements, according to the *Journal of the American Medical Association*. Making homes nearly air-tight to conserve energy also poses other serious health risks, the AMA *Journal* warned in a 1981 editorial.

Energy Tax Breaks

Now for the good news. Saving energy also can save you money on taxes. The federal government allows you to take tax credits for installing certain energy improvements. Tax credits are better than deductions because you subtract them directly from your tax bill.

Under the 1978 tax bill, you can claim a credit of 15 percent of the first $2,000, or a maximum of $300, for items installed in your principal residence—including rental apartments, between April 20, 1977, and December 31, 1985. Most newly built homes finished after April 20, 1977, aren't eligible. Covered items include:

- Insulation.
- Furnace replacement burner.
- Automatic flue opener modifier.
- Exterior storm or thermal doors and windows.
- Automatic setback thermostat.
- Electric energy usage display meter.
- Exterior caulking or weatherstripping.

The IRS had refused to include as benefits such items as siding with insulation, drapes, carpeting, heat pumps, wood paneling, and enclosed fireplaces. For a full list of what is and isn't covered, get, from the IRS, IRS publication No. 903, "Energy Credits for Individuals."

You also can get federal tax credits for installing solar, wind, or geothermal energy devices. This credit was raised in 1980 to 40 percent of the first $10,000 of such outlays, plus 20 percent for the next $8,000, or a maximum of $4,000. The credit includes homes built before and after 1977.

You can get state tax breaks for energy-saving improvements, too. California, for instance, offers a credit equal to 55 percent of the cost of certain improvements. Colorado has a credit equal to 55 percent of the cost of a solar installation. And in Ohio there's a property-tax exemption for energy-saving conversion devices.

Home-improvement Ripoffs

One risk of getting your home fixed up is that the home-improvement industry is rife with ripoff artists. Older people are prime targets for the remodeling-and-repair con artists. While most home-improvement firms are honest, if you get stuck with a dishonest one you not only can wind up with shoddy or unneeded work, you could even lose your house.

"Home-improvement fraud is the largest category of cases we have," said Clair Villane, director of the district attorney's consumer-fraud office in Denver. "And it's increasing wildly."[2]

The most worrisome kind of fraud these days involves so-called lien-sales contracts. These allow a contractor to foreclose on a customer's house, often without going to court, if the customer doesn't pay the bill or misses a payment. Contractors insist that since they can't use the improvement alone as collateral once it's part of the house, they require an interest in the entire property. But others say that many abuse that right.

So beware of signing home-improvement contracts that contain a lien on your house, including the more common mechanic's lien, which requires you to pay the contractor's suppliers if the contractor doesn't.

Lien sales "could be the home-improvement fraud of the 1980s," said Stephen Brobeck, executive director of the Consumer Federation of America. "There are tens of billions of dollars tied up in home equity. This lets the crooks tap into that."

Solar Frauds

A lot of crooks also are hoping to tap into the sun. "Solar energy is the new area for fraud because people are so vulnerable," said Adam Levin, director of New Jersey's Division of Consumer Affairs. "People panic when they look at fuel bills and a lot of new companies appear out of nowhere, promising enormous energy reductions. People fall for it."

According to a report by the Consumer Federation of America, unscrupulous contractors also have taken advantage of state and federal tax credits for solar installations. For example, a contractor offers to sell a customer a $3,000 solar system for $4,000 to increase the customer's claim for a tax credit. The contractor then will throw in a "free" $1,000 monitoring system. The result, the report says, is "a higher price to the consumer, only partially offset by the tax credit, extra profit for the contractor," and a monitoring system that may be worth less than $1,000.

Common Frauds

The Consumer Federation of America (CFA) asserted that in terms of dollar amount, home-improvement abuse is the nation's No. 1 consumer fraud. And elderly homeowners are victimized frequently by home-improvement frauds because "their homes are older and in need of repairs, especially necessary ones like re-roofing," the federation's study said.

The most vicious abuse, "home-equity ripoffs," can involve all kinds of improvements, from siding and carpeting to air conditioning and burglar alarms. Typically, the products are overpriced and are sold with financing at an unusually high interest rate. "Burglar alarm systems worth less than $750, for instance, have been sold for prices exceeding $5,000," the CFA report said.

The Consumer Federation of America report also warned of these common abuses:

Basement waterproofing. The salesperson tells you that the only way your wet basement can be fixed is with a special soil-injection technique or a special pressure pump process that will cost you anywhere from $1,500 to over $4,000. Otherwise you may be in for "disastrous" structural damage to your entire house, you are told. In fact, most leakage problems can be solved with less-expensive repairs, and both the soil-technique and pressure pump methods offer dubious effectiveness, experts say.

Roofing ripoffs. The most common problems are unneeded roof replacements, unfinished work, down payments taken by contractors who never do the work, poor workmanship, and contractors working without a license or a bond.

The CFA report cited this example: "One elderly couple contracted to have their home re-roofed for a total of $2,118. They were given a five-year warranty. But when the roof started to leak within the first year, the contractor refused to make the repairs without an additional $500. Meanwhile, leaks and water stains ruined the paint in several rooms."

Protecting Yourself

Before you sign on the dotted line for a costly home improvement, investigate carefully. Note these precautions:

Door-to-door repair people. Be leery of door-to-door repair people who tell you that repairs are urgently needed. Get a second and third opinion from reputable home improvers.

"Bait-and-switch." Beware of "bait-and-switch" tactics. This is when a product, such as carpeting or siding, is advertised at an unbelievably low price and the salesperson tries to switch you to a costlier version after explaining how inferior the cheaper advertised product is.

Check the contractor. Check the contractor's past performance by contacting previous customers, local consumer-protection agencies, and the Better Business Bureau.

Written estimates. Get two or three written estimates for the work you want done. Be skeptical of bids that seem too much lower than the others. "Quality is not guaranteed by cost, but exceptionally low bids often indicate that corners will be cut somewhere," the CFA report said.

Based on model laws in some states, the report recommends that your home improvement contract contain these provisions:

1. A description of the work to be performed: The Wisconsin Home Improvement Trade Practices Act, one of the two or three most comprehensive in this area, requires the name and address of the salesperson, detailed information about the principal products and materials, description of any mortgage or security interest to be taken in connection with the financing or sale of improvement, among other provisions.
2. Starting and completion date.
3. A schedule of payments: California's home-improvement law affords consumers the most protection here. It generally limits down payments to $100 or 1 percent of the contract price, whichever is greater. It also specifies that additional payments reflect the cost of the work done.
4. Cooling-off period. Contractors arranging financing for improvements must comply with the federal Truth-in-Lending law which allows cancellation of the contract without penalty within three days after it is signed if the buyer's house is being used as loan collateral.
5. Limits on liquidated damages: Liquidated damages provisions, requiring the payment of penalty with the contract is cancelled after the cooling-off period, are illegal in Michigan. In several other states, there are ceilings on the amount of damages contractors can demand.
6. Protection against liens. Homeowners in Hawaii and Louisiana have a right to demand that contractors post bond affording protection against any liens.
7. Proof of insurance. Some states require contractors to carry insurance covering their liability.

Some states also require the licensing of contractors or the regulation of certificates of completion. Check to see whether contractors in your state must be licensed or bonded. Never sign a completion certificate statement until the work has been finished to your satisfaction.

Controlling Costs

In addition to getting your house in good shape, there are other steps you can take to help control the cost of keeping your house.

Year-round budget plans. Arrange with your utility companies to pay your heating and cooling bills and electric bills on year-round budget plans. By spreading your payments over the full year, you can avoid the shock of huge monthly bills during peak periods of usage.

Property-tax breaks. Check the property-tax breaks for older homeowners in your state and locality. Keep track of values in your neighborhood and challenge your property-tax assessment if it seems out of line. If your home is over-valued by tax authorities, then you will pay higher property taxes than you should.

Also, look for other ways to get help with your property taxes. In Hartford, Connecticut, older homeowners can receive credits toward their property taxes by working for various local-government offices.

Minor home repairs. Learn to do minor home repairs yourself. Take a home-repair course or read up on repairs in books from the library. You can save money on repair bills.

Local home maintenance repair programs. Check to see if your locality has a program to help older people maintain their homes, or if one can be started. Such programs already exist in several communities. In Brevard County, Florida, for example, the Community Service Council operates a Home Maintenance and Repair Program for homeowners over age 60. The program is financed 90 percent by the federal government and 10 percent by the county.

"Our goal is to help people stay in their homes," said Maurice Gantz, the volunteer administrator. The council primarily sends out small work crews to provide needed basic repairs. "I would broadly describe our work as a cut above the handyman level and certainly not equal to a general contractor's abilities. A job can be as minor as repairing some screens which are torn or a job may consist of . . . replacement of rotting wood, minor plumbing and electrical repairs, repairing sagging ceilings, and painting to protect against deterioration."

"Any of these services help make a place livable, and as importantly, lets people know that they are not alone, that someone does care. That is probably more important than the house work itself," Mr. Gantz said.

"In one instance, we simply shored up a sagging center beam under a mobile home. Less than one-half day's work for two men," he said. "But the couple living there had a combined income of under $450 a month and much of that went for medical needs. They simply could not afford professional help."

Renting Help

One way to help cover the costs of maintaining a house that may be larger than you need, but want to keep, is to rent part of the place as an apartment or sleeping rooms. Rental potential, some older people suggest, is something to keep in mind when remodeling or deciding whether to stay or move elsewhere. But be advised that setting up apartments (or businesses) in a home sometimes is restricted by zoning laws.

"Several years before retirement I looked carefully at my housing and decided that I would be better off in my home than in an apartment, having watched several of my friends making such a move and later regretting it," said Trunette Olsen of Seattle, Washington. *"I considered several factors: proximity to public transportation; access to some sort of recreation (the beach); location of food stores; availability of a drugstore; the neighborhood in general; and the possibility of renting a room to augment my pension.*

"My home meets the above requirements," Mrs. Olsen concluded. *"I am able to rent my basement bedroom and bath while providing a sort of cooking facility in the laundry—thus making it a sort of apartment attractive to young bachelors. Were I to become incapacitated, I would hope to rent the basement to a couple who would care for me; or I would move into it myself, leaving a pleasant home for them."*

By renting out part of their houses, some older people say they are able to stay in the house and neighborhood where they feel most comfortable.

"I am 65 years old and feel I have an ideal housing situation," said Rosalee Engle of Richfield, Minnesota. *"When my children were young, we bought a three-bedroom rambler in a first-ring suburb of Minneapolis in a very nice residential neighborhood. When my husband died at age 40, I decided to rent out part of my home.*

"The apartment reduced my expenses and it is nice to see a light in the house when I come home at night, and even to know there is someone within calling distance if I should ever need them," Mrs. Engle said. *"I can take a trip in the winter without having to worry about the furnace going out, or other catastrophes. Yet I can still enjoy a familiar neighborhood in which I feel comfortable."*

Some retirees use parts of their homes to provide rental space and an office for their part-time careers.

Retirees are often advised, and often consider, a move into smaller living quarters. Occupying a large house which may once have been appropriate for a family becomes unnecessary and not economical for most retired couples. Renting unused rooms or unoccupied stories is an option for retired persons who can no longer utilize the space of a family home, yet who are unable or unwilling to move to another location.

Home improvement serves to keep retirees active and to expand the potential for utilizing unused space. Basements are particularly suited for renovation; they can be finished and partitioned, and several working areas can be constructed from the original room. Offices can be designed by retiring professionals—such as tutors and counselors—who wish to continue practicing their livelihood on a part-time basis. Local organizations and civic groups may also find such office space useful (a fact which carries with it the benefit of tax considerations from rental property). These practical applications of available space make the choice of remaining in the family home both economically sound and personally rewarding.

Rooms to Rent

One alternative for some retirees is to rent sleeping rooms. But it is best to check with your local officials to make certain you are not violating zoning laws.

"We involuntarily retired nearly 15 years ago because numerous small strokes incapacitated my husband. Because our four-bedroom house was vacant most of the time, we rented sleeping rooms to pay our housing costs," said Ann Schneider of Boonville, Indiana.

"As our physical condition deteriorated (I have rheumatoid arthritis) we moved to this location, nearer to our daughter, and a larger house with more income—with four sleeping rooms," she said. *"The rooms rent for $20 to $25 a week. We gross between $3,300 and $4,200 a year.*

"Our rents pay our housing costs even though we are still paying for it. Its valuation has doubled in 12 years," said Mrs. Schneider, who added: *"I think more emphasis should be put on making retirees sufficiently independent to live alone as long as possible in their community. I am appalled by the numbers of widows I talk to who live alone in a big house complaining about the taxes and expenses, yet who would never consider renting a portion of their house."*

Dorothy and William Center Takach own a large house near Drake University in Des Moines, Iowa, and also rent rooms to pay for their housing expenses.

"We occupy the six rooms and bath on the first floor, the basement, and the entirely finished attic," Mrs. Takach said. *"There are four sleeping rooms and bath on the second floor. Presently they rent for a total of $80 a week. Our house payment is $125 a month, plus taxes and insurance.*

"I prefer sleeping rooms to an apartment because there are four possible sources of income rather than one," she said. *"We rent by the week. Vacancy rates last a week or less, two weeks at the most. We rent only to working adult males."*

"I have often wondered as I talk to older people who are in large houses on small incomes why they haven't planned for such an exigency?" Mrs. Takach added. "By planning ahead they are prepared for the changeover. They also have the advantage of being in familiar surroundings. Sleeping rooms come under single-family dwelling codes since there is not a second kitchen."

Housesharing

Another arrangement older people ought to consider is sharing the house with others, either older, younger, or the same age and/or sex," Mrs. Takach suggested. "There are several single-family dwellings in this area that are rented to groups of singles, who share kitchen and bath and living room facilities."

In fact, sharing a home is gaining increased popularity in the Minneapolis-St. Paul area, Boston, Los Angeles, and elsewhere as a way for older people to keep their homes while providing shelter for others.

In the Minneapolis-St. Paul area, the Share-a-Home Program is run by the Lutheran Social Service of Minnesota, 2414 Park Avenue, Minneapolis, or 1201 Payne Avenue, St. Paul.

"The Share-a-Home program is designed to help older people remain in their homes," said U.S. Senator Rudy Boschwitz of Minnesota. "Through the program, these older adults are matched up with younger people—college students, young singles, young families—who are in need of housing or enjoy a sense of family.

"For example, you have an older adult wanting to stay in their own home, but unable to meet some of the demands of doing so—rising fuel costs, the physical labor involved in maintaining their home, and so forth. This person could be matched up with a young person wanting to attend college, but unable to meet the financial requirement for housing.

"The two could help meet each other's needs—the student easing the financial and physical burdens of the older adult, and that person easing the financial burden of the student," Senator Boschwitz said.

One advocate of housesharing is Maggie Kuhn, founder of the Gray Panthers. She practices what she preaches.

"In our house, there are nine persons," she told a Gray Panthers conference in Chevy Chase, Maryland, "and I'm the oldest." She said her Germantown, Pennsylvania, home also included "three cats, a poodle, a pair of parakeets, and two tanks of tropical fish."

For a complete, practical guide to housesharing, we recommend the book *Living with Tenants: How to Happily Share Your House with Renters for Profit and Security* by Doreen Bierbrier. To order, send $7.00 ($5.50 plus $1.50 for handling and postage) to: The Housing Connection, P.O. Box 5536, Arlington, VA 22205.

Retirement Communities-The "Good Life"?

An elderly lady was filling out an application for residency in a new retirement village. She put down her current address and after "ZIP" she printed firmly: "Normal for my age."

Lane Olinghouse
in The Wall Street Journal

For many older Americans, retirement communities are heaven on earth. With alluring names like Sun City and Leisure World, retirement villages are self-contained communities that offer older people tranquility, security, companionship, and loads of leisure activities with others their own age. These "adults-only" communities are limited to residents over a certain age who can buy or rent all types of housing. The community often has its own stores, theaters, libraries, and even medical facilities. Usually there are swimming pools, tennis courts, and golf courses for residents, plus an endless schedule of activities from bridge and bingo to drama lessons and disco dancing.

For some older Americans, however, these heavenly retirement communities are the work of the devil. They see such villages as too costly, too crowded, and too much like ghettos for old people segregated from the mainstream of life.

About the only accurate generalization that can be made about retirement communities is this: Older people feel very strongly about such places—they either love 'em or they hate 'em.

"It's a Great Life"

"I cannot sing enough praises for retirement community living," said Ray Mendenhalls, who with his wife, Della, lives in the retirement community of Green Valley, Arizona. "It is a very quiet and relaxing place to live without the noise of the younger generation," Mr. Mendenhalls said.

"As a four-year resident of the Mainlands Eight section of Tamarac, Florida, a retired adult-type community, I would like to say 'It's a Great Life' here," volunteered Mrs. W. Friedman. "We have people ages 50 to 85 in our community with such a wonderful, helpful neighborly feeling that we have never had before in various communities.

"We lived in New York State before retiring here. There are so many activities available, one could never be bored," she said.

Another enthusiast lives in a retirement community in Oregon—and very happily:

"If I had a million dollars, I would not live anyplace else," said Deila I. Whitman of Portland, Oregon. "My husband and I [both retired teachers] looked from the Canadian border to the Mexican border before we chose this place, Rosa Villa.

"We moved in in 1966 in spite of the fact that our friends thought we had lost the few marbles we had. I can't remember one disappointment," said Mrs. Whitman, who moved into a studio apartment at Rosa Villa after her husband died.

Retirement communities, such enthusiasts argue, offer an active, family-like atmosphere that older people often can't match elsewhere. At Sun City, Arizona, the largest of the retirement communities, with a population of about 60,000, "the recreation facilities are superior to any we have seen," said Winifred C. Marsh, who with her sister left the Bay Area of San Francisco in 1977 and retired to Sun City.

"This place has more than five centers for sports like swimming, mini-golf, shuffleboard, tennis, man-made lakes, and many golf courses suitable for beginners and real professionals," Miss Marsh said.

"Many shopping centers serve our needs," she added. "We play cards and go to an excellent library. We enjoy the library, cards, and congenial people the most in Sun City, Arizona."

Dissent in Paradise

But not everyone who moves to retirement communities is happy with them.

"I was 54 and my husband 64 when we moved into Panorama Village, a retirement community in Hemet, California. For me, the move has been a disaster," wrote one woman.

"I am sure that many of these places are fine for some people," she stressed. "But I find that so many 'old' people together just have too many problems. That is, we hear of death, sickness, sudden heart attacks, etc. And it is like a small town with gossip and jealousy. I am sure some of my neighbors called on me the first week I lived here to see what kind of furniture I had.

"If you play bridge or golf, you are OK. If not, it is difficult," she said. "There are many rules and regulations, and I just don't feel as free as I would like."

Her conclusion: "If you want lots of regulations, golf, bridge, and gossip, this is the place. But if like me, you want to be free to make your own choices, then people should think very carefully before making a move."

A major criticism of retirement communities by many older people is that residing in such places amounts to segregated living.

"Retirement communities are not a good place to live because they confine the activities and thoughts of the elderly only to the elderly," said Mrs. Sam W. Bauer of Carson, California.

And while planned activities are a good way for some to keep busy, others find them stagnating.

Suggested Gail R. Willett, who lives in a retirement community in Vincentown, New Jersey, "Yes, they do provide 'lots to do'—if all you want to do is fill time.

"We visited 16 before we bought," Mrs. Willett said. "After seven years I find out talking to people here, about 20 percent would like to be in a more alive area—another 20 percent are undecided and 60 percent are very satisfied."

Plenty to Do

To give you an idea of life in one retirement community, here is a look at a big one in Port Charlotte, Florida:

"It's 7 o'clock on a Thursday night, and the evening's entertainment is well under way at American Legion Post 110. About 175 people hunch over square white cards while a male voice calls out, "B-11 . . . O-66 . . ."[1]

Bingo is a serious pursuit here. Players shoo away a visitor who tries to question them while the game is on. "Kiddo, in Port Charlotte, there's two or three bingo games almost every night," says Legionnaire Marsh Wautelet, a retiree who helps run this one. "People put aside money to play whether they can really afford it or not."

Port Charlotte ranks firmly in the middle of the spectrum of Florida retirement communities. It is a community of landscaped mobile home parks and pastel-colored, single-family homes, most of them built by General Development Corp., the biggest developer in the area.

Opportunities for fishing, golf, tennis and shuffleboard abound, and retirees form clubs around every conceivable interest. For example, there are clubs for square-dancers, Navy Seabee veterans, and former New York City transit employees.

The hub of social life is the Port Charlotte Cultural Center. The $4.5 million facility, built largely through retirees' fund-raising efforts, houses among other things what is popularly known as Port Charlotte University, an adult-education center that offers more than 200 courses.

"Want to get busy? Retire," says Kay Pearl, a hearty 64-year-old who participates in many activities at the center. "You're never bored," added Dorothy Bilanchone, a 68-year-old retiree from Waterbury, Connecticut, who sings in the frequent musical productions at the center.

An estimated 500,000 or more older Americans live in fulltime retirement communities, most of them in the Sunbelt. And their numbers are growing and the retirement communities are popping up in all parts of the country. "By the latter half of this decade, they will be the growing segment of the housing industry," predicted the president of U.S. Home Corp., the nation's largest builder.

But for some, retirement-community living isn't easy, at least initially. "Our biggest battle is loneliness," said the coordinator of Charlotte County's adult and community education. "A lot of people dream about paradise. They sell their homes and move here. After the drapes are up and the carpets are down, paradise can turn into a living hell if they don't find something to do."

Most people, though, find plenty to do and seem happy. An associate of the National Council on Aging in Washington said: "This kind of environment supports positive mental health."

Advantages of Retirement Communities

Is a retirement community your cup of tea? To decide, you need to weigh the pros and cons of retirement-community living and match them with the lifestyle you want. Here in the next few pages is a list of advantages and disadvantages of retirement communities. First are the advantages:

Community spirit. Many older people enjoy living and socializing in a homogeneous community.

"Friendships and acquaintances are easily made due to the fact that we are practically all of the same age group and our interests are generally shared," said Mrs. Richard G. Hayn of Hemet, California. *"My husband and I have lived in two retirement communities for the past seven years and have nothing but the highest praise and kudos for such wonderful communities."*

"My husband and I have found a retirement community an excellent place to live," agreed Dorothy B. Julius of Vista Village in Olympia, Washington. *"The freedom to come and go as one chooses, the safety of 'home' in the community while one is away, the availability of neighbors and especially the sense of belonging to the 'family' makes an ideal set-up for us,"* Mrs. Julius said.

While some people condemn retirement communities because of the lack of young people, many residents praise the serenity of adult-only living. Indeed, Ann Erickson of Sun City, California, complains that developers there may open the area to people of all ages.

"We came here because it was a retirement area," Mrs. Erickson said. *"I resent having it now being considered for a full-family area and pushing out those who came here to be away from young, noisy people. Let us seniors have our little corner of peace and quiet. Those who need more excitement should not retire here, but in larger family areas. There are so many of them, we have so few.*

"I want to live in a retirement community," she continued. *"We watch over and know each other. We move slower, we do not need speeding cars, motor bikes, and skate boards.*

"We older folks will be able to cope with inflation, if not disturbed by eager beavers trying to make a fast buck and then leave us with their housing, sewer, school, and other urban problems. There ought to be a law!"

Not that such folks are anti-kids.

Mrs. Hayn of Hemet noted that children and grandchildren *"are welcomed to visit whenever they wish to do so"* and *"we're certainly not deprived of children's voices."*

"On the whole, we all love living in our retirement communities with our peers and yet not be excluded from mingling with the younger generation for daily variety," Mrs. Hayn said. But *"We hope we never again have to live in conventional neighborhoods of mixed age groups. Retirement community—we love it!"*

Plenty of activities. Retirement communities offer plenty to do for those who want to do more than sit and watch TV.

"All of my needs have been met here" at Oceana in Oceanside, California, said Mildred V. Riebel. *"A built-in social life, every kind of activity from bridge to swimming, amateur theatricals, musical events, all sorts of crafts and more."*

Indeed, at most retirement communities there is no shortage of things to do. At Century Village East, a large retirement community in West Palm Beach, Florida, a typical resident spends six hours a day in organized activity. The staff consists of a large athletic contingent (golf pro, tennis instructor, exercise experts), plus teachers of archeology, anthropology, bridge, lapidary, music, writing, painting, sewing, ceramics, and on and on.

Just because all these activities are available, though, residents don't have to use them.

"One can be as active or inactive as one chooses," said Hilda Bender of Seal Beach, California. *"For elderly people who can adapt to them, these places are ideal to live and we need many, many more of them."*

Recreation facilities. For the athletically inclined, there's everything from swimming pools and tennis courts to jogging and shuffleboard.

At Sun City, Arizona, a small annual fee entitles residents to use seven swimming pools (indoor and outdoor), air-conditioned shuffleboard courts, and other athletic facilities. Jogging and physical fitness are the current rage.

"We've gone to dynamic retirement—positive aging," said a vice president of the development company. "People aren't to be looked upon as old and inactive physically in their 70s. Our attitudes are changing in Sun City."

Mildred Gladwell of Leisure Village in Lakewood, New Jersey, agrees.

"I am still a healthy 79 and swim all summer in our pools or do a daily walk," she said.

Carefree living. Many maintenance and medical services are provided, and most communities provide shopping and transportation facilities, religious services, and some even cemetery plots.

"You name it, we have it," said Mrs. Whitman of Rose Villa in Portland, Oregon. *"Our medical program is second to none. A jiggle of our phone and it will bring a nurse."*

"I would like to report 13 years of pleasant living in Leisure Village," said Mrs. Gladwell of Lakewood, New Jersey. *"The past few years I*

have been widowed here, but feel safe and find pleasant companionship. The few minor repairs needed have been done under a monthly maintenance fee, efficiently and quickly. What a relief not to have to wait days or even months for repairmen to not come when needed."

Many retirement communities do take care of repair problems, either as part of the community fee or for an extra charge.

Security. For many, safety from crime is the No. 1 reason that older people move to retirement communities.

Many communities have 24-hour security services. Visitors are checked when they enter, and security forces keep watch on the residences.

"The main thing that brings people to these places is the promise of security, and it is a fact that crime is at a minimum," said Hilda Bender of Seal Beach.

"Many residents here are refugees from strife and mug-ridden cities where we were not safe to even walk the sidewalks in the day-light, let alone at night," said one woman in Leisure Village in New Jersey.

"I don't think I could have made a better move than to get a home in a retirement community," said Frances B. Allen of Walnut Creek, California. *"In this community, we have 24-hour security and I think it is the security service that is perhaps the most important to a person living alone.*

"For instance, when I left a pot on the stove and it burned, it set off the smoke alarm," Mrs. Allen said. *"It was a security man who came and knew how to turn the alarm off. When I slipped and broke my leg, it was 'security' who came first, evaluated, and called my doctor and stayed until they took me away in an ambulance."*

Homes are a good investment. Generally, homes purchased in retirement communities seem to have increased in value.

"Due to sundry reasons, when the need to sell a home arises, these homes usually are sold within a 4- to 8-week period if the house is priced within reason despite inflationary increases," said Mrs. Richard G. Hayn of Hemet, California. *"I can honestly state that homes have more than doubled in price since we bought ours in 1975."*

In Green Valley, Arizona, the townhouse that Ray and Della Mendenhalls bought for $39,900 in 1977 was going for more than $70,000 in the 1980s. And in Oceana, an over-40 condominium community in California, home values went from about $14,000 to $28,000 in 1971 to $45,000 to $80,000 in the 1980s.

Drawbacks of Retirement Communities

One thing is clear: The people who enjoy living in retirement communities feel very strongly about the benefits of their lifestyle. But there are disadvantages to consider—many of which are on the other side of the advantages coin.

Cost. The biggest one is that many retirement communities are becoming increasingly costly and, in some cases, increasingly crowded.

"Throughout the country, many retirement communities have been built, but economically they have gone beyond the reach of middle-income persons who wish to buy a home," complained Lillian Calabrese of Haslett, Michigan.

The changing situation also affects people who live in these communities.

Thomas Murray, a retired mechanical officer on the St. Louis-San Francisco Railway Company and his wife, Elsie, thought they had found utopia when they moved to Rancho Bernardo, California, from Missouri in 1964.[2]

Their two-bedroom house was ideal, and the community, with its planned mix of half retirees and half general population, had won awards. Located 23 miles north of San Diego, Rancho Bernardo was far enough inland to be relatively free of fog, but ocean breezes still sweep the air close in.

"It was like living in the country with city conveniences," Mr. Murray recalled of the early days there.

But in the 1970s, as Rancho Bernardo gained population and San Diego's urban sprawl began to surround it, the Murrays soured on their retirement home and moved back to Springfield, Missouri.

R. Barry McComic, president of Avco Community Developers, Inc., conceded that Avco's Rancho Bernardo—once envisioned as a haven for the middle class—had become a preserve for the wealthy retiree. The average home price is now more than $100,000, and the average retired resident has a retirement income of more than $31,000 a year. Mr. McComic believes a retiree can live "comfortably" there on $24,000 a year.

Crowded. Some people also find that Sun City, Arizona, 12 miles northwest of Phoenix, has become too urbanized. It has grown to over 60,000 residents since it was established in 1960.

Sun City officials conceded that the increasing population deters some potential retirees. But they said that Sun City's size enables it to support a 261-bed hospital, a large shopping center, and beautiful recreation centers and golf courses.

Sun City's ambiance obviously appeals to a lot of people. The community's urban sprawl keeps increasing and officials hope to add 75,000 residents in Sun City and its new Sun City West.

That doesn't bother people like Sam Higginbotham, 70, who has lived in six different Sun City houses since 1960. He said people haven't any right to complain because the developer has said all along that a large city was planned.

Other residents are concerned that friends and relatives won't be able to join them in retirement because of sharply rising home prices. William Gresko, a 66-year-old retired aircraft supervisor, said that today he couldn't afford to buy the same three-bedroom, two-bath home he bought for $38,500 in 1974. Two-bedroom homes now start at about $60,000 (property taxes are a relatively low $400 to $500 a year, however, because there aren't any schools to support).

Segregated living. Some critics condemn retirement communities as ghettos for the aging.

"I condemn retirement communities per se for the simple reason that there is no counterbalance of young folks," said Louis J. Stack, a retiree in Albany, Georgia. "There is wit, wisdom, knowledge, and experience to be derived from the old, but also vitalization of life, purpose, ideas, and dreams from the young," said Mr. Stack, an ex-marine.

"What is more invigorating to an older person than a bright, shiny, smiling face?" he asked.

"The most common reason I hear retired people give for not living in a retirement community is [that] segregation by age is just as distasteful as segregation by sex, color, or any other method," said Warren D. Cummings of Newton, New Jersey. "As a retired teacher who spent his life with 16-year-olds, I need some young people around.

"That the all-the-same-age people in any one such community are all at about the same income level makes the prospect even more dreary," Mr. Cummings added. "Being another pea in the pod is not my idea of living."

Our surveys of older people show that the majority would prefer to live with a mix of young people as well as older people. But it should be noted that children are allowed to visit most retirement communities, and some developments do include sections for younger families.

Too many planned activities. The same planned activities and lessons that attract many retirees to retirement communities turn others off.

"My wife and I have investigated retirement communities, but find them unsuitable for our tastes," said a New Jersey man. "They seem to always have people involved in busy activities—bridge, which we dislike; golf, which I like in moderation; and crafts, in which neither of us are interested."

John Finnegan of New Hyde Park, New York, said he and his wife were frustrated in their search for a retirement community by the sellers' emphasis on planned activities.

"From talking with many retirees, others agree with us that they do not need someone to arrange their lives," Mr. Finnegan said. "They have lived much longer and have been through much more than these people who are trying to regulate lives.

"We feel that most of the elderlies just want some slower, relaxed living," he said. "We want to do what we want, when we want to, and not feel that unless we do it on cue, we will be looked down on."

As one upset California woman said:

"Why, they even tried to tell me when to get up for a morning meeting."

The emphasis on activities also can apply to recreation facilities.

"Special facilities depend on the individual," said Carl F. Hyder of Whiting, New Jersey. "Some must have a golf course and a swimming pool. Special facilities mean added cost of living. Can one afford it?"

Sometimes those fancy facilities get little use. Marika Sumichrast noted that at the retirement community where she was a vice president, "We built a golf course, and less than 15 percent of the residents used it. It's nice but terribly costly. We could have built several community buildings, or reduced the monthly recreation fees."

Remoteness. Many retirement communities are long distances from urban centers.

Away from the cities is where land is cheaper. But getting to shopping areas or to visit friends and relatives can be difficult for residents who don't have cars—and even for those who do.

Raymond J. Erfle of Philadelphia moved back to the city after owning a home in Leisuretown, 26 miles from the City of Brotherly Love.

"In our particular case, our children were in the Philadelphia area, and we were making a 50- to 60-mile round trip each week, which together with the lawn work got to be too much," Mr. Erfle said.

"Typically, they are too remote from the cultural centers," said a New Jersey man. "We like plays, concerts, ballets, well-supplied libraries, and art galleries. Some are not near medical centers for us, looking down the future a few years."

Dejection. Some find retirement communities too depressing.

"My main dislike, if you will, is getting to know people well, then having them become ill or die. I am 72 and among the youngest residents," wrote one woman in a Michigan retirement community.

"I lived in a retirement community for eight years and after 13 deaths on our block (my husband's among them) it became too depressing and I moved out," wrote a Prescott, Arizona, woman.

A former resident of Sun City, Elmer Beckman, found that the pros of safety and cleanliness in a retirement community were outweighed by the cons of stereotyped lifestyle, racial and social intolerance, and "a high level of social-material-economic one-upmanship," as well as "sterile attitudes" and the "World's Worst Vehicle Drivers."

Not Only for the Wealthy

The choice is up to you. If retirement communities sound like they might appeal to you, there are plenty to choose from. The big ones, like Sun City and Century Village, have plenty to offer, and they still have housing for moderate-income retirees.

"We retired to Sun City, California, from Ohio three years ago and we are very happy with it," said Ann Erickson, despite her apprehension about youthful encroachments. "We bought a new doublewide mobile home. We feel it is the most economical way for retirees to go."

Many retirement communities are specifically geared to people of moderate means. At Crestwood Village in Whiting, New Jersey, near the Atlantic Ocean, home prices in 1983 ranged from $47,490 for a basic two-bedroom house to $85,760 for a deluxe two-bedroom/two-bath model with garage.

During the community's nearly 20 years, builder Mike Kokus has earned a reputation for keeping housing and operational costs within the budgets of middle-income retirees. The community hasn't any social directors, recreation directors, or a large staff. And since the ocean and public tennis courts, swimming pools, golf courses, and shopping facilities are less than 10 minutes away, a lot of monumental and costly facilities aren't needed.

Leisure Technology, run by Mike Tenzer, another developer of retirement villages in New Jersey, Florida, California, and other states, tries to cater to the somewhat more affluent. At three of their communities in New Jersey, new units start in the mid-$50's: *Leisure Village West* at Lakehurst, *Leisure Knoll* at Manchester and *Leisure Towne* at Vincentown, New Jersey. Mike Tenzer typically stays with single-family detached homes, superbly designed and well marketed.

The Smaller and the "Piggyback" Communities

There are plenty more such retirement villages. Some are located in smaller communities.

"I am an enthusiastic resident of a small retirement community in the Tennessee mountains," said Gretchen King of Pleasant Hill, Tennessee. "Because I have no children, I wanted a place where I would be secure as I grow older. I didn't want my nieces and nephews to have to sit in conclave on the question of 'What are we going to have to do about old Aunty Gretchen, now that she's in her dotage?'

"This particular place, Uplands, offers three levels of living," Miss King said. "(1) A resident can life-lease a lot and build his own house or buy one a former resident is selling. (2) A resident can rent an apartment (which I do) for $75 to $200 a month. Or (3) there is 'Sheltered Care.'

"Meals are available to all of us if we want them, at an extra charge, of course," she said. "A nurse is on call 24 hours a day."

At Leisure World in Seal Beach, California, one resident was roundly satisfied:

"The cost of living is very reasonable and a two-bedroom apartment costs us approximately $190 a month, which includes utilities and insurance," said Hilda Bender. "It is extremely well run, very stable financially, and has an enormous number of activities of every description, plus security."

Not all retirement communities are in the Sunbelt or in resort areas.

"I have lived in Canterbury Village in Grand Rapids, Michigan, for over five years. This is a comfortable place, occupied by people over 60," said M. Carolyn Sturges. "It is in no way subsidized. Rentals now range from $280 to $350 a month, plus $7 for carports. It is a friendly atmosphere. We enjoy many group activities."

A new trend is the development of lower-cost, "piggyback" retirement communities near the older and larger communities. These are smaller communities with lower-priced homes and without the amenities of the nearby retirement havens. But many residents have friends in the larger retirement community and are able to use the recreational and other facilities as "guests" at minimum cost. You just have to know the right older folks in the bigger and plusher communities.

Shopping for the Right Place

Finding the right retirement community for your needs and your pocketbook can take a lot of hard looking and research.

"We visited, visited, visited retirement communities, talked to residents, attended some of their activities, looked at homes under construction," said A. E. Roos of Whiting, New Jersey. *"The factors we felt were important and helped us select Crestwood Village were:*

- Wooden floors—easier on body when walking in home.
- Insulation, city water and sewer.
- Quality of drinking water.
- Storage space, closets, and attic area.
- Reputation of builder to stay with the community and feel responsible for construction.
- Air pollution (little) in area.
- Minimum number of steps—we all get older.
- Quality and quantity of activities available.
- Feeling toward volunteers—here they are important; we all need to feel wanted and useful.
- Transportation and medical services.

"We are very happy with our life at Crestwood Village," Mrs. Roos concluded.

But others haven't been as fortunate.

"We have been looking for a place to move and have covered half the East Coast from North Carolina to Florida," said John Finnegan of New Hyde Park, New York. *"In 90 percent of the retirement communities that we visited, the people who were in charge are not senior citizens. Their main purpose is to sell houses and condominiums. The sales pitch is always the same—'We have planned activities—shuffleboard, tennis, darts, and crafts, etc., etc.'*

"Another hassle in buying a home in these retirement communities, as elsewhere, is that the salesperson is forever trying to sell 2 bedrooms, 2 baths plus a living room and a Florida room," Mr. Finnegan complained. *"I would venture to say that 95 percent of us do not need all this much house. We need less space and more time to enjoy it.*

"The sales pitch we have heard all along is, 'the resale of your home is much easier if you have all this'—even before you buy it, they are selling it for you."

Owner Power

Many other older buyers share Mr. Finnegan's frustration. These buyers tend to know what they want and have a good sense of quality—after all, they likely have lived in many houses, and at least have many years of experience taking care of a home. Sometimes what they are offered by retirement-community salespeople is not only offensive but aggravating. The sales approach to prospective buyers—and the service approach to current residents—is a good clue about the development's sensitivity to the real needs of older people.

In shopping for a home in a retirement community, you need to bring the same kind of sharp eye, and sharp questions, that you would bring to any other home purchase. Remember, too, that you may share ownership of other parts of the community, besides your own home; you certainly will if it is a condominium community. Sometimes control of the community is turned over to an owners' association that hires a management firm to run the place. In any case, the demands of residents can help shape the community's policies.

For example, as residents grow older in some established retirement communities, they are raising new kinds of demands. More of them want the community to add chapels, nursing-care facilities, and even cemeteries. These can add to costs and create sometimes bitter disputes among younger retirees and older ones. And when it comes to helping to pay for a church, some condominium residents claim there should be a separation of church and condo.

A Buyer's Checklist

The moral about finances and health care and unheavenly problems is to find out as much as you can about a retirement community itself, as well as the housing, before you decide to move in. To help you go shopping for a retirement community to live in, there follows a checklist provided by Marika Sumichrast, based on her experiences while working as the Vice President of Marketing and Sales of a large retirement community in Maryland. You can make up your own list of questions based on your personal needs and requirements, but don't be bashful; ask questions; probe and quiz before you make any move.

Now take a look at the following checklist.

Cost. Don't believe what they tell you. Chances are when you add it all up, it will cost more. Make sure you have some idea how much more.

1. Can you afford it? Can you afford to carry the mortgage, if you have one? Do you have a changeable interest rate in your mortgage?

2. Can you afford to pay the fee required to live in the community? What is the condominium fee, if you live in a condo? Who controls the fees—the developer or an owners' association? In estimating monthly expenses, add 10 percent to 20 percent to what you read in the brochure, just to be on the safe side.

3. Is the sales price comparable to other available housing? The cost per square foot should be about the same as for similar housing, or possibly 5 percent to 10 percent higher because of special provisions for older people.

4. Can you resell the units and get comparable appreciation with other housing? How have the houses appreciated in value over the years, if it is in an older development? How are they selling now?

5. Will your heat and $$$ go up the chimney? Is the home you are about to buy fully energy efficient? Insist on knowing the insulation value (R-value), type of windows and doors, and cost of utilities.

6. Find out who has to fix what. You are not a handyman. That is something you want to get away from. Find out what your maintenance responsibilities are and what the owners' association will take care of for you.

Builder. Check him out.

7. Check the builder's reputation. Find out from others (people living there, the homeowners' association or condo association, or resale agents) things like: Has he ever built a retirement community before? Has he built anything before? Is he solvent? Does he pay his bills? What do financial people think of him?

8. Does the developer take care of warranty work? What is his reputation for taking care of complaints promptly and fairly?

One of the biggest problems for buyers is that many developers simply do not finish the units to the customers' satisfaction. They do not take care of the warranty.

9. Is the developer running the management, or is the management of the community independent from the developer? If a management is independent, find out its reputation for running the community and responding to resident requests and complaints.

Don't buy from paper. Don't buy without seeing a model or making an actual visit to a house. If this is a condo or a co-op, and the building is poorly built, you will have to help foot the bill if elevators, roof, concrete work, and so on need repairing or replacing.

10. What is the quality of the product? What do people who live in the community think about their homes? Are they satisfied or do they complain about a lot of inferior or unfinished work?

11. Are individual buyers or the community suing the developer for inferior work or unfinished work? How difficult is it to get anything done that was supposed to be done in the first place?

12. What is the durability of the housing and common facilities? Will there have to be a lot of renovation in, say, the next two or three years? What is the life expectancy of roofs, carpets, appliances, elevators, heating and air conditioning equipment, and other items?

13. What kind of security does the community provide? Is it real, or only on paper?

14. Insist on inspecting your home at least 14 days before settlement. Make a list of needed work. Go back again before settlement to see whether the work was done. Never go to settlement without all items being taken care of to your satisfaction.

Design. Don't crowd me in!

15. What are your space requirements? Are cherished possessions going to fit into the housing unit you buy? Are you ready to give up your furniture, if you have to?

16. Think twice about one-bedroom units. If there are two people, you may like to have privacy. Or children or other visitors might come. Or you may need nursing help someday.

17. Get a small kitchen—you won't have to be a full-time cook. You will enjoy more leisure and won't have to use your kitchen the way you used to. What you need is a small kitchen with an eating space—so you don't have to carry things around.

It has been suggested that older people can live without dishwashers because they don't use too many dishes. But a dishwasher may become essential, because as people grow older they often suffer from arthritis, and washing becomes a chore.

Other do's and don'ts.

18. Is retirement-community living for you? Will you be able to live with other older people?

19. Can you part with friends, relatives, children, and the environment that you were used to?

20. Can you easily get from your car to the house? Is there public transportation close by in case you are unable to drive?

21. What is the distance to shopping facilities? Are they close so you could walk to get a few things at the grocery store, or must you drive?

22. Is the community very far from cultural activities? How far are you willing to travel to see a movie, theater, opera, or go to a good restaurant?

23. Are you willing to help pay for all the clubs and the recreational activities and facilities that you may not use much?

24. What is the developer going to turn over to the owners' association after he leaves? What does that mean in terms of increased payments?

25. What restrictions are there on your activities and interests?

What are the rules on inviting children and friends, on pets, on freedom to change the unit, on playing music? Can you still do the things you were used to doing without somebody telling you what you can and cannot do?

Can you live with the rules? Is it worth it?

Continuing-care Living

For older people who want or need a retirement home that provides more personal care than most retirement communities offer, there are "continuing-care" retirement homes and villages. At a minimum, they provide room, meals, and medical care. They are for those older people who are ready to give up some lifelong chores.

"I believe all people who can afford a retirement home should enter before they are too old—especially women," said the Rev. G. Barrett Rich of Bridgeport, Connecticut. "My wife cooked and kept house for 50 years and that was enough. There comes a time in a woman's life when she is tired of cooking and unable to do so.

"Now here at 3030 Park Avenue, she does not have to cook, keep house or shop," Rev. Rich said. "She has a cleaning woman, a nurse, a doctor on call, and a hospital connected with the building."

Housing at such homes can range from furnished rooms and apartments to cottages and houses. Such communities usually provide medical care for life. And some are quite luxurious.

Residents in most such communities are offered a wide variety of services but retain their independence.

"I never dreamed while I was on my way to becoming an older senior citizen that I would be able to live out my days in such luxury with such pampered care and attention," said Dorice M. Myers, who lives in a continuing-care retirement village.

Religious organizations, unions and other groups sponsor some continuing-care communities.

"Terwilliger Plaza in Portland, Oregon, is a retirement home that the teachers of Oregon have sponsored for more than 18 years, and it is one of the most satisfactory retirement homes that I have ever visited," wrote E. J. Dalbey, who lives there. "Inasmuch as there is a great deal of volunteer service, and the members of the board of management are residents here, the cost is reasonable, though it may not be as plush as some. It is not restricted to teachers. It does not offer as many health services as some retirement homes, which helps keep the cost down," she said.

Continuing-care homes aren't nursing homes. Like conventional retirement communities, they offer lots of things to do.

"We have many activities such as bridge, golf, movies, illustrated lectures, gardens, musicals, etc.," said Rev. Rich in Bridgeport, Connecticut. "The meals are excellent and we have menus of many choices."

Continuing Care; A Growing Market

Continuing-care housing has usually been provided by church groups or other nonprofit organizations. Typically, residents live in individual apartments or cottages and have at least one meal a day prepared for them; laundry, housekeeping, and social functions are a part of the routine services.

The uniqueness of continuing care is the anticipation that as residents age their needs will change, requiring more personal care or medical attention. The goal is to provide the whole range of services—even extended nursing-home care—on one campus as the needs of residents dictate. To avoid the expensive health care costs, some communities have limited the number of days at which care in the health facility can be provided without increasing the resident's monthly fees. Prospective residents should be thoroughly informed about just what services, including health care, are covered.

Because of growing demand for such housing and because more people are living longer, private developers and investors are expanding into continuing-care housing. Lewis Goodkin, a Fort Lauderdale, Florida marketing adviser, puts the nationwide market for continuing-care housing at 1.5 million buyers, and he expects the market to increase.

The typical continuing-care apartment or cottage contains 500 to 700 square feet. Entrance fees typically run $38,000 to $80,000 with a monthly charge of $525 to more than $1,000 for a couple.

A number of developers are entering the market. Michael Tenzer, president of Leisure Technology Corporation, sees continuing-care housing as a natural progression of his firm. "We believe there is a strong market there," he said.

In the May/June 1983 issue of the *Lew Goodkin Newsletter*, Mr. Goodkin offers the following consumer profile of continuing-care, or life-care, residents and costs in Florida:

The sex and marital status profile shows that the largest market segment is the female who outlived her husband and is in need of modest daily living assistance and companionship.

Age:
- 16% between 60–69 years of age,
- 25% between 70–79,
- 51% between 80–89, and
- 8% age 90 and above

Income (After Retirement):
- 50% have incomes less than $10,000
- 30% have incomes $10,000–$20,000
- 20% have incomes over $20,000

Distance Moved to Facility:
- 35% from within same county
- 53% from outside the county but within the same state
- Average distance moved is under 100 miles

Marital Status:
- 70% Widowed
- 22% Never married or divorced/separated
- 8% Married

Sex:
- 83% Female
- 17% Male

Tenure Prior to Moving In:
- 55% Owned
- 45% Rented

Reasons for Choosing Life Care: (In order of importance)
- Health (mental and physical)
- Security
- Companionship

The **real** income for these consumers is a difficult element to measure when determining market size or ability to afford. Home equity, pensions, stock and bond portfolios and the like are not reported as wage and salary income but are obviously dollars that can be used to consume life care housing. And no doubt the recent dramatic surge in the equity markets has boosted the net worth of the potential life care consumer considerably.

Pricing structures can be in the form of an entrance fee with a monthly payment or refundable trust plans. (A refundable approach is made necessary by the present IRS ruling on entry fee income.) We are increasingly bullish on the refundable approaches.

The spectrum of services and the type and size of units offered in each project are quite diverse—the pricing structure below is meant for general comparisons only. It should be noted that due to the similarity between life care/congregate facilities and hotel facilities

General Pricing Structures
(Single Residences Only)

		Trust Refundable	
Unit Type	Sq. Ft.	Price	Monthly fee
Studio/efficiency	350	$37,000	$460
One bedroom	600	61,000	610
Two bedroom	900	89,000	920

and because many communities incorporate nursing homes on site, a life care community may qualify for tax free industrial development bonding.

Unheavenly Problems

Some larger continuing-care communities may require entrance fees up to as much as $100,000. Many of these communities have religiously oriented names, although they may not have established any church affiliations. For a few of these communities, including some that are church connected, the investments are not always made in heaven.

For various reasons, ranging from inadequate management to fraud, financial difficulties have overtaken a few church-sponsored continuing-care homes, even homes with church-type names. Some older people have lost both their investments and their housing as a result.

That doesn't mean that all such housing is risky. It just means that they should be checked carefully before you put down your money. Many of these communities provide pleasant living for older people. And some facilities can be quite inexpensive.

Continuing-care Finances

Many continuing-care facilities, of course, are financially sound and well managed. But "the desirability of living in them goes back to the question, Is it a safe investment?" cautioned R. L. Thistlethwaite, a retired financial consultant who himself lives in a continuing-care community in Summit, Missouri.

Mr. Thistlethwaite offers this advice to prospective continuing-care residents, so ask these questions:

A. Endowment of buy-in dollars.
   1. What does this lump sum pay for?
   2. Prior to moving in, are my endowment dollars escrowed.
   3. If I change my mind prior to moving in, what amount do I forfeit?
   4. If I decide to leave the community after a year or two, what refunds are made?
   5. Who is the principal lender to the community and are principal and interest payments current? (You don't want to buy a piece of potential bankruptcy.)
   6. What evidences are there of internal auditing? What provisions are made for an external audit of endowment funds?

7. How qualified are the financial officers of the retirement community? Is the policy-making board fiscally competent to sit in judgment on management budgets, audits, projections, etc.?
B. Operating budget and control of income and expenses.
 1. What do monthly fees cover?
 2. What state laws assure the potential resident of responsible management?
 3. Are there any activities or projects supported by the retirement village that are financially questionable? Examples—golf course, meeting place, recreation rooms.
 4. How have the increases in monthly fees compared with the rise in cost of living? What is the projected fee five years hence?
C. Questions about management.
 1. Will the turnover of residential units support debt service (interest and principal)?
 2. What annuity tables, charts, graphs, trend lines support management judgment?

"Benefits concerning basic health care, transportation, food, leisure, maintenance, all hinge on an operational cash flow," Mr. Thistlethwaite said. "And the capital structure is often tied up with a debt service which impairs peace of mind of many residents because of potential or actual bankruptcy."

Living with Continuing-care

Experts also note that some retirees may find continuing-care too institutionalized and with too many regulations for those used to being independent. Those who can adjust can benefit from the new activities and companionship.

One retired couple in Kitty Hawk, North Carolina, decided, with some pangs of guilt, that the wife's aging mother would be better off in a continuing-care facility. She had been living with the couple and, at first, was unhappy about being moved to the home. Then she got caught up in the many activities, including talent shows and fashion shows by the residents. Before long she loved her "new home."

Indeed, during one visit with her daughter and son-in-law, the mother sat around impatiently for a while, and then demanded:

"Take me home. It's too boring around here."

Adventures In Retirement Living

Even though we can no longer hop around with abandon, we still want to be where the action is, not isolated in some high-rise condominium.
Mary Harlow
Delray Beach, Florida

10

For many older people, retirement isn't just the end of their working years, but a start of new adventures.

"We are two of thousands over the United States who have sold their real estate and are living full time in travel trailers," said Alice M. Horton of Apache Junction, Arizona. "We love the whole concept of mobile living, meeting new people with similar interests, seeing the greatness of these United States, the chances to try new activities and not sit by the fire and stagnate."

Retirement living, as Mrs. Horton indicated, isn't limited to a conventional house, a condominium, or an apartment. The options are limited only by your imagination. Retirees live in motor homes and travel trailers, in cabins in the woods, on houseboats and sailboats, in remodeled old buildings, on sun-drenched islands, in scenic hotels in Europe, and in any number of other surroundings.

Here are some insights into just a few of the offbeat options undertaken by some retirees.

On the Road

For Leone and Bob Estus of Austin, Texas, home is a 31-foot-long travel trailer at wherever they happen to be as they motor from Mexico to Canada and across the United States. And for the Estuses, retirement living on wheels can't be beat. Wrote Mrs. Estus:

"Some 10 years prior to our retirement date, after having had considerable experience with a travel trailer on vacations and weekends, we began to think of the possibility of making a trailer our full-time home when our working days came to an end. . . .

"By the time our retirement actually arrived, there were two other factors, at least, which moved us in that direction: one was the increasingly excessive cost of utilities in our all-electric house, which had come to exceed the amount of our monthly payment; the second was the burden of caring for our large yard, which came to be more work than pleasure."

So when retirement time arrived in 1978, the Estuses sold their house in Austin, bought a travel trailer and a van to pull it, and hit the road. They are now in their third travel trailer, with an A-frame on the front. Inside, it is a real home, 8 feet wide and 29 feet long. Mrs. Estus added:

> It might be roughly described as a miniature two-room-and-bath apartment. We have a living room and kitchen area at the front, a bedroom with a full size and very comfortable bed in the rear, and a hallway, bath, and closet area between.
>
> The [trailer] is what is known as a conventional or straight-sided trailer, rather than the curved airplane-type construction seen on some popular makes. We find its construction preferable because it gives much more storage space in the overhead cabinets plus a greater feeling of roominess for persons of normal size moving about within it.
>
> We were fortunate in being able to order this trailer and take delivery on it directly from the factory. We began with all the options we wanted for full-time living. We have since made some additions—such as a microwave oven and a large outside awning that expands our living space during good weather and protects our entry door from rain.
>
> We have room for virtually all the items that we would want to have in a conventional home, such as books, photo albums, and slides, plus our projector. We carry a portable typewriter and a portable sewing machine. Our tow vehicle, a van, accommodates all the necessary tools, spare parts, fishing equipment, folding chairs, and so forth, even including a 13-foot inflatable boat and a small motorbike.

Covering the Country

Since beginning this gypsy life in the summer of 1978, we have pretty well covered the United States, plus five Canadian provinces and an excursion into Mexico as part of a tour that included putting our trailer and tow vehicle onto a flat car for a four-day trip over the Sierra Madre Mountains to the coast and then traveling by highway as far south as Puerto Vallarta. . . .

Initially, our intention was to follow the seasons in reverse—north in the summer and south in the winter. But events have frequently altered these plans. We may be accused of being somewhat aimless, but we enjoy the feeling of utter freedom, moving where and how we please. Our trailer is very adequately insulated and heated, so we could be comfortable even in much worse weather than we are likely to encounter. . . .

We might add that we have been very successful in finding practitioners of all sorts in all areas of the country, including doctors, dentists, opticians, mechanics, and repair people where required—and also veterinarians and groomers for the third member of our family, the poodle Princess. We carry medical records from the Austin physician who last gave each of us a complete physical examination. And we are able to order drugs as needed by mail from an outlet of the American Association of Retired Persons.

Travel Trailer Tips

Here is Mrs. Estus's advice for on-the-road retirees:

First and foremost, for couples, be sure that you are good friends! Two people living in such close quarters *must* be able to get along with a minimum of friction; there is literally no room for quarrels or hard feelings!

Secondly, each partner must be aware of what he or she is giving up. If either one has many, many outside interests, social groups, civic obligations, and the like, which they are not prepared to relinquish, the mobile life is not for them.

Likewise, if her home is a woman's pride and joy, and if entertaining gives her much satisfaction, some serious adjustments will be required. Social life does not cease, of course, and there is plenty of opportunity for entertainment. But it is all on a very, very casual basis, if done at all.

A close-knit family that is geographically concentrated is another consideration. But if the family is well-scattered, the possibilities for visiting are enhanced.

Our best advice, then, is simply to be aware of what must be given up or left behind. And one last word—no one should embark on this sort of living without some thorough and rather lengthy experience with a trailer. We have known of people who buy their very first trailer when they retire. We think they will have a lot of bad moments getting acquainted with their new way of life—enough to discourage all but the very hardy souls.

Motor Home Concerns

In addition to travel trailers, many retirees live in recreational vehicles (RVs), which have built-in engines and cabs, and cost between $20,000 and $30,000.

To hold down gasoline bills, more energy-efficient recreational vehicles are being produced, and newer towing vans also guzzle less gasoline than their predecessors. As a result, a "condominium on wheels"—travel trailers costing $8,000 up and RVs costing $20,000 up—still cost less than a home for many retirees, said Wayne L. Peay, a dealer in Albuquerque, New Mexico.

Another potential problem with motor homes is where to park them when you aren't traveling. George Bunzer of Murphy, North Carolina, has come up with one possible solution: a home for motor homes. Mr. Bunzer designed and built a chalet where his motor home can be parked and used during the off-season.

"We have a 35-foot travel trailer within out home and everything about it is just great," Mr. Bunzer said. *"The chalet provides a 'home base' when not traveling. Your RV hooks up to become a working part of the house, thus avoiding the expensive duplication of facilities, such as the kitchen and bathroom. This allows use of the unit all year.*

"When your traveling days are over," he added, *"you can always raise the floor in the garage area, build in a full kitchen, half-bath, and one or two bedrooms, and convert the chalet into a conventional home."*

Mr. Bunzer sells plans for his Bunzer's RV chalets. You can write him at Route 6, Box 384, Dept. S, Murphy, NC 28906.

The Simple Life

William and Phoebe Lowell's idea of an ideal retirement is to get off the fast lane of life and back to the land, in Coos Bay, Oregon.

"We are happy with our small, remodeled old garage with a shed-like addition (three ample rooms in all). We can afford it, and we can maintain it easily, and the surroundings, on four acres, are very enjoyable," Mrs. Lowell said.

"There are pastures, a garden area, a wood lot for our wood burning stove (used for both heating and cooking), our own well and septic system" she said. And while the Lowells shun many modern conveniences, *"we aren't totally 'back woods.' We have the best of both lifestyles: our electric range, washer and dryer for rainy weather and a small freezer.*

"Now why and how did we end up away up here in Coos Bay, Oregon—two oldsters originally from Maine? Well, I'll tell you why and how," Mrs. Lowell continued. *"Maine weather was too harsh for Mr. Lowell after back surgery."* So the Lowells moved to Southern California in 1953. *"But Southern California turned into an awful rat race after nearly 20 years.*

"Our brand new, custom-built modern, all-paid-for home lost its appeal. It was becoming increasingly expensive to travel, or camp out, and also very crowded. There was no more hunting within hundreds of miles, no more fishing. Our children were grown, through school, and we didn't need to work so thoroughly."

What happened was, the Lowells sold out and moved to Sacramento, California, in a country setting. They bought a house for themselves and one for their daughter and three granddaughters.

"But land developers moved in, taxes increased each year, just about everything increased and without warning. Our Social Security just wouldn't cover it all and our savings were dwindling. It was like a 'Writing on the Wall,' saying 'Look Ahead.'

"We had a chance to buy this unusually great place in Oregon—cash sale. So we sold again, both places, and moved again. Great Move!

"Each move was to a smaller house with less upkeep, less taxes at first and fewer services at first," Mrs. Lowell said. But "There are more incentives here for active, retired 'youngsters.' The sea we love, lakes, rivers, sloughs for crabbing, clamming, fishing, and boating; forests for hunting, garden areas to raise our own produce, and pastures to raise our beef and chickens.

"And the second reason we are happy with our present housing situation," Mrs. Lowell concluded, "is because our property has two homes on it. Our daughter and granddaughters have a beautiful ranch-style home on the rise above us."

A Cabin in the Woods

For Grace Huggard, a former real estate agent in Long Island, the ideal retirement home is in a cabin overlooking majestic mountains near Johnsburg, New York.

"I have lived alone for many years, and when I was able to retire from business I indulged my heart's desire for mountains and space," she said. "I sold my suburban Long Island home and bought over 100 acres of woodland and an old farmhouse, sound but neglected.

"Then, years later, in my 70s, the large house was becoming somewhat of a physical chore," she said. "Happily for me, my son and his family now occupy and love the house. And, happily for me, too, I am still on the 100 acres, ensconced in a small, cabin-type house 20 feet by 32 feet. It is adequate for my needs, easy to care for, and economical to heat. We all have wood stoves up here in the land of the trees.

"Redeeming features are the floor-to-ceiling glass doors overlooking the mountains and an 8-foot deck across the front and kitchen side of the house. I would prefer the house to be a little larger, even for me, and if it were to be for two people, I'd suggest another den-type room be added."

But Mrs. Huggard said the location can't be beat.

"Location of the home should be the first and foremost consideration. One can change the house—even move it—but the land stays."

Retirement Restoration

For some, retirement is the adventure of keeping busy by restoring an old and often-historic house. While still living in Hinsdale, Illinois, Mr. and Mrs. Raymond Whitener bought an old house near relatives in Marquand, Missouri, and began to remodel it for their retirement home.

"The house, which was bought in 1971, was about 100 years old," Mr. Whitener said. "Two great-uncles once owned the house. The land had been obtained through a Spanish land grant and settled by my ancestors in 1804. The house had the simple facilities of running water, one bath on the first floor, propane gas space heaters on the first floor, and a small wood stove in the two bedrooms on the second floor.

"When we bought the house, we bought most of the old furnishings, which we used when we came here on vacation and to visit relatives. In 1973, while still living in Hinsdale, we decided to start modernizing the house. We asked a friend and co-worker, who was an architect, to draw plans which could do the following:

1. Save as much of the old house as possible.
2. Since there was an old barn on the property, we wished to use as much of the old material as possible.
3. The south and west sides of the property (the back of the house) are bound by streams. We asked the architect to make this side the "loafing" area. This is why we have the sun deck over the family room and balcony overlooking the stream on this side.

"The front of the house faces Main Street of a small town with a population of about 400. The Post Office and stores are about one block away. We are surrounded by national forests near the Ozarks. The two big social events are farm auctions and wakes," Mr. Whitener said.

"The old part of the house that was the dining and kitchen areas was moved back far enough to make a garage. The fireplace in the family room was built from the foundation stone from the barn. The beams in the kitchen and dining areas were sawed from the barn wood," he said, and wood from the barn was used in the ceiling, the kitchen cabinets, and the deck.

"The outhouse has been preserved," he added.

"The house is furnished with antique furniture which my wife has bought—and I have repaired and refinished. My wife has used old pictures of the town and former residences as decorations."

The Whiteners now live in their restored, ancestral house. But Mr. Whitener noted that the work continues.

"Restoring an old house, then keeping everything in ship-shape," he said, "is not retirement."

A Stained-glass Home

Cooper and June Evans of Mercer, Pennsylvania, also bought an old building and remodeled it for their retirement home. But their home is not a house.

"Several years ago, while I was executive secretary for our local chamber of commerce, we purchased an abandoned church located in the central part of our town," Mrs. Evans wrote.

"Our first objective was to participate in our local project of restoration and also to have investment property," she said. "We paid $3,000 for the church—our stained glass windows now insured by the square inch, are worth far more than the original investment.

"The building, constructed in 1852, includes two entrance halls and one large room for worship. A false ceiling had been installed and when this was removed, we found there was enough height for two floors. Our original plans were then altered to include the rental area on the first floor (now a doctor's office) and the apartment for ourselves on the second floor.

"At the time of purchase, we owned and were living in a 15-room house, which we realized would require too much upkeep as we grew older," said Mrs. Evans. Both she and Mr. Evans are in their 60s.

"Although we have spent more than 10 times our original investment for remodeling we think we have made a wise investment," she said. "The income from our rental areas can be used to pay for utilities, taxes, etc.

"Our apartment includes a living room 12 feet by 21 feet, den combination 12 feet by 15 feet, kitchen 12 feet by 13 feet, two bedrooms 12 feet by 13 feet each, bath, utility room, plenty of closet space, and a 9-foot by 8-foot reception hall below the balcony. Our only mistake was not including a powder room, and we are now making plans to install one beneath the steps.

"We feel that we have a perfect solution to housing for ourselves as retirees," Mrs. Evans said. In fact, you might say that their church home is the answer to a retired couple's prayers.

On the Waterfront

For Dr. Richard Cameron, home has been a houseboat on the Washington, D.C., waterfront.

"There are two joys of living on a houseboat—one is that you are called Captain and the other is that your friends think you are doing a great thing," Dr. Cameron said.

"Boat people (as a breed) have existed for a long time in the warmer climes of our fair land, but only recently has a hardened strain moved to Washington, D.C. Can you imagine living in the nation's capital on a boat and being practically downtown? . . .

"Houseboats range in cost from $13,000 for a used 40-foot one to nearly $100,000 for the best grade, 60-foot brand-new version," Dr. Cameron said. "The slip fee here is approximately $3 per foot per month. For my old 40-foot houseboat, it cost $120 per month. This includes water and a parking space for one car. Not bad in Washington where you can pay $80 a month to park your car downtown (and over $100,000 for an average-priced house).

"Living on a houseboat can be fun," he added. "Designed for summer warmth, most houseboats are not insulated and lose great amounts of heat. But Washingtonian boaters continue to struggle down the windswept docks in winter to sleep in these cold boats. Water pipes freeze frequently and you shower with friends in the apartments downtown. Most boaters look for friends with fireplaces. Space is at a premium—you shower in a broom closet and you store your real belongings at self-storage rental places in the suburbs.

"But it is fun. It is your little refuge in the big city. You own it, and it is not to become a condominium. Your neighbors are nice, and the boaters' unwritten rule is to respect each other's privacy. For low-cost good life, it can't be beat.

"Of course, these units also are mobile, as they have engines," Dr. Cameron added. "One winter when I had enough of the cold, I decided to head down the channel to the Potomac and to the Atlantic

Ocean, south to the Panama Canal and into the broad Pacific where I could be picked up by the U.S. Navy's 7th Fleet so as 'boat people' I could be resettled in sunny, warm California.

"But, alas, I couldn't get my engines started."

Caribbean Living

Many people dream of retiring to a Caribbean island. Mr. and Mrs. Richard W. Case not only dreamed, they did it. They advise others to follow that dream.

"In the winter of 1969–70, I made a three-island trip to the lower part of the Caribbean—visiting Granada, Antigua, and Barbados," Mr. Case said. "I put a down payment on a small, on-the-cliff ocean-front lot in Barbados, West Indies. . . .

"I brought my wife with me the next winter and we decided the original 65-foot lot was a bit small," he said. "So, a year later, we bought a 100-foot-wide, half-acre piece of land with a much more interesting view, combining the Atlantic Ocean and a view of the upper east coast of Barbados.

"In February 1974, we contracted to have a two-bedroom two-bath house built with a living room, kitchen, and storage room for $16,000," Mr. Case said. "It turned out that our house was to be the first complete house our contractor had ever built, and we were 2,000 miles away in the States! In Barbados, you must submit complete plans—floor plans, side elevations, site map, etc.—for what is called Town and Country Planning. T&CP is a good thing.

"The house was to be about 1,350 square feet. It was built with the local 'cement' block consisting of coral stone dust, sand, and cement. The rain never comes from the west here, so on the west side we used what is called here decorative block, instead of awning windows. The reason for the decorative block was to let the easterly breeze pass through the house.

"Electricity is best here (gas is costly and hard to get in remote areas)," Mr. Case said. "In our location, where we catch the easterly breezes, one would hardly ever need air conditioning, and with the average daily temperatures of around 86 degrees, it would be expensive.

"Oh, yes," Mr. Case added, "the contractor ran into rising prices in the 1974 oil crisis and the house wound up costing me about $20,000 in U.S. money." But the value of planning ahead, he said, is that "at today's prices, the house would cost about $50,000."

A Continental Retirement

The ideas for adventuresome retirement are endless. Mary Harlow of Delray Beach, Florida, called for low-budget, resort-type hotels and motels for traveling retirees, such as already exist in Europe.

"Having lived on four continents, I've encountered many lively retirees-in-orbit living off-season in waterfront or scenic motels with kitchenettes," she said. "Why doesn't some innovative builder set up a chain of budget motels in the U.S.A. and Spain or Morocco for the geriatric set? The guests could be rotated at will on a space-available basis, every three to six months.

"The ideal motel for retirees would be semicircular, so that they are bound to encounter one another in a casual setting, similar to life aboard a ship," she said. "There should be a coffee shop or cafeteria and a mini-market nearby, if not actually on the premises. To avoid segregation, the retirees' rooms should not be all together—other guests, coming and going, would provide interest sharing their travel experiences.

"Having spent two years in a bargain international motel on the Portuguese Riviera, I speak from experience," she added. "My neighbors included a retired diamond cutter from Norway, a Ph.D from the University of Vienna, an herbalist from Cape Cod, even Rudolph Valentino's nephew and his Spanish starlet spouse, plus the Russian Circus for three-and-a-half memorable weeks.

"I went for two weeks, but stayed two years. Do you need a better testimonial?"

Unfinished Business

It is too late to consider the usual housing for retirees without a revolution in home building.
William Heinrich
Retiree in Lakeland, Florida

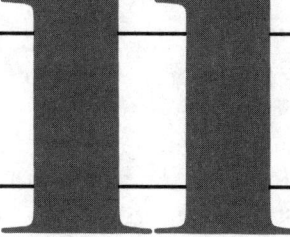

11

The United States is heading for a crisis in housing for older Americans.

That is the message from many older people and various experts on housing and aging. With proper planning, you can do much to protect yourself. But unless industry and government pay more attention to this growing group of maturing Americans, many older people will be squeezed by the costs of keeping up their old homes and be unable to afford the high prices and rents of other housing if they want to move.

"The growing scarcity of adequate and affordable housing poses at least as great a threat to society" as the energy crisis, said the president of the United Association of Journeymen and Apprentices of the Plumbing and Pipefitting Industry. "Many Americans, especially the elderly, have been put in a squeeze. They can't afford to buy a home, and they are being forced out of increasingly scarce numbers of apartments."

In short, when it comes to housing older people, there is a lot of unfinished business.

The fact is that there are going to be a lot more older people in the next 20 years. The people who are going to be the oldsters of tomorrow are already here. All you have to do is look around. They are the men and women in their late 40s and in their 50s who now fill our corporate offices, work in our factories, repair our cars, and provide other services. They are many of the people we see in supermarkets with disbelief in their eyes when looking at the price of food.

There are plenty of good ideas for ways to head off a housing crunch. Some of the proposals involve more government help for the elderly who are poor or frail. Other suggestions would update and ease certain government restraints. But most ideas call for simply awakening industry and government to the burgeoning housing market for older consumers whose needs are not being met.

More, much more, needs to be done. Drawing on the views of many of today's retirees, here are some proposals for better housing tomorrow.

A Housing Agenda

1. **Build smaller houses.** The housing industry needs to recognize the growing market for smaller houses on smaller lots with smaller price tags. Older people simply don't need the 2,000-foot behemoths being built today. And too few builders are constructing the houses that the older generation wants and needs.

There is more than a social purpose here. It is a question of whether the free market will respond to a significant consumer demand. Builders can think big by thinking smaller because older people will make up a huge market in coming years. These are consumers who know what they want. And as the auto industry has discovered, you can't sell a big Chrysler to a customer who wants a small Datsun.

By building smaller houses together or as part of a subdivision of bigger houses, developers actually could tap two markets: older people and young first-time buyers who are not priced out of the market. A bonus would be the mixing of young and old in a single community.

2. **Design houses for what people say *they* need.** Too many houses are designed by planners who think they know what is best for the customer. Clearly, they don't know what is best for the *older* customer. New, smaller houses for older people should be designed to meet their needs for access, one-level, convenient-to-use rooms and, don't forget, lower (or adjustable) shelves and counters.

"Hopefully, in the future, planners of housing for the older age group will be not just architects and builders, but people with training in making space more human, such as home economists trained in housing and home furnishings," said Helen Wilson of Harper Woods, Michigan.

And, we might add, the planners should include some older people.

3. Expand the variety of multifamily housing. With energy and land costs climbing, apartment-type housing will be an increasingly efficient option. More condominiums and townhouses will be needed for home buyers, and the potential cost advantages of cooperatives should be given closer attention. Rental apartments likely will be scarcer because relatively few new buildings will be constructed.

One restraint to many of these larger, multifamily developments is that people fear they will disrupt their communities. And many older people don't like big high-rises.

Doubling Up

The alternative is to put more emphasis on smaller multifamily buildings. One type popular with many older people is the old "double," or duplex. The duplex looks much like a single-family home, but has double the housing impact. An older person could own the duplex and rent the other side to another oldster or to a younger family. The rental side also could be used to provide room and board to someone who would watch over an aging owner.

The tenant unit could be "for the person who takes care of the one in the adjoining apartment, getting meals, cleaning, and doing the laundry for the older person," suggested Adeline Wenke, a retiree in Ellinwood, Kansas.

Instead of big high-rises, low-rise buildings with a relatively small number of apartments—and perhaps services—for older people could be built.

"There are thousands of people like me who can pay their way (but are not rich), but can't be completely alone," said Mrs. Alice Curley of Annapolis, Maryland. "Nothing is being built for us: buildings for 10 or 12 with the privacy of your own apartment where you can have your own pets."

4. Make better use of existing land. This would be tied to the increased use of smaller, multifamily housing units.

"Thousands of vacant lots throughout cities remain unsold and unused year after year. Owners, like myself, must pay taxes on them with no hope of financial return," said Mrs. Gordon Walsh of Lovettsville, Virginia. "Instead of building massive projects, if the federal government would enlarge its scope to include multiple dwellings such as four-family houses, the countryside would maintain its residential quality," she said.

There is room for private enterprise, too. Gladys Scott, of Philadelphia, suggested a high-rise retirement community.

"Some day I hope there will be retirement communities for those of us who live and thrive on city activity," she said. *"Because of land expense, they could be garden-type. But why not a total-care high-rise—complete with dining room and recreation room and a roof that you can take a folding chair up to and relax?"*

5. Make more use of manufactured housing. What we once knew as trailers and then mobile homes have become an important low-cost housing alternative. Ironically, the many older people who live in mobile homes know best how out-dated the old concepts are. Yet many local-government officials and voters, with old-fashioned ideas about tinny trailers and seedy trailer parks, refuse to consider the advances in this kind of housing. By easing restrictions on manufactured homes, many communities could open up whole areas for moderate-priced housing.

Zap the Zoning

6. Change a lot of the outdated zoning laws. One reason—a major one—why more innovative housing can't be built for older people, and others, is that zoning and building codes in most communities are written to require big lots and big houses. Under many zoning laws, it costs about $1.25 per square foot of land for a single-family house. By a stroke of the pen—or rezoning for higher density, such as a townhouse—the cost of the same piece of land goes to $7.50 per square foot. So you pay $18,000 for 12,000 square feet of ground for a single-family house, but you pay $22,500 for 3,000 square feet for a townhouse. Similar complexities make it hard to build smaller single-family houses on smaller lots.

One way to hold costs and prices down would be to change the zoning laws. But that steps on too many toes, and city councils will fight you to the last square foot. Most communities probably wouldn't want to drop all zoning—though Houston gets by without any—but they ought to see whether some requirements hurt the community more than they help.

7. Cut regulations. A Rutgers University study shows that about 20 percent of the sales price of a house goes for all kinds of regulations. Some are necessary, but some aren't. By weeding out the unnecessary ones, you can help hold down costs and prices and allow construction of more homes needed by older people.

Help at Home

8. Find better ways to help older people stay in their homes. Many older people want to stay in the houses they own, but in doing so, they are sitting on golden nest eggs of assets in houses that have greatly appreciated in value. This is money they could use for repairs or living expenses, rather than leaving the house and its assets to their heirs.

Research should be supported to develop reverse mortgages that allow older homeowners to draw on the assets of their house, but with safeguards to protect them against losing their home if they should live to a ripe old age. The assets should at least be usable for needed home repairs. More states should allow older homeowners to defer property taxes until the house is sold.

9. Allow older homeowners to rent out parts of their homes. If older people could turn part of a big old house into an apartment to help pay the upkeep, it would be easier for them to keep their houses. Or they could share their house with other people, young or old. But many localities prohibit such uses of homes.

10. Provide at-home care. More elderly could remain in their homes if they were able to receive certain needed care at home as they grow older and require services short of full continuing-care aid. It might be cheaper for older people to receive such part-time services or to use Medicaid funds, rather than to pay the cost of full-time care in nursing homes or other facilities.

"I have a lady to come in and take care of the house and cook. In fact, she takes care of all my needs now," said Grace Kelso of Clovis, New Mexico. "I feel a lot of older people would be happier living in their own home if they had someone to take care of them.

"If the government would hire someone to care for these people, it might be less costly than building homes," Mrs. Kelso said.

Retiree Resources

11. Local governments should encourage scattered-site housing for older people. One resource would be by using government funds, if necessary, in their communities.

Older people don't want handouts. But they do want to be part of a community, and it may be up to the community to provide some help to insure that there is adequate housing for older residents of moderate means. Asserted Isabelle P. Murray of Whiting, New Jersey:

"It would be far better for communities to provide suitable (physically and financially) living facilities for its elders who can be a vital source for volunteers in hospitals, pre-school baby sitting, and educational experiences for a growing community."

12. Use pension-fund power to provide more housing for older people. Pension funds invest billions of dollars to provide pension income for retirees. Avenues should be explored to invest in, and to help provide, housing for the pension holders.

While pension-fund assets have grown in recent years to the point where they now constitute the largest single capital pool in our economy, they have been largely absent from the trillion-dollar-plus residential mortgage market. By increasing pension investment in mortgages, the mortgage market would become more competitive, result in declining mortgage rates and make more housing available to all people—including older people.

Some progress is being made. The deregulation of the nation's financial institutions is attracting new investors in pools of mortgages, including pension funds. What is needed is for the pension-fund investors to also focus on the housing needs of their members. As an official of the Deferred Compensation Administrators has proposed, the pension goal of providing income security "could be significantly enhanced if in addition to providing direct income payments, the pension fund also invested in home-equity conversion plans that allowed retirees to use the principal in their homes—an otherwise frozen asset."

Homes and Family

There are still more housing options that need to be explored. One is to find better ways to help older people live with, or near, their families. Most older people resist the idea of living with their children—they want independence and they don't want to interfere with the lives of their offspring. But as we have seen, with a separate "wing for mother" or other arrangements, it is possible to combine independence with family living.

E. Schumacher of St. Louis further suggested that one way older people could relieve themselves of the burdens of a big house would be to let their children or a younger family, who couldn't afford a house, move into the house, and for the older person to move to smaller quarters on the same property.

"Many older Americans find their large homes too expensive to maintain, but difficult to leave," he said. *"Whenever possible, separate*

quarters added to the larger house, or lot permitting, the addition of a one-bedroom cottage, could be considered. Thus, older generations could continue to live within their secure surroundings and vacate the larger building to growing families able to assume maintenance."

Nguyen Ngat, an immigrant from South Vietnam now living near Chicago, said he and his wife were shocked by what he called "the houses where the old men live"—retirement and convalescent homes.

"In Vietnam, when parents grow old, they live with their children and their children take care of them," he said with feeling. "Children like their parents; they don't separate."

Many older Americans, of course, are active and involved and independent. But the longer life span—and almost 2.3 million Americans are now over 85—the greater the chance that the death of a spouse, an accident, or changes in health or financial status will turn an independent parent into one requiring help, from children or someone else.[1]

Most children, in fact, do come to the aid of aged parents when problems of failing health and infirmities arise, social workers say. And 50 percent to 70 percent of all day-to-day care provided by these elderly parents is provided by the children.

For families with other problems of their own, taking on the care of an elderly parent can be agonizing. As Joseph Califano, Jr., former Secretary of Health, Education and Welfare, told Senate hearings on aging, choosing to help elderly parents can severely stretch a family's physical, emotional and financial resources, "sometimes to the limit."

Services to help families through this period are often inadequate or hard to locate. And caring for aged parents is often a very difficult job. "Maybe that's why there's a Commandment about it—because it's so difficult to do," said Anna Zimmer, director of a Community Service Society of New York program that helps families who are caring for older relatives.

The search for housing solutions for older Americans thus must be separated into the needs of "young old" and the "old old," and their families.

The Old Neighborhood May Be Best

Many of those proposals are shared by many experts on housing for older people. But too often such housing is discussed in terms of new homes for people who want to move away to the Sunbelt or other areas, said Leo E. Baldwin, housing program coordinator for the 15-million-member American Association of Retired Persons (AARP).

"Most older people do not want to move away from their neighborhoods," Mr. Baldwin said. And more planning should be focused on finding ways to help them stay.

Currently, one problem is that about the only way that older homeowners can capitalize on the increased values of their houses is to sell the house and move elsewhere. "There's no good mechanism they can use so they can utilize their assets and continue to occupy the house," Mr. Baldwin said. "That is the single biggest problem."

The AARP official advocated reverse mortgage plans with more safeguards for older homeowners. Such plans should guarantee lifetime income and occupancy in the home, he said. They also should be overseen by a third party—such as retiree groups or local government—that would guard the rights of the older homeowner. Otherwise, "I'm afraid that some people might get involved who would exploit the elderly," Mr. Baldwin said.

The reverse mortgage plans can be used to allow older homeowners to use part of their assets to obtain money for maintenance. This, coupled with programs that allow them to defer property taxes, would enable many of them to keep their homes, Mr. Baldwin noted. Because older people tend to own older houses, "home maintenance and the inability to afford the upkeep are two leading reasons why older people leave their homes before they are ready to give them up," he said.

"A Little Reverse Discrimination"

There are other ways to help older people keep their homes. One solution, suggested by AARP communication counsel Barry Robinson, would be for localities to practice "a little reverse discrimination." Without changing local zoning or building codes, city councils could grant special variances, allowing apartments in houses where the owner has lived a specified number of years. By making the required time of ownership long enough, only older homeowners would qualify.

But such plans aren't the answer for many older homeowners who want to stay in their neighborhoods. "It doesn't solve the problem of being saddled with a house they probably shouldn't be in in the first place," Mr. Baldwin said. "You've got to find other housing options, but within a few blocks of where they live now." But, again, too often "zoning restrictions cut off the options."

For example, the growing number of neighborhood schools that are being closed because of declining school populations in many communities could be put to use for older people. "Remodel the schools as senior centers and build houses on the playgrounds," Mr. Baldwin urged. This, in fact, has been done in Michigan. But getting zoning rules changed to allow such options "is like pulling teeth," he said.

Another option, Mr. Baldwin suggested, is to "bring in small, manufactured housing units—duplexes, triplexes, and bigger two-story units—to provide new housing on existing land in neighborhoods," rather than to tear down existing buildings and construct huge high-rises. This would provide "modest housing that conforms to the neighborhood" and "protects the character and value of the neighborhood," Mr. Baldwin said.

One possible concept would be a "mini-condo" development using small areas of land for attractively designed buildings with 8 to 12 condominium or rental units, with an inside court and some services for older residents. These could be constructed, Mr. Baldwin suggested, in various parts of a city to provide 80 to 120 housing units with one overall manager.

What About Granny Flats?

There is even a potential housing option for individuals who could move from a big house when they get older, but who could stay on their property. It is called a "granny flat," and it is widely used in Australia, France, and some other countries.

A granny flat basically is a small, temporary house that can be placed on the grounds of an existing house and then removed when it is no longer needed. A young family that owns a house, for example, can have the small unit placed in their yard as a place for a parent, or a "granny," to live semi-independently.

The granny flat "is so popular in France that the government subsidizes the price of the housing to develop it and sell it," Mr. Baldwin said. But in the United States so far, "city councils say 'we can't do it.'"

The advantage of such housing is that there isn't the expense of new sewer or utility systems because the houses can connect into existing systems. Also, nonprofit corporations could be formed to obtain and rent the houses cheaply. Well-designed, manufactured housing already exists that could be used, Mr. Baldwin said. These are houses with 650 square feet of living space, a 15-year life expectancy, completely furnished, which could be amortized at a cost of $120 a month, he said. And the corporation wouldn't have to buy land or make site improvements because existing sites would be used with the landowner's approval.

His suggestion is that the nonprofit corporations own the houses and rent them to older occupants. The corporation would take responsibility for maintaining the houses and removing them when no longer needed, if local communities would grant the zoning variances needed to allow such units.

The main advantage of such housing, Mr. Baldwin said, is that "it reconnects the family responsibilities. If the younger people, man and wife, are both working, grandma can look after the kids during the day, have dinner with the family in the evening, and then go to her own house to watch TV. If grandma gets sick, somebody is nearby to take care of her."

When it comes to the housing needs of older people, "there are answers if we challenge people to look for them," Mr. Baldwin said. And older people have the growing muscle to get changes made, to respond to their responsible suggestions.

A Housing Blueprint for the 1980s

The housing needs of older people was the subject of a Mini Conference on Housing for the Elderly conducted in October 1980 in Washington, D.C. More than 300 housing developers, reformers, consumers, and advocates attended the Mini Conference, which was sponsored by the National Council of Senior Citizens. The mini conference prepared recommendations on housing for the 1981 White House Conference on Aging.

The group concluded the three-day session by proposing more than a score of recommendations designed to form "a housing blueprint for the 1980s."

The blueprint stressed five major areas:

1. Greater help for homeowners against rising costs.
2. Increased protection for renters against displacement.
3. Expanded construction of assisted units for the poor.
4. Broader choices for the frail of housing types and services.
5. Greater information for all about programs and services; better co-ordination among providers; and increased consumer participation in programs, planning and management.

"There was a general consensus," the mini conference concluded, "that . . . supply of all housing types needs to be expanded. Furthermore, for older people, attention must always be paid to the fact that their homes are more than a shelter; the adequacy of the housing environment is a key ingredient to their overall health and life satisfaction. Hence, for them, housing and services must be treated as an integrated set of concerns."

A Word for the Women

Special attention should be given to the housing needs of older women. The reason is that women tend to outlive men and often end up living alone. Indeed, more than one third of all households headed by people over age 65 are comprised of women living alone.

The need for changes in housing, pensions, and other areas where women are often short-changed were discussed at another Mini White House Conference on Older Women, which was held in Des Moines, Iowa, in 1980.

On housing, the group came up with these proposals:

> More "families of choice" in which older women would share their homes with unrelated people, young or old.
> More programs designed to instruct older women on how to turn their homes into "boarding houses" for the elderly.
> "Respite care" in which homemakers would provide primary care for the frail elderly or disabled persons.

The meeting also saw the birth of a new group to press the views of older women. It is called, appropriately enough, the Older Women's League. And its first president, Tish Summers of Oakland, California, put into perspective the power of older women to forge changes.

"We are not over the hill," she said. *"We are women with one third of our lives left. And if we get together, we can have some social impact."*

A Call to Action

There are a lot of ideas for dealing with the housing problems of older people. Some are practical, some aren't. It is time to sort out the good ones and get on with the job. To do that, two final actions are needed:

1. A national conference on housing for older people. Builders, developers, designers, lenders, government officials, senior citizen groups, and older people themselves should meet to set an agenda for improving the housing opportunities of older Americans.

What's needed is to find strategies for unleashing the marketplace to meet what will be a growing consumer demand for new types of housing.

2. Most of all, we need to listen to the people who know best what is needed—the older people themselves. People like Mrs. Barbara L. McGloin of Andover, Massachusetts. She and her husband, like many others in their late 50s and older, have plenty of thoughtful ideas.

"If some decision could be made by local residents as to what their own needs are, I believe housing would not be such a problem," Mrs. McGloin said. *"If organized correctly, a community situation could be planned to house young and old together (perhaps in attached units at a reasonable rental) as little children benefit from the wisdom of the elderly.*

"All the elderly need to keep a sense of dignity and have a purpose, not just exist."

Ordering Federal Publications on Housing

Most federal publications on housing are available from the U.S. General Services Administration's Consumer Information Center in Pueblo, Colorado. There is a $1 user fee for processing an order with two or more free titles.

Send your orders to:
>Consumer Information Center
>Department IRS
>Pueblo, CO 81009

If you are ordering free publications, please address your order to:
>Attn: S. James

If you are ordering any publications that are for sale, please address your order to:
>Attn: R. Woods

Notes

Chapter 2. Where Will the Living Be Easiest?

1. "Aging Americans," by Earl C. Gottschalk, Jr., *The Wall Street Journal,* November 13, 1979.
2. "Regions," by Sam Allis, *The Wall Street Journal,* July 1980.
3. "Aging Americans," by Earl C. Gottschalk, Jr., *The Wall Street Journal,* November 13, 1979.
4. "Older Americans," by Neil Maxwell, *The Wall Street Journal,* March 4, 1983.

Chapter 3. Cashing In Your Housing Assets

1. "Creative Financing," by Marilyn Chase, *The Wall Street Journal,* May 1, 1980.
2. "Real Estate" by Paul A. Gigot, *The Wall Street Journal,* April 15, 1981.

Chapter 5. Housing Options—A Home of Your Own

1. "Your Retirement Housing Guide," American Association of Retired Persons, 1975, pp. 5–6.

Chapter 6. More Housing Options—Renting

1. *"Housing for the 1980s,"* by Michael Sumichrast, Mimeo, National Association of Home Builders, 1980.
2. "Renters Lament," by James C. Hyatt, *The Wall Street Journal,* June 4, 1979.

Chapter 8. Keeping Up the Old Homestead

1. "Tax Report," *The Wall Street Journal*, January 7, 1981.
2. "Real Estate," by Lawrence Rout, *The Wall Street Journal*, December 10, 1980.

Chapter 9. Retirement Communities—The "Good Life?"

1. "Older Americans," by Jody Long, *The Wall Street Journal*, March 2, 1983.
2. "Aging Americans," by Earl C. Gottschalk, Jr., *The Wall Street Journal*, November 13, 1979.

Chapter 11. Unfinished Business

1. "Aging Americans," by Amanda Bennett, *The Wall Street Journal*, November 16, 1979.

Index

A

AARP. *See* American Association of Retired Persons
Abel, Lucille B., 96
Agler, Gary (Mrs.), 138
Alton, Margaret, 1
American Association of Retired Persons, 2, 72, 100, 118, 125, 245
Amrep Corporation, 84
Anderson, Carl P., 122
Andrus Gerontology Center, 132
Apartments. *See also* Condominiums; Renting
  advantages, 121–22
  condominium conversions, 126–29
  disadvantages, 122–24
  subsidized, 129–30
  waiting list, 130–31
Appliances, life expectancy of, 186–87
Arizona, as retirement site, 12–13
Arkansas, as retirement site, 14
Ash, Oliver K., 149

B

Bait-and-switch tactics, 200
Baldwin, Leo E., 39, 245–47
Barnetson, Margaret, 105
Basement waterproofing, 200
Bathrooms, 145–46
Bauer, Sam W. (Mrs.), 209
Beckman, Elmer, 217
Bedrooms, 144–45
Beeman, Geraldine, 126, 148
Bender, Hilda, 212, 213
Bergere, Richard, 5, 19, 94, 95, 193
Biedenkopf, T. H. (Mrs.), 116
Bierbrier, Doreen, 206
Biggar, Jeanne, 14
Bilohlavek, Linda, 116, 119
Bilohlavek, Ray, 116
Bingham, Hiram, 147
Blanke, Edward, 60
Blanke, Suzette, 60
Boegner, Otto G. (Mrs.), 42
Bordewisch, Erma C., 114
Boschwitz, Rudy, 205
Braun, Sonja, 65
Brobeck, Stephen, 199
Brown, Alberta, 112
Brums, Nancy, 88
Bunzer, George, 231
Burglar-proofing, 189
Butcher, Lee, 109
Butler, Robert, 3, 39
"Buying Lots from Developers," 88

C

Cabinets, life expectancy of, 185
Calabrese, Lillian, 214
Calcara, Frank, 88–89
Cameron, Richard, 235
Canterbury Village, 218
Capital gains, 59–60
Caribbean, as retirement site, 236
Case, Richard W., 236
Castro, Ruth M., 133
Caulking, 194
Century Village, 105, 217
Cesak, Elsie H., 112
Chase Econometrics, 19–20
Christ, Dean, 180
Cities, attraction of, 18–19
Climate, 16, 38
Coleman, Minnie, 41
Colorado, as retirement site, 12
Complete Book of Home Buying, The (Sumichrast, Shafer, and Sumichrast), 100
Concept House, 168–72
Condominium Book, The (Butcher), 109
Condominium Buyers Guide, 109
Condominiums, 104–9. See also Apartments; Renting; Retirement communities
  advantages, 105–6
  buying, 106–9
  conversions, 126–29
Consumer Federation of America, 199, 200
Consumer Reports, 197
Continuing care, 223–27
  church-sponsored, 226
  finances, 226–27
Cooling hours, 39, 48–53
Cooperatives (Co-ops), 109–12. See also Retirement communities
Coopersmith, Lucille B., 117
Corte, Marina, 140
Costikyan, Thelma, 129
Cost of living, 16, 20, 22–26
Costs, of retirement communities, 214
Cousins, Stanley, 91
Cox, Mary Louise, 145
Craig, Jacquelin, 104
Crestwood (New Jersey), 172, 173
Crestwood Village (Maryland), 174
Crestwood Village (New Jersey), 217, 219
Crime, 8, 38, 189
Crispen, Robert, 5
Crowding, in retirement communities, 215

Crowell, S. H. (Mrs.), 143
Culture, 16
Cummings, Warren D., 215
Curley, Alice, 240

D

Dahlstrom, Melvin, 115
Dalbey, E. J., 223
de Geus, Leonard, 17
Design of housing, 3, 134–39, 153–76, 239. See also Energy; Housing
  bathrooms, 145–46
  bedrooms, 144–45
  for disabilities, 148
  family rooms, 143–44
  "Great Rooms," 143–44
  kitchens, 139–42
  laundry, 147
  of retirement communities, 222
  parking, 147
  recreation, 147
Dickinson, Peter A., 13, 16
Disabilities, 148
Dolat, Rose, 130
Donn, Helen, 108
Donn, Herman, 108
Donnelly, John, 77
Donnelly, Julie, 77
Doors, life expectancy of, 183
Downie, Helen, 40
Downie, John, 40

E

Eaglewood, 175
Electrical wiring, 188
  wiring, life expectancy of, 181–82
Energy, 99, 148–50
  fraud, 198–99
  savings, 193–97
  solar, 149
  tax deductions, 197–98
Engle, Rosalee, 203
Erfle, Raymond, 19, 216
Erickson, Ann, 211
Estus, Bob, 228
Estus, Leone, 228
Europe, as retirement site, 237
EVAC house, 150
Evans, Cooper, 234
Evans, June, 234
Exterior paint, life expectancy of, 184
Exterior trim, life expectancy of, 184

F

"Fact Sheet on Home Equity Conversion," 72
Family rooms, 143-44
Federal National Mortgage Association (Fannie Mae), 69, 116, 136, 153
Field, K. S., 150
Finnegan, John, 4, 216, 219
Fireplaces, 195
Fire protection, 189
Flooring, life expectancy of, 185
Florida, as retirement site, 12, 30, 105
Folwick, Goldie, 71
Folwick, Orlin, 71
Foundations, life expectancy of, 181
Frank, Dick, 106
Frank, Juanita, 106
Fraud, and home improvements, 198-99
Friedman, W. (Mrs.), 208
Fuel costs, 99
Furnaces, 195

G

Gantz, Maurice, 190
Gardens, 147
General Development Corporation, 85
Gibson, Bethune, 12, 36, 38
Gick, Flora C., 195
Gladwell, Mildred, 212
Goodkin, Lewis, 224
Goodkin, Sanford R., 16
Goodkin Research Corp., 16
Goody, George, 22, 66
"Granny Flats," 246-47
Grant, Alice Lloyd, 33
Grapentin, Elsie, 2, 146
Gray Panthers, 205
"Great Rooms," 143-44
Gresko, William, 215
Griffin, Tom, 68
Grimes, Charles A., 153
"Guide to Planning Your Retirement Finances," 8

H

Haire, Grace M., 121
Harlow, Mary, 237
Harmening, Dorothy L., 113
Hayn, Richard G., 40
Hayn, Richard G. (Mrs.), 211, 213
Heating, life expectancy of, 182
Heating degree days, 39, 48-53
Heat pumps, 195
Heinrich, William, 35
Hendrickson, H. (Mrs.), 147
Higginbotham, Sam, 215
High-rise buildings, 3
Home buying, 65-68, 96-103
"Home Energy Savers Workbook," 197
Home-improvement costs, 190-93
Home improvements, fraud, 198-99
Home ownership, as hedge against inflation, 7
Horizon Corporation, 84
Horton, Alice M., 228
Houseboats, 235-36
House items, life expectancies of, 181-87
Housesharing, 132, 205-6
House size, 239
Housing. *See also* Design of housing; Repairs
  costs, 27-33, 99
  defects, 97-98
  design, 134-76
  fuel costs, 99
  high-rise, 3
  regulations, 241
  scarcity, 2, 238-39
  single-family, 4, 96-97
  size, 96-97
  in small towns, 18
Housing Management Corporation, 131
"How to Crimeproof Your Home," 189
Huggard, Grace, 232
Hughes, Russell, 151
Hyder, Carl F., 39, 216

I

Income property, 88-91
Income taxes, 32
Inflation, 7
INFORM, Inc., 85-88
"Insiders Guide to Owning Land in Subdivisions, The," 86-88
Installment sales of homes, 60-63
"Insulate by the Number" (poster), 197
Insulation, 196-97
  life expectancy of, 184
International Developers, Inc., 129
"In the Bank . . . or Up the Chimney," 197
Isaman, Dollie M., 139, 140

J

Johnson, Clarice, 32
Julius, Dorothy B., 211

K

Kass, Benny, 81
Kelso, Grace, 94, 242
Keskulla, Carolyn, 37
King, Gretchen, 218
King, O. L., 97
Kipp, R. Earl, 36, 135
Kitchens, 139–42
Kneip, Carl, 42
Koehl, Lilo, 35
Koslowski (Mrs.), 145
Kuhn, Maggie, 205

L

Lajda, Brano, 75
Land buying, 82–86
Land use, 240
Laundry appliances, 147
Layman, Lena, 5
Lease purchase agreements, 62
Leche, Arthur, 18
Leisure activities, 37
Leisure Knoll, 217
Leisure Technology, 217
Leisure Technology Corporation, 224
Leisure Towne, 217
Leisure Village West, 217
Leisure World, 218
Levin, Adam, 199
Lew Goodkin Newsletter, 224
"Life Expectancies of Various Parts of the House," 180
Life expectancy of house items, 180–87
Lingard, Aldro, 136, 144, 145
Litwin, Walter J., 160
Living Costs, 20, 22–26
Living with Tenants: How to Happily Share Your House with Renters for Profit and Security (Bierbrier), 206
Long, Lois J., 64
Lowell, Phoebe, 231
Lowell, William, 231
Lutheran Social Service, 205

M

Manufactured housing, 117, 241
Manufactured Housing Institute, 117
Marsh, Winifred C., 208
Masonry, life expectancy of, 183
Massachusetts Institute of Technology, 136
McComic, R. Barry, 214
McConnell, Stephen R., 132
McGloin, Barbara L., 249

Medical facilities, 16, 36
Meeker, Marvin (Mrs.), 139, 152
Mellon Institute, 193
Mendenhalls, Della, 207
Mendenhalls, Ray, 207
Millspaugh, Delight, 76
Mini White House Conference on Older Women, 248
Missouri, as retirement site, 14
Mobile homes, 112–15, 241. *See also* Motor homes
  financing problems, 116–17
  rules for buying, 117–20
Money Magazine, 19
Montgomery, Robert (Mrs.), 105
Mortgages
  lease purchase, 62
  older buyers, 69
  pension funds, 243
  refinancing, 70–71
  reverse equity loans, 71–73
  second, 61–62, 71
  taking back, 61
  wrap-around, 62
Motor homes, 6. *See also* Mobile homes
Moving from old home, compared to staying, 9–10. *See also* Retirement sites
Mueller, Theresa, 15
Multifamily housing, 240
Munro, Florence, 114
Murray, Isabelle, 135, 242
Murray, Thomas, 214
Myers, Dorice M., 223

N

National Association of Home Builders, 2, 4, 84, 109, 180, 194
National Association of Housing Cooperatives, 111–12
National Center for Home Equity Conversion, 74
National Council of Senior Citizens, Inc., 131
New Jersey, as retirement site, 14
New Mexico, as retirement site, 12
Ngat, Nguyen, 244
Nicola, Fr., 90
Nursing homes, 3

O

Oczytko, Vina S., 139, 147
Older homes, 187
  restoration, 233–35

Olsen, Trunette, 203
Olson, Lester, 13
Olson, Mary Ruth, 13
"Options" house, 154-56
Orendorff, Joseph H., 153

P

Pacific Northwest, as retirement site, 14
Paint, exterior, life expectancy of, 184
Palmer, William R., 118
Parker, Jack, 2
Park Fairfax, 129
Parking, 147
Parsons, Roger A., 149
Pastula, Rose, 147
Pauley, Ruth, 6, 82
Paulsboe, Dorothy, 142
Pearl, Kay, 210
Pease, Evelyn S., 149
Peay, Wayne L., 231
Penny, Lydia King, 135, 145, 189
Pension funds, in mortgage market, 243
Pets, 42
Plumbing, life expectancy of, 182
Porter, Sylvia, 85
Potraty, Virginia, 140
Product Safety Commission, 188
Property taxes, 27-29, 32, 99, 201-2
"Protecting Your Housing Investment," 189
Purpura, Anne, 6
Purvines, Stuart, 60

Q

Questions and Answers about Condominiums, 109

R

"Ranking States According to Their Attractiveness for Retirement," 19
Recreational vehicles (RVs), 230-31
Recreation facilities, 16, 147, 212, 215-16
Reed, John T., 91
Relatives, as factor in retirement location, 39
Relocating, at retirement, 9. *See also* Retirement sites
Remodeling. *See also* Repairs
  costs, 190-93
  electrical wiring, 188
  old home restoration, 233-35
Renter taxes, 33
Renting
  advantages, 121-22

condominium conversions, 126-29
  costs, 27
  disadvantages, 122-24
  as retirement income source, 63-65, 202-5, 242
  as retirement site, 88-91
  taxes, 33
"Rent or Buy," 124
Repairs, 179-80, 202
Retirement communities, 5-6, 207-9, 218-22
  advantages, 210-13
  buyers checklist, 220-22
  church-sponsored, 226
  continuing-care, 223-27
  costs, 214
  crowding, 215
  disadvantages, 214-17
  life-care, 223-27
  recreation facilities, 212, 215-16
  security, 213
Retirement sites, 9-12
  Arizona, 12-13
  Arkansas, 14
  big city, 18-19
  Caribbean, 236
  Colorado, 12
  Europe, 237
  Florida, 12, 30, 105
  housing costs, 27-33
  investigating before retirement, 33-38
  living costs, 20, 22-26
  Missouri, 14
  New Jersey, 14
  New Mexico, 12
  Pacific Northwest, 14
  rural, 15-16
  small town, 17-18
  Sunbelt, 12-14
  Texas, 12
Rich, G. Barrett, 223
Riebel, Mildred V., 212
Robinson, Barry, 99, 148
Roofing, 200
Roofs, life expectancy of, 182
Roos, A. E., 219
Rose, G. M. (Mrs.), 65
Rossmoor Corporation, 176
Rovillo, Marjorie, 97
Rudnick, Marion G., 3, 134, 143
Rural living, 15-16
Ryan, Marianne, 77
Ryan, Philip, 77

S

Sale-leaseback, 73
Sales tax, 32
Schenke, Raymond, 157
Schneider, Ann, 204
Schumacher, E., 243
Scott, Gladys, 18, 241
Sea Colony, 78
Second mortgages, 61–62, 71
Security, 189, 213
Seibel, Margaret D., 119
Share-a-Home Program, 205
Sicurella, Belle M., 38
Single-family homes, 4, 96–97
SmallTown USA (de Geus), 17
Smith, Betty, 115
"Smoke Detectors," 189
Smyczynski, Jeanne, 96
Stack, Louis J., 215
Stanbro, Ada, 36
Stasick, Joseph, 5, 97
Stevens Neighborhood Housing Improvement Program, 132
Storm windows, 194
Strang, Dorothea M., 40, 137, 146
Strickler, John F., Jr., 150
Studnicky, Jack P., 128
Sturges, M. Carolyn, 218
Sturrock, Eva L., 4
Subsidized apartments, 129–30
Sumichrast, Marika, 220
Summers, Tish, 248
Sunbelt retirement, 12–14
Sunbelt Retirement (Dickinson), 16
Sun City, 217

T

Takach, Dorothy, 204
Takach, William Center, 204
Tax deductions and exemptions
 energy, 197–98
 primary residence sale, 55–58
Taxes
 capital gains, 59–60
 income, 32
 property, 32, 99
 renter, 33
 sales, 32
 vacation homes, 79–80
Tenzer, Michael, 138, 217, 224
Terwilliger Plaza, 223
Texas, as retirement site, 12
Thistlethwaite, R. L., 226
Thomas, H. W. (Mrs.), 38
Thuemmel, C. H. (Mrs.), 94
Tile, life expectancy of, 185
Townhouses, 104–9
Trailers, 241
Transportation, 36–37
Travel trailers, 228–31. See also Mobile homes
Trim, exterior, life expectancy of, 184
Trimble, Jean S., 92
Trommershausser, J. (Mrs.), 80
"Turning Home Equity into Income for Older Homeowners," 74

U

Underground houses, 150
Underwood, Joanna, 85
United Association of Journeymen and Apprentices of the Plumbing and Pipefitting Industry, 238

V

Vacation homes, 77–79
 construction, 80–82
 renting out, 79–80
 selling, 80
 taxes, 79–80
Villane, Clair, 198
Vredevoogd, E. Eleanor, 81

W

Waddington, Gwen, 92
Wallace, Florence, 151
Walsh, Gordon (Mrs.), 240
Walsh, Nola A., 1
Warm Hearth Village, 178
Water heaters, 194
Wautelet, Marsh, 209
Weiss, Jane M., 142
Wenke, Adeline, 240
White, Betty, 37
White, Kathryn, 68
White, Wilber, 68
Whitener, Raymond, 233
Whitfield, Gladys, 93
Whitford, Jean, 189
Whitman, Deila I., 208

Wigley, T. B. (Mrs.), 152
Wilson, Helen, 239
Windows, life expectancy of, 183
Wintermute, Tim, 131
Women
　housing needs, 248
　White House Conference on, 248
Wrap-around mortgages, 62
Writer Corporation, 106

Y

Yards, 147
York, Herman, 153, 157

Z

Zappulla, Tom, 139
Zimmer, Anna, 244
Zito, Frank, 100
Zoning laws, 241, 245

Ronald G. Shafer, Marika Sumichrast, Michael Sumichrast

About the Authors

Michael Sumichrast, Ph.D., is chief economist and senior staff vice-president of the National Association of Home Builders. He is a widely-quoted, international authority on housing, a frequent advisor on housing issues to the United States Government, and has been actively involved in home, industrial, and commercial construction. He has written numerous articles, newspaper columns, and studies on a wide range of housing issues. Dr. Sumichrast is co-author of several books, including *The Complete Book of Home Buying*.

Ronald G. Shafer is a feature editor in the Washington bureau of *The Wall Street Journal*. As a Journal staff reporter since 1963 in Chicago, Detroit, and Washington, he has specialized in such subjects as transportation, consumer protection, and housing. He is a journalism graduate of Ohio State University. Mr. Shafer is co-author of *The Complete Book of Home Buying*.

Marika Sumichrast, Ph.D., has wide experience in all facets of real estate. She has done research as a private consultant for the National Academy of Sciences and the Building Research Advisory Board; for three years she was a vice-president of Rossmoor Leisure World retirement community in Washington, D.C. Dr. Sumichrast has extensive knowledge of retirement communities and has lectured throughout the United States on the subject of retirement housing.